A Self-governing Dominion

A
Self-governing Dominion

CALIFORNIA, 1849-1860

By William Henry Ellison

UNIVERSITY OF CALIFORNIA PRESS

Berkeley   Los Angeles   London

University of California Press
Berkeley and Los Angeles, California

University of California Press, Ltd.
London, England

Copyright, 1950, by
The Regents of the University of California

California Library Reprint Series Edition 1978
ISBN: 0-520-03713-8

Printed in the United States of America

1 2 3 4 5 6 7 8 9

To ELIZABETH

Preface

THIS WORK begins with the evolvement of California's first constitution. It ends on the eve of the Civil War with the fall of William M. Gwin and David C. Broderick, whose rivalry for political control was the dominant note of the late 1850's. The events that accompanied this rivalry and of which it was a part brought the people of California to see their dependence on the Union and firmly welded the commonwealth into the federation of states. Each of the chapters might stand alone as an essay on the subject treated; all have political connotations. Their recurrent theme is the principle of self-government of particular localities and of the state as a whole, which continually found expression in the assumption that Californians were a people apart, in their units and as a unit independent of outside authority. Throughout the 'fifties the people of California, as a result of either their own efforts or the operation of historical forces, were a people unto themselves. In a broad sense, the state sought to be, or by fortuitous circumstances came to be, a self-governing dominion.

Three assumptions underlie the writing of the book: first, that fortuitous circumstances played an important part in the California story; second, that the business of the historian is not only to tell how events and developments came to pass but also to explain, as far as he is able, why they occurred when they did; and, third, that since the meaning of the past for the people of each decade or century is modified by their own experiences, it is important that each generation write for itself a history of the past. This book, written on the eve of the centennial of California's founding as an American state is, therefore, an attempt to rewrite and reinterpret a period in the state's history from the standpoint of today.

Approximately half of the volume is based on original sources, the rest on books and studies that are recognized as authoritative. In parts of the book, therefore, the citations are of original sources and with full documentation; in others they are of secondary sources, with minimum documentation but with references sufficiently numerous to validate quotations and important events and show the sources that were used.

Permission has been generously given by the publishers to include in chapter vi an abbreviation and modification of my article, "The Federal Indian Policy in California, 1846–1860," published in the *Mississippi Valley Historical Review*, Volume IX, No. 1 (June, 1922); a part of the article, "Rejection of California Indian Treaties—A Study of Social Influence on National Policy," which appeared in the *Grizzly Bear* for May, June, and July, 1925; and, in chapter vii, an adaptation of my essay, "The Movement for State Division in California, 1849–1860," published in Volume XVII, No. 2 (October, 1913), of the *Southwestern Historical Quarterly*, of the Texas State Historical Association. In a different way, the "Memoirs" of William M. Gwin, which I edited and which the California Historical Society published serially in Volume IX (1940) of its *Quarterly*, have been an important source of information and help in the study.

I am indebted to Miss Dorothy Gates for secretarial assistance in the preparation of the book, and to Elizabeth Pellett (Mrs. Robert Pellett), who, in addition to typing the first eight chapters, gave invaluable help in assembling and arranging the material. My daughter Margaret (Mrs. Roy C. Beckman) and Robin Adams (Mrs. Henry Adams) read the manuscript critically, making numerous corrections and improvements. Finally,

I have profited greatly from the valuable suggestions and assistance of my wife.

My thanks go to Mr. August Frugé, Acting Manager of the Publishing Department, and to Miss Dorothy Huggins of the editorial staff, University of California Press, for their long-continued courtesies and assistance.

Santa Barbara, California WILLIAM H. ELLISON
February 18, 1949

Contents

I

Steps toward Self-government

Gentlemen are talking of natural boundaries. Sir, our natural boundary is the Pacific Ocean. The swelling tide of our population must roll on until that mighty ocean interposes its waters, and limits our territorial empire.—Francis Baylies of Massachusetts, 1823

THE STUDY of California as a self-governing dominion properly begins with the making of its first constitution. But that epoch-making process cannot be separated from a series of actions taken previously by the United States to express its authority over California and its people, or from attempts by some of the American citizens in the new land, as well as by the government in Washington, to prepare the way for American political control in California.

The political philosophy stated in the Declaration of Independence had nowhere found expression before 1776. Even today, the idealism embodied in that document of freedom is not fully exemplified in professedly democratic states. It is therefore not surprising to find that the citizens of the United

States who one hundred years ago made the initial attempts to take government in California into their hands and to impose their institutions upon the Californians were not greatly concerned about protecting the inalienable rights of life, liberty, and the pursuit of happiness by instituting a government deriving its just powers from the consent of the governed. Their primary purpose was to govern, and to promote and protect their own interests, without regard to the rights of men in general.

The first attempt to create a self-governing American unit in California was the unlawful seizure of Mariano Guadalupe Vallejo, by a band of United States citizens, at Sonoma on June 14, 1846. These men, most of whom were "dressed in leather hunting shirts, many of them very greasy," surrounded the home of the respected Vallejo, put him under arrest, and attempted to set up a government. Their actions were natural, but arbitrary and undemocratic. These rough-looking men were clearly not protagonists of the equality of man.

In spite of this, for more than a century an exaggerated nationalistic patriotism has glorified the illegal and highhanded "Bear Flag Revolt" because Americans carried it through and sanctified it by putting forth a statement tinctured with political idealism. A "proclamation" [1] signed by William B. Ide, one of the leaders of the movement, asserted that the aim of those who launched the attack was to set up a "republican government" in place of a "military despotism" which, Ide charged, had been ruthless and oppressive. Without consulting the Californians, the newcomers assumed authority over them, made a crude flag, and gave the people glowing promises of liberties and privileges that would be theirs under the government that was about to be set up. Ide's proclamation further invited "all peaceable and good citizens of California who are friendly to the maintenance of good order and equal rights" to

---

[1] Copies of Ide's proclamation are printed in California Historical Society *Quarterly*, I (1922), 72–79. H. H. Bancroft, *History of California*, V, 151–153, prints a copy of the corrected proclamation, with notes on the several versions, and tells where the various copies may be found.

repair to the camp at Sonoma "to assist in establishing and perpetuating a 'Republican government' which shall secure to all civil and religious liberty," on the theory that "a Government to be prosperous and happyfying in its tendencies must originate with its people."

These words of Ide, who acted as leader of the rugged band who had miraculously become "the people," sounded beneficent, but the actions of the group spoke to the Californians so loudly that they drowned out the high-sounding phrases. Thomas O. Larkin and other American settlers who had been longer in the country than the "Bear Flaggers" saw no excuse for the movement. It resulted in violence that otherwise would have been avoided, sowed the seeds of ill will, and blighted the hopes of Larkin and others who were nurturing the idea of peaceful annexation of California by the United States. No one can know what would have been the course of the revolt had not the official news of the Mexican War arrived a few days after the Bear Flag was raised. It is possible that the province might have been carried on to independence as a preliminary to its annexation by the United States; or ideas engendered at this time might have come to fruition in a Pacific Republic on the western coast—the objective of a movement which developed later.

This preliminary attempt at political action, known as the "Bear Flag Revolt," grew, in part, out of dissatisfaction with the local Mexican government, which the Americans considered bad because of its dissimilarity to that to which they had been accustomed in their home communities. It must not be forgotten, however, that, for a century, American frontier settlers had been in the habit of making their own government wherever they went. Theoretically, the Americans of the California frontier wanted to set up self-government in California—that is, government by Americans—but their ideas of democracy were as yet not developed sufficiently to make them feel obligated to respect the wishes of the majority, the Californians.

The first assertion by the United States of its authority over California came through Commodore John D. Sloat when, on July 7, 1846, he took possession of Monterey, raised the United States flag, and issued a statement to the people of California. In his conciliatory proclamation,[2] although he asserted unequivocally that "henceforward California will be a portion of the United States," he affirmed, "although I come in arms with a powerful force, I do not come among them as an enemy to California; on the contrary, I come as their best friend." He informed the inhabitants that henceforward California would be a part of the United States, but he assured them that their civil rights of conscience, property, and suffrage would be respected; that their clergy would remain in possession of the churches; that United States produce and manufactured goods would be admitted free of duty, and one-fourth of former rates would be charged on foreign merchandise. He stated also that any person who did not wish to live under the new government as one of its citizens would be afforded every facility for selling his property and removing himself from the country. And, in order that "the public tranquility may not be disturbed," he invited the prefects of districts and alcaldes of municipalities to retain their offices and to continue to exercise their customary functions.

Commodore Robert F. Stockton arrived at Monterey on July 15 and received the transfer of authority from Sloat on July 23. When Sloat left California on July 29, all the area north of Santa Barbara was in the possession of the United States. Stockton immediately inaugurated a more vigorous policy. First, he enlisted the Bear Flag men as volunteers in the United States Army, forming them into the "California Battalion of Mounted Riflemen," and appointed John C. Frémont as major and Archibald H. Gillespie as captain. Next, and just before sailing south to extend the conquest there, Stockton

---

[2] Sloat's proclamation "To the Inhabitants of California" is printed in 30th Cong., 2d sess., House Ex. Doc. No. 1, pp. 1010 f.; California Historical Society *Quarterly*, II (1924), 188–190; Bancroft, *op. cit.*, pp. 234–237.

issued a new proclamation [3] to the people—a document that was bombastic, accusatory, and menacing. In it he stated that United States forces had been threatened. Disregarding the fact that Frémont, with military forces, had invaded a province of the Mexican nation, he charged that José Castro, the commander in chief of the military forces of California, had violated principles of national hospitality and international law by pursuing him, and he asserted that he would make war upon any civil or military leaders who opposed the authority of the United States. Toward the Californian population Stockton showed some magnanimity in stating that all who acknowledged the authority of existing laws and obeyed his orders should be "treated in the same manner as other citizens of the United States."

The conquest of southern California was quickly accomplished. Frémont first went with his men to San Diego, while Stockton landed at San Pedro. Then, in coöperation with Frémont, who had come up and joined the other forces, Stockton marched into and took possession of Los Angeles, without opposition, on August 13. Four days later he issued a second proclamation.[4] In this he announced that the flag of the United States was flying from every commanding position in the territory, and that the country, now free from Mexican dominion, belonged to the United States. It would, "as soon as circumstances permit," he asserted, be governed by officers and laws similar to those of other territories of the United States. Until territorial organization could be effected, military law would be in force and the commander in chief would be the governor. Stockton requested the people to elect officials to fill the places of officeholders who declined to serve under the new government; if the people did not fill these

[3] For Stockton's undated "Address to the People of California," probably issued July 29, see Bancroft, *op. cit.*, pp. 255–257; 30th Cong., 2d sess., House Ex. Doc. No. 1, pp. 1035–1037.

[4] This proclamation is in 29th Cong., 2d sess., House Ex. Doc. No. 4, pp. 669–670. See also Edwin Bryant, *What I Saw in California, Being the Journal of a Tour . . . in the Years 1846, 1847* (New York, 1848) pp. 298–299.

vacancies by election, the governor would appoint persons to fill them. Everyone who adhered to the new government, he said, would be considered a citizen and would be protected. The laws would be administered according to the former usages of the country. Persons found carrying arms, without permission, outside their own houses would be considered as enemies and would be shipped out of the country. Thieves would be put to hard labor on the public works. Persons must stay in their houses from ten o'clock at night until sunrise. While the territory remained under martial law, the California Battalion would serve as a sort of military police force.

Acting as commander in chief of military and naval forces and as governor of California, Stockton declared Upper and Lower California to be the territory of the United States by right of conquest. He decreed that executive power should be vested in a governor, who should reside in the territory of California, be commander in chief of the army, act as superintendent of Indian affairs, approve laws passed by the legislative council, grant administrative pardons, and commission officers. There should be a secretary, holding office in like manner, who should record and preserve the laws and proceedings of the executive and legislative departments and annually report them to the President and Congress. In the absence of the governor, the secretary should execute the powers and duties of the governor's office. Legislative power should be vested in the governor and a legislative council of seven members. The governor should appoint this council for the first two years, and thereafter the people should annually elect its members. The governor should designate the time and place of its first meeting. Legislative power should extend to all rightful subjects of legislation. No law should be passed "interfering with the primary disposal of the soil." Property of the United States would not be taxed. No law disapproved by the governor would be valid. Municipal offices already existing should continue, and their proceedings should be regulated by the laws of Mexico until other laws replaced them. Elections of the usual city, town, and district officers should be held every year.

Stockton, on August 22, stated that he intended to withdraw with his naval forces from California as soon as he could safely do so. The withdrawal, he said, was for the purpose of protecting American commerce in other parts of the Pacific. He declared that before leaving the territory he would appoint Frémont governor and Gillespie secretary, and that he would name a council of state and other officers that might be needed. He made an appointment to meet Frémont in San Francisco on October 25, "to complete the whole arrangement" and to place him in office as governor of California.

In keeping with Stockton's plans, Captain Gillespie was placed in command of Los Angeles, and Frémont, with the remainder of the California Battalion, marched northward in order to recruit for his forces and to place soldiers in command of municipalities.

Alcaldes, as the proclamations of Sloat and of Stockton had decreed, continued their functions as administrators of government. And since, as Stockton had proclaimed, vacancies in the office of alcalde were to be filled by election, he ordered an election for September 15. At Monterey, where there were seven candidates, 368 votes were cast, of which Walter Colton received 68—a plurality over any of his competitors. The office of alcalde at Monterey was very important, since the alcalde there had jurisdiction in cases involving breaches of the peace, crimes, business obligations, and disputes over titles to land, "arising within the middle department of California." It was, in fact, an appellate alcalde's court for the district. Colton, in his attempt to achieve justice, blended, in imperfect fashion, California customs and common-law rules of the United States.

Frémont, however, was not to become governor as early as Stockton had planned. On the night of September 29, 1846, less than a month after Stockton had reported the war at an end, "Juan Flaco" (John Brown) arrived at Monterey after the remarkable feat of covering the 460 miles from Los Angeles in fifty-two hours. He brought the news that the southern Californians had revolted and that Gillespie's garrison at Los Angeles was hard pressed. Finding that Stockton had sailed for San Francisco, Brown, after refreshing himself with food and drink and a scant three hours' sleep, continued his journey 140 miles farther. Reports of the success of the Californians in Los Angeles and vicinity aroused excitement and hope among the Californians at Monterey and other places and caused Stockton some apprehension. He at once made plans for reconquest and, after sending a vessel with troops to San Pedro, he himself proceeded to San Diego.

Toward the end of the year, General Stephen W. Kearny arrived in California with part of his original army. After conquering New Mexico, Kearny had left the greater part of his command as a garrison in Santa Fé. On his way to California with three hundred dragoons he had met Kit Carson with dispatches from Commodore Stockton stating that American control was already established there. Kearny thereupon sent all but one hundred dragoons back to Santa Fé, and, with Carson as guide, continued toward California. When he got there he found the Californians again in control. At San Pascual Kearny fought the bloodiest battle of the conquest. Two hundred marines and soldiers sent out by Stockton convoyed his depleted forces to San Diego.

Frémont, meanwhile, made his famous march from the region of Monterey to Los Angeles. The forces of Stockton and Kearny headed toward Los Angeles, while, ahead of them, the Californian forces, returning northward, proceeded to the Rancho de Cahuenga near San Fernando. There they were met on January 12, 1847, by Frémont and the California Battalion coming from the north. Frémont had expected a fight and was therefore surprised that the first thing the Californians did was to make a peace offer. Terms were soon agreed upon, and articles of capitulation were drawn up and were signed on January 13, 1847.

The Californians agreed to surrender their entire force to Frémont, to give up their arms and return peaceably to their homes, and to conform to the laws and regulations of the United States. And Frémont agreed that, pending a treaty of peace between the United States and Mexico, any Californian or Mexican citizen who so desired should be permitted to leave the country, and every citizen of California should enjoy the same privileges and rights as those enjoyed by citizens of the United States. He also guaranteed protection to all residents of the country.

After the Americans had finished their conquest of California, there followed a period of unfortunate strife among the military chiefs, Stockton, Kearny, and Frémont, each of whom sought all the control he could get and undoubtedly aspired to be the first to establish a civil government in California. Kearny had been instructed by the Secretary of War to march to California, take possession of it, and establish a civil government. On his arrival he had found that possession had already been taken in the name of the United States, and a hybrid form of government, partly civil and partly military, had been put into operation. Stockton claimed authority as commander in chief because he had directed the conquest and was holding the country with the assistance of Frémont and his army. Under his assumed authority, Stockton named Frémont military commander and governor. Frémont assumed the civil governorship on January 19, 1847, with William H. Russell as secretary of state. A legislative council, appointed by Stockton, was summoned to convene in Los Angeles on March 1. The controversy over the governorship prevented it from doing so. Frémont remained at Los Angeles as governor but without any valid authority or anything to govern, and his contest with Kearny continued.

While this unfortunate conflict between Kearny, on the one hand, and Stockton and Frémont on the other, was in process, Commodore William Branford Shubrick arrived at the port of Monterey under orders from the Navy Department to take command of the naval forces there. The relations between Shubrick and Kearny were cordial. In coöperative action they fixed upon Monterey as the capital and seat of government, and this decision they jointly announced on March 1, 1847. Together they issued a document which stated that the President of the United States, in order to give the people of California civil government and protect them from internal disorder and foreign attack, had invested Shubrick and Kearny with separate powers, civil and military, for effecting that end. Stockton and Frémont, as has been noted, had decided to make Los Angeles the capital, and from there Frémont tried to carry out the functions of government. In the end, he found himself obliged to disband his California Battalion and report to Kearny, his superior officer, at Monterey. There he received orders to accompany the general, who was then preparing to leave California for "the States." Frémont's subsequent court-martial is another story. Stockton, soon after issuing his commission to Frémont as governor of California, went to Lower California on a naval mission. Upon his return to San Francisco, having been superseded in naval command by Shubrick, he gave up the command of the *Congress,* and in July set out on his return to the United States.

With the departure from California of Kearny, Frémont, and Stockton, the person left to command the land forces and to act as governor was Colonel Richard B. Mason. Mason, who in the previous November had received orders to proceed to California and to assume certain responsibilities when occasion warranted, had arrived at Monterey on February 12, 1847. On May 31, he took command of the land forces and assumed the office of governor. Many problems confronted him. Among them were the disrespect which some of the people had for his office because of the unsavory disputes of his predecessors, insistent individual claims against the government that had to be satisfied, the absorption of newcomers from many nations and from places with divergent institutions, and the somewhat difficult adjustment of two peoples who had so recently opposed each other in a war.

Mason immediately made it known by proclamation that he

was commissioned as civil governor in California, and he at once gave attention to various details of administration that needed regulation. Numbers of immigrants were taking up land wherever they pleased. This led to the appointment of surveyors. On May 7, 1847, Mason appointed William B. Ide surveyor of the northern department, the district lying north of San Francisco. About a month later, he designated Jasper O'Farrell to serve as an additional surveyor for the same department, and Jacob R. Snyder as surveyor for the middle department. Land titles created many problems, for at the time neither the Mexican government nor the government of the United States was in a position to deal with this question. Mason, therefore, refused to make any grants but insisted that titles should remain as nearly as possible as they were when the American flag was raised on July 7, 1846.

Another subject of interest was that of the authority and jurisdiction of the American alcaldes. There was, of course, much dissatisfaction with this hybrid system of government and a great deal of railing against these officials. Dr. Robert Semple, for example, in the *California Star*, February 13, 1847, charged that "we have alcaldes all over the country assuming the power of legislatures, issuing and promulgating their bandos, laws, orders, and oppressing the people." He asserted, too, that the "most nefarious scheming, trickery and speculating have been practised by some." [5] Even as early as February, 1847, these complaints were used as a basis for urging that a convention be called to form a constitution for the territory. Mason's recognition of the authority of the alcalde is indicated in his direction to the newly elected town council which he found when he visited San Francisco in October. On leaving, he addressed a communication to the council. In it he reminded the members that their jurisdiction was restricted by the territory embraced within the limits of their town, he directed the alcalde to determine these limits with as little delay as possible,

[5] Quoted in Cardinal Goodwin, *The Establishment of State Government in California*, p. 63.

and he imposed certain restrictions upon the authority exercised by the council.

Dissatisfaction with what was referred to as the "ineffectual mongrel military rule" continued to increase. The governor failed to provide higher tribunals, thus forcing alcaldes to adjudicate in cases involving any amount of money, or to disregard the cases. Naturally, the authority which they exercised, combining in their persons executive, legislative, and judicial functions, became more powerful as time went on, and more liable to abuse. The situation could not be remedied until peace was signed, the military rule suspended, and civil government set up.

It had been a rather general practice for an occupying force to continue the law system of the occupied territory if it did not conflict with accepted ideas of justice held by the invaders. Difficulties hindered the observance of this practice in California. The laws were in a foreign language, they were not widely disseminated, and the procedures as well as the laws themselves seemed to Americans quite arbitrary. In the nature of things, a system which fitted the pastoral social scheme of California did not satisfy Americans, whose background was widely different. In characteristic American fashion they showed contempt of Mexican laws and procedures which differed markedly from their own.

Partly because the California system of law and judicial procedure was at variance with American practices, in some measure because the old order was unsuited to what was developing, and even more because it is a trait of Americans to want to run things according to their own pattern, the growth of American law in California was rather rapid. In the application of common-law procedure, Walter Colton, about a month after he became American alcalde of Monterey, empaneled the first jury ever summoned in California. The case was that of Charles Roussillon, whom Isaac Graham had accused of stealing a quantity of lumber. A jury was called for September 4, and the trial was held on that day. A third of the jury were Mexicans, another third Californians, and the rest Americans. The prosecutor used the English language, the defendant French, and the jury, except the Americans, Spanish. W. E. P. Hartnell, an Englishman, acted as interpreter. The jury deliberated for an hour and returned a verdict acquitting the accused, with certain recommendations in regard to the cost of the trial. This was the beginning of the administration of Anglo-Saxon justice in California. Very soon this method became a common practice of the country, although there was no law providing for it until California became a state. It was not long before American settlers claimed jury trial as a right, and the Californians themselves were forced to adopt it. As early as December 29, 1847, Mason issued a general order for trials by jury in all cases in which the amount involved was more than one hundred dollars.

The difficulties of the governmental situation in California were further complicated by the discovery of gold on January 24, 1848. The depopulation of towns which had some machinery of government, and in which the ordinary restraints of community life and custom existed, made serious problems in law enforcement and social control. Editorials and communications in the *California Star* and the *Californian* reflect the sentiment of the people in a demand for new laws and for law enforcement.

Governor Mason was aware of the public dissatisfaction and of the difficulties occasioned by the lack of an adequate law system; by the middle of April he was working toward a solution of the problem. Both newspapers made this clear in their editorials. But they were impatient of delay, and in an editorial in the *California Star* of May 20, Sam Brannan sharply pointed out the need for action. On the very next day, in a letter written to Captain Joseph L. Folsom at San Francisco, Governor Mason indicated that he had drawn up some laws. "I send Mr. Hartnell, the government interpreter, to San Francisco," he wrote, "to attend to the correct printing of the Spanish translation of some laws, &c., that I intend to publish." In other communications on May 31, and June 1, he indicated that the laws were being printed.[6] There is much mystery about the laws that Governor Mason drew up and had printed. Nearly two months elapsed without a trace of them. This may have been because of difficulty in finding a printer, since so many persons had gone to the mines, and both the *Californian* and the *California Star* had ceased publication for the time being. That the laws were printed is confirmed by the following notice in the *Californian* of August 14, 1848:

LAWS.—Governor Mason has had printed both in the English and Spanish languages, a code of laws for the better government of the territory of California—the preservation of order, and the protection of the rights of the inhabitants, during the military occupation of the country by the U.S. forces.

It seems certain that the laws were never offered for sale and that they were never circulated. Possibly the only copy published and bound was the one acquired by the Huntington Library in March, 1923.[7] The rarity of the book is no doubt explained by an inscription written from bottom to top of the title page: "Not published in consequence of the news of peace—J. L. Folsom." The notice in the *Californian* of August 14, referred to above, states that the laws which Governor Mason had had printed were for the preservation of order, and so forth, "during the military occupation of the country by the U.S. forces." Notification of the ratification of the Treaty of Guadalupe Hidalgo had arrived on August 6. The laws accordingly found their way into print too late.

The volume of California laws drawn up by Governor Mason for the better government of California consists of sixty-seven pages. The code contains twenty-seven headings, with numerous sections under each heading. Since it was intended

[6] Mason's letter of May 21, 1848, is in 31st Cong., 1st sess., House Ex. Doc. No. 17, p. 555; his letter of May 31 is in *ibid.*, p. 558; his letter of June 1, in *ibid.*, p. 559.

[7] The article by Lyndley Bynum, "Laws for the Better Government of California, 1848," in the *Pacific Historical Review*, II (1933), 279–291, is the basis for the statements here about the laws drawn up by Governor Mason.

for use during the military occupation only, it contains no provision for executive and legislative functions. These rested with the military governor and an almost nonfunctioning council. Except for a few provisions relating to finance, the document provides only for the administration of justice, civil and criminal. The sections on justice, which form the greater part of it, set up a system of American jurisprudence. The office of alcalde is retained, but its executive and legislative powers have been taken away, leaving only the judicial, thus making the alcalde a counterpart of the Anglo-Saxon justice of the peace.

The distance of California from the seat of federal government caused delays and confusion in the administration of the territory. In October, 1848, Brigadier General Bennett Riley was directed to relieve Colonel Mason as governor of California, and in November, Brigadier General Persifor F. Smith was appointed to the command of the United States Army on the Pacific Coast. On February 26, 1849, five days after the attempt in San Francisco to set up self-government by the election of assemblymen, the mail steamer *California* came into port carrying General Smith, who superseded Colonel Mason as commander of the military division in California. General Riley arrived at Monterey on April 12, 1849, and on April 13 he relieved Mason as governor. Mason left California on May 1. In the summer of 1850, in St. Louis, he died of cholera at the age of 61 years.

Colonel Mason in his position as governor had been much criticized by the Americans in California. In fact, they had been openly antagonistic toward him. This was in the natural order of things, because Americans are prone to criticize authority, especially if it is military, for they reason that military government has no place in time of peace. This attitude had been particularly sharp toward Colonel Mason because many of the American group were engaged in every sort of project to make money, and he would not use his position to further their ends or to fill his own purse. Mason had amply demonstrated that he had a strong, native intellect and that his knowledge of the principles of civil government and law was greater than that with which he had been credited. As a military man he not only obeyed instructions implicitly but acted in all matters with scrupulous regard for the honor of his office. Although in the midst of bold, enterprising, and speculative men, and urged by them to use his position to make a fortune for himself and his friends, he never lent his power to any deal for his personal advantage. The record of his administration in California shows that his respect for order and justice was so exemplary as to dull markedly the sharp criticisms of his detractors. He deserves high praise for having so administered the affairs of the country that when his successor arrived, adjustment to a civil form of government was relatively easy.

As soon as the conquest had been completed, American residents in California had begun to agitate for the establishment of a civil government controlled by them and under the protection of the United States. These people who desired self-government were a minority, oblivious of the rights of the majority. Their wishes, however, could not be realized until the war was ended officially by a treaty of peace. When news of the peace reached California on August 6, 1848, objection to military government became more intense, and demands for setting up civil authority markedly increased. President Polk, in his special message to Congress of July 6, 1848, took note of the situation and urged that steps be taken immediately to provide a territorial organization for California. Because of the questions thrust upon the country by the introduction of the Wilmot Proviso, Congress adjourned without making any provision for the recommended organization. The President came to the question again in his annual message at the opening of the second session of the Thirtieth Congress, on December 5, 1848. Including with his message the important report of Mason and the letters of Larkin on the gold mines, he referred again to the subject of government for California and submitted that the condition of the country demanded immediate territorial organization.

In answer to President Polk's message of July 6, 1848, recommending the adoption of a territorial government, a Senate committee, to which the subject had been referred, reported a bill designed to provide a territorial government for Oregon, California, and New Mexico, leaving adjudication of the slavery question to the Supreme Court of the United States. This bill passed the Senate but was rejected by the House. After the President issued his message in December, 1848, the matter was taken up in much the same manner as before. The judiciary committee, to which the subject had been referred, recommended that, instead of one new state, two territories should be erected. The question was wildly debated; some members of the committee lamented the discovery of gold, others pronounced it a bubble, and still others proposed to cede back the country to Mexico. Nothing came of this bill; and even the civil and diplomatic appropriation bill was almost defeated because certain amendments had been engrafted upon it, extending the scope of the revenue laws of the United States to include California. California was left, therefore, without any legal authority except that exercised by the governor, who had been appointed by the President, and the much-criticized government the governor had set up. Yet it gained something in this session of Congress in the extension of the revenue laws of the United States over all the territory seized from Mexico; the designation of San Francisco as a port of entry, and of Monterey and San Diego as ports of delivery; the authorization for the appointment of a collector of customs; and the appointment, on November 1, 1848, of William Van Voorhies as an agent for the establishment of post offices and the transmission of mails in the territory.

In the meantime, the Americans in California, disturbed by Congress' delay in providing for them, began to plan to do for themselves what Congress had failed to do for them. A meeting for this purpose was held at San Jose on December 11, 1848, at which a recommendation was passed for the assembling of a constitutional convention in the following January. At larger meetings in San Francisco on December 21 and 23, it was urged that delegates should be elected from the district to a constitutional convention to be held at San Jose in March; and on January 8, 1848, five delegates were elected to this convention. Other meetings and other elections were held, but lack of unanimity of action and, in many places, delay in electing delegates, caused postponement of the assembling of the convention from March until May. It should be noted that, at gatherings of prominent citizens in San Francisco on February 17 and 24, 1849, the delegates who were elected to the convention were instructed to oppose by every honorable means the introduction of domestic slavery into the territory of California.[8]

Before General Smith and General Riley arrived in California, definite steps had been taken to set up self-government in San Francisco. While the municipal affairs of the town were in great confusion in consequence of a dispute over the results of two elections to choose councilmen for the year 1849—one on December 27, 1848, and the second on January 15, 1849—a public meeting was called to work out a new plan of municipal government. An assembly in Portsmouth Square on February 12 adopted a plan for municipal government that had been drawn up by George Hyde. This plan created a "Legislative Assembly for the District of San Francisco," which would consist of fifteen members presided over by a speaker. The plan provided also for the election of three justices of the peace, who would have judicial power. All elected persons would serve for one year from the date of their commissions. The election was accordingly held, and on March 5 the so-called legislative assembly met.

Francis J. Lippitt was elected speaker by this assembly. A committee was at once appointed to report a code of laws,

---

[8] Frank Soulé, John H. Gihon, and James Nisbet, *Annals of San Francisco*, p. 208; Bancroft, *op. cit.*, VI, 269–270.

and another was appointed to wait upon General Persifor F. Smith, who commanded the military forces of the United States, and Commodore Thomas ap Catesby Jones, who commanded the naval forces, to ask for their recognition of the organization. In the letter drawn up and presented to General Smith by the committee it was averred that at the moment the Treaty of Guadalupe Hidalgo took effect the Constitution of the United States and its principles were extended over the territory of California. Under this theory, known as the "Settlers'" or "Benton" theory—the latter because of its strong advocacy by Thomas Hart Benton, famous Senator from Missouri and the father-in-law of John C. Frémont—it was contended that military government derived its power from war, and that with the conclusion of war there was left only a presumed consent of the people.

In his reply to the committee General Smith stated that he deemed it unnecessary to do more than state the opinion of the President of the United States and his Cabinet, which was that, after the ratification of the treaty on May 30, 1848, the government then in force should continue as a *de facto* government until it was changed by the proper authority, which was Congress. Therefore, a governmental organization such as the San Francisco legislative assembly was illegal. The theory stated by Smith was called the "Administration" or "Buchanan" theory. In spite of this opinion, which had the support of eminent jurists, neither the citizens of San Francisco nor the advocates of a constitutional convention were willing to abandon their plans. They did, however, agree to postpone again the meeting of the proposed convention, from May until August, and to change the place of meeting to Monterey.[9]

As has been noted, General Riley had assumed the administration of civil affairs in California, as the executive of the existing civil government, on April 13, 1849. Riley, who was

---

[9] Detail on the San Francisco legislative assembly may be found in 31st Cong., 1st sess., House Ex. Doc. No. 17, pp. 729–737; Bancroft, *op. cit.*, pp. 261–274; Goodwin, *op. cit.*, pp. 66–70.

sixty-one years of age, has been described by some of his contemporaries as "a grim old fellow," and "a fine, free swearer." Although he had had little firsthand acquaintance with civil affairs, subsequent events indicated that he had intelligently studied questions of law and government as they pertained to California. Because he was a soldier, accustomed to obeying orders as well as to giving them, it was natural that he should try to carry out his orders to the letter. On taking office in California, he claimed the same powers as Mason had possessed, and he indicated his intention of following Mason's practices.

Governor Riley found in California an unsettled state of mind about both law observance and government. Much confusion had resulted from the immigration of numbers of foreigners, particularly Americans, who not only knew little about the Spanish laws but cared less about their observance. Elisha Crosby in his *Memoirs* says:

> Every man carried his code of laws on his hip and administered it according to his own pleasure. There was no safety of life or property   so far as the intervention of law was concerned there was no police. Spanish law was in operation here then and the only way it could be enforced was through the Military Governor and the Prefects and Alcaldes holding office under him. It was an unknown system to our people and we were absolutely in a state of chaos, society was entirely unorganized . . .[10]

In the difficult situation into which Riley had been projected, he found himself handicapped in his powers to carry out the laws, because of desertion of his soldiers, who, like many others, had been too strongly tempted by reports of gold in the hills.

When Mason turned over the office of governor to Riley he advised him to call a constitutional convention to provide a state government for California. Riley was favorable to this method of instituting a government, and on learning, on June 1, that Congress had adjourned without making any provision

[10] Elisha Oscar Crosby, *Memoirs*, p. 42.

for governmental organization in California, he decided to issue a proclamation calling for a convention to make such organization. This he did on June 3.[11] In this lengthy document he described the institutions and laws as they then existed, and pointed out the necessity of completing the organization of the civil government, and the need for a convention to provide a state or a territorial government in California subject to the approval of Congress. In explanation of what was proposed, he listed the various officials and outlined their functions. His scheme of civil government recognized Spanish forms fully, but it gave an American character to the administration by making the officers of the law elective instead of appointive. In the document, Riley ordered an election to be held on August 1, in which officials would be chosen to serve until January 1, 1850. He named the same date for an election of delegates to a convention the purpose of which was to draw up a state constitution or to organize a territorial government, and he specified that thirty-seven delegates should be elected from the several districts, to meet at Monterey on September 1.

[11] For the "Proclamation of the Governor," see J. Ross Browne, *Report of the Debates in the Convention of California, on the Formation of the State Constitution, . . . 1849,* pp. 3–5.

II

Constitution Making in the Land of Gold

That to secure these rights, Governments are instituted among Men, deriving their just powers from the consent of the governed . . . —DECLARATION OF INDEPENDENCE

IN HIS *Diary*, March 5, 1848, James K. Polk records that as he and General Taylor, accompanied by William W. Seaton, the mayor of Washington, and Robert C. Winthrop, the recent Speaker of the House, rode to the Capitol at the time of Taylor's inauguration, Taylor expressed views about California which greatly surprised him. These views, as recorded by Polk, were "to the effect, that California and Oregon were too distant to become members of the Union, and that it would be better for them to be an Independent Government." After commenting that these were alarming opinions to be entertained by the President of the United States, Polk added: "I have entertained serious apprehensions, and have expressed them in this diary, that if no Government was provided for in California at the late Session of Congress there was danger that that fine territory would be lost to the Union by the establishment of an Independent Government." [1]

A dramatic contrast to Taylor's opinion and Polk's apprehension is presented by another who witnessed the inaugural parade—a man who was to play a major role in the convention that framed the first California constitution. In his "Memoirs," and speaking in the third person, William M. Gwin tells of resigning the office of commissioner of the new customhouse at New Orleans and going to Washington to settle his accounts preparatory to leaving for California. He arrived in the capital on Sunday morning, March 4, 1849. On the next day, as the inaugural procession was passing Willard's Hotel,

Mr. Gwin, returning from the Treasury Department, where [he] had been settling his accounts, met Stephen A. Douglas in front of the hotel, and while looking at the procession as it passed, remarked to the Senator that the next morning he intended to leave the city en route for California. He said that the failure of Congress to give that country a territorial government would force its inhabitants to create a state government, that he intended to advocate that policy and to advocate it with success, and announced himself then and there a candidate for United States senator from California, and [said] that within one year from that time he would ask him [Douglas] to present his credentials as a senator from the State of California.[2]

The superior prescience and political understanding of Gwin were proved when, eleven months after making the statement, and nine months after his landing in San Francisco on June 4, he handed his credentials as Senator from California to Judge Douglas for presentation to the Senate, having been regularly elected to that office under the provisions of California's recently ratified constitution.

When Gwin arrived in California, the legislative assembly

[1] *The Diary of James K. Polk,* ed. by Milo Milton Quaife (4 vols.; Chicago, 1910), IV, 375-376.
[2] "Memoirs of Hon. William M. Gwin," ed. by William H. Ellison, California Historical Society *Quarterly,* XIX, 3. Gwin wrote his "Memoirs" in the third person.

of San Francisco was in sharp conflict with Governor Riley and General Smith. Clearly, Riley's proclamation of June 3 and the plans for making a new government were contrary to the theory on which the assembly of San Francisco was based, and on which its delegates to a constitutional convention had been elected. In spite of General Smith's declaration that the actions of the assembly were invalid, Governor Riley's statement, in a special proclamation, that its proceedings were null and void, and his appeal to the people to sustain the legally constituted authority of the land, the San Francisco assembly denounced the governor, drew up laws, declared their body to be a legally constituted one, and asserted that since its members held office by the authority of the people they would continue to do so until they were deprived of that right by those who had elected them.

While these sharp exchanges flew back and forth, the citizens of San Francisco called a mass meeting for June 12, in Portsmouth Square, to consider the part of Riley's proclamation that had reference to a constitutional convention. Although the meeting was addressed by William M. Gwin, Peter H. Burnett, Thomas Butler King, and others who favored Riley's plan, it passed resolutions declaring that the people had a right to organize this government for their protection, that the people were the authority for choosing their delegates, and that Governor Riley's call was not binding upon them. A committee of five was appointed to confer with other districts on the election of delegates to a convention. The meeting then adjourned.

Soon after the adjournment, calm reasoning began to replace angry feelings. Public opinion turned more and more toward the securing of a government that represented the people irrespective of whether it was set up under the "Settlers'" or under the "Administration" plan. Influenced by the changing sentiment, the committee which had been appointed on June 12 issued on June 18 an address which, while not admitting the power or right of Riley to lay down the plan for a convention, recommended that the terms of his proclamation should be followed as a matter of expediency. Opinion turned rapidly in favor of Riley's plan, and interest in the district legislature declined. Loss of interest in the controversy was shown by the small vote on the subject in an election on July 9. The district legislature thereupon dissolved.

In the meantime, agitation for the convention was carried on throughout the territory, with King, Gwin, and others making speeches in the various districts. Governor Riley also visited many points in the territory, partly to find out the conditions existing and partly with the organization of government in mind. Before the middle of July it was fully settled that there should be a constitutional convention as proposed in Governor Riley's proclamation of June 3, that the election of delegates should take place on August 1, that the convention should meet at Monterey on September 1, and that, until a constitution could be drawn up and adopted, the *de facto* government should continue to operate. The election to choose delegates to the constitutional convention took place on August 1 without disturbance. Riley in his proclamation had stated that there should be thirty-seven delegates, but because the districts of San Jose, San Francisco, Sacramento, and the San Joaquin had grown rapidly in population since the date of the proclamation, the convention membership was increased to forty-eight.[3]

On September 1, 1849, the delegates began to assemble. Most of them were strangers to one another. Only three-quarters of them were citizens of the United States by birth. Nine of the delegates were under thirty years of age, twenty-three were over thirty and under forty, twelve were aged forty to forty-nine, one was fifty-one, two were fifty-two, and the oldest member was fifty-three. Twenty-two of the assembly were from northern or free states, fifteen were from slave states, seven were native Californians, and four were born outside the present limits of the United States. A surpris-

[3] For factual and colorful detail of these happenings, see Bancroft, *History of California*, VI, 275–284; Samuel H. Willey, *The Transition Period in California*, pp. 84–92; Bayard Taylor, *Eldorado*, pp. 147–149.

ing number of the convention members had already held high positions; others later rose to levels of distinction.[4] This unusual body, which the people, motivated by their own needs, had called together for the purpose of framing a system of government, faced the monumental task of forming a state out of unorganized territory acquired from a people who had only recently been subjugated by United States forces. The native Californians, who at the time of the election of the delegates still made up a substantial part of the population, were expected to coöperate in making a constitution that would embody the political theories of their conquerors.

In the little Spanish town of Monterey, these delegates of diverse origins gathered to do their work. The place has been described favorably and beautifully by Bayard Taylor.[5] After giving a picturesque description of its situation and climate, and speaking of its society as remarkably pleasant, Taylor added: "There is a circle of families, American and native, residing there, whose genial and refined social character makes one forget his previous ideas of California life."

The sparse accommodations of the town made the housing of the delegates and visitors quite a problem, but here hospitable citizenry took a hand. They hastily constructed a makeshift hotel and provided a few restaurants. Materials with which to carry on the work of the convention were almost entirely lacking. Colton Hall, in which the delegates met, was, however, a neat and spacious two-story edifice of yellow stone, which had been built by Alcalde Walter Colton as a town hall and schoolhouse. Classes were dismissed, and carpenters made the second story of the building ready for the convention assembly.

No newspapers were published in Monterey—the nearest was in San Francisco—and scarcely any books were available

[4] A complete list of members of the convention, the origin of each, the state in which he last resided, and his occupation are given in J. Ross Browne, *Report of the Debates in the Convention of California, on the Formation of the State Constitution . . . 1849*, pp. 478–479.
[5] See Taylor, *op. cit.*, pp. 133–143.

to which the members could refer for authority in performing their constitutional work. Gwin had with him copies of the constitutions of Iowa and New York, but, except for these, almost the only equipment for making a fundamental body of laws consisted of the abilities and knowledge of an unusual group of men. The lack of a printing press had led Gwin, on the advice of several delegates, to have copies of the constitution of Iowa printed in San Francisco, so that every member might have it before him. The constitution of that state had been selected because it was one of the shortest and most recently adopted.

Lack of a quorum·on September 1 delayed the organization of the convention until Monday, September 3. On September 4, Robert Semple, a pioneer printer of Monterey, was chosen president; William G. Marcy was named as secretary; and William E. P. Hartnell, a linguist of English birth, was selected as interpreter. On September 6, J. Ross Browne, who later became a prolific writer, was elected "Reporter to the Convention." He took down the complete proceedings of the convention and at its end, as directed by the convention, carried through their publication, a task which, as will be seen, he performed with intelligence and thoroughness. Organization was completed by the naming of chaplains: Samuel H. Willey, a Protestant, was to alternate with two Catholic ministers in offering the invocation.

As the convention began its labors, the question at once arose whether a state or a territorial government should be formed. A few delegates from the southern part of the country favored the territorial form, but this advocacy was not strong. In his proclamation calling for the election of delegates, Governor Riley had said, "a convention . . . shall meet and frame a State constitution or a Territorial organization," but it was well known in Monterey that he strongly favored a state constitution. Since most of the delegates also were in favor of statehood, a resolution was quickly adopted, directing the convention to proceed with the formation of a state government. It was decided, also, that instead of a number of committees, which some thought would be desirable, there should be one large standing committee on the constitution, each district being represented on it by two members.[6]

The committee on the constitution was appointed on the afternoon of September 6. It worked expeditiously, and on the next day, Myron Norton, its chairman, reported on Article I, which was the declaration of rights. This, as it was presented, consisted of sixteen sections, eight taken from the constitution of New York and all the rest from that of Iowa. Several days were spent in discussing and amending this declaration. Certain of the sections of the constitution of New York were stricken out and sections from that of Iowa were substituted or added before the declaration of rights reached its final form. Although it was not finally passed until October 10, it is worthy of note that these delegates of the new frontier made a bill of rights the first burden of their thoughts and actions.

In the discussions of several fundamental questions, carried on while the bill of rights was under consideration, the young constitution makers of California demonstrated their versatility, ability, and unexpectedly good mental equipment. Men of twenty-five to thirty years of age argued like seasoned political scientists. This is particularly true with respect to the arguments and the action of the convention in following the stated principles that a bill of rights, when appended to a constitution, should be only declaratory of general fundamental principles, that the objective of the constitution was to organize the government and prescribe the nature and extent of the powers of its several departments, and that legislative enactments could not properly be included in such a document. Again, when they debated at length on the delicate question of the right of suffrage, the delegates clearly showed their superior qualities.

[6] Details of the organization of the convention are recorded in Browne, *op. cit.*, pp. 7–30.

The discussion of the suffrage question brought out sharp differences of opinion in the interpretation of the term "citizen." A statement in Article II of the proposed constitution providing that every white male citizen of the United States "shall be entitled to vote," raised the questions whether this would include Indians, and who were Indians. This led to argument over whether the word "white" should be inserted before the words "male citizens of Mexico," some of the delegates being determined to introduce the race question and exclude Indians. This caused delegate Pablo de la Guerra, an eminent Californian, to insist that some of the first men in the Mexican republic were of the Indian race. But in the end, after various amendments were introduced, debated, stricken out, or retained, it was agreed, in the completed suffrage section, that:

Every white male citizen of the United States, and every white male citizen of Mexico, who shall have elected to become a citizen of the United States, under the treaty of peace exchanged and ratified at Queretaro, on the 30th day of May, 1848, at the age of twenty-one years, who shall have been a resident of the State six months next preceding the election, and the county or district in which he claims his vote thirty days, shall be entitled to vote at all elections which are now or hereafter may be authorized by law: Provided, that nothing herein contained, shall be construed to prevent the Legislature, by a two-thirds concurrent vote, from admitting to the right of suffrage, Indians or the descendants of Indians, in such special cases as such a proportion of the legislative body may deem just and proper.[7]

As important in its implications as any issue raised while the bill of rights was under discussion was the Negro question. The matter came up in connection with and following the adoption of a section on property rights of foreigners who were or might become residents of the state. At the time this section

[7] Full discussion of the subject of suffrage is recorded in *ibid.*, pp. 61-76, 305-307, 323, 340, 341.

was being amended, a delegate moved to insert, as an additional section, one which, from the national standpoint, proved to be the most important statement of the constitution: "Neither slavery, nor involuntary servitude, unless for the punishment of crimes, shall ever be tolerated in this State." Before the section was discussed, an amendment was offered: "nor shall the introduction of free Negroes under indentures or otherwise, be allowed." After debate over the propriety of combining the two questions into a single section, the amendment was withdrawn. Considering what resulted from the prohibition of slavery in California, it is remarkable that the only debate on the slavery exclusion section concerned the part of the constitution in which the particular provision should appear. When its inclusion in the bill of rights was assured, the proposed section excluding slavery was unanimously adopted. This action was a surprise to some, because of current reports that Gwin and others in the convention who had been born in the South were definitely in favor of slavery.

Although the question whether slavery should be allowed in California had been settled, the question whether free Negroes should be permitted to live here was still to be considered. There had been no debate on the slavery issue, but extensive discussion arose over admission of free Negroes. An amendment introduced on this subject on September 11, for inclusion in the bill of rights, was debated for several days. It proposed that "The Legislature shall, at its first session, pass such laws as will effectually prohibit free persons of color from emigrating to and settling in this State, and to effectually prevent the owners of slaves from bringing them into this State for the purpose of setting them free." After attempts at amendment, and a great flow of oratory in which considerable feeling was expressed, the provision was rejected by a vote of thirty-one to eight. Although many definitely were in favor of keeping free Negroes out of California, a general fear existed that an article excluding them might imperil the approval of the constitution by Congress. A strong group, therefore, adhered to the principle that exclusion should be accomplished by law and not through the constitution.[8]

The policy of excluding from the constitution provisions which had no relation to principles of governmental organization was disregarded in the inclusion of a provision forbidding dueling. The section was first included in the declaration of rights, but after much discussion and amendment, it was removed and inserted in the body of the constitution under "Miscellaneous Provisions." It provided that any citizen of the state who should, after the adoption of the constitution, "fight a duel with deadly weapons, or send, or accept a challenge to fight a duel, . . . or knowingly aid or assist in any manner those thus offending," should "not be allowed to hold any office of profit, or to enjoy the right of suffrage." In support of the section it was argued that its inclusion would lift the standards of citizenship, take away a certain license for street fights and other evils, and tend to destroy the belief that dueling and honor were synonymous. The opposition held that a clause in the constitution would not prevent a man from fighting a duel in defense of his honor; that a man would be damned by the public if he would not fight; that the prohibitory clause might deprive the state of the services of good men and great leaders like Clay, Jackson, Benton, and others, who fought duels; and that a man willing to risk his life when his honor was assailed would risk all his rights of citizenship on the same ground. The trite arguments pro and con amount to little in themselves, but they serve to interpret the political and moral mind of lawmakers on a frontier that has had no counterpart in any other area or time in American history.

Lengthy arguments on such a subject, continuing through days, brought out clearly the variance in the mores of the country, as persons from areas with differing codes tried to place in the constitution the standards which prevailed in their sections. In the peculiar frontier community of California, while the

[8] For discussions of the questions of slavery and the free Negro see Browne, *op. cit.*, pp. 43–50, 137–145, 331–340.

transition was taking place in the application of honor codes, inability to harmonize differences resulted in confusion. Although the section forbidding dueling was placed in the constitution, numerous duels were fought in the state after the adoption of the constitution. Even Gwin, an ardent spokesman for the prohibition of duels, participated in one in 1853. The law and the mores were clearly in conflict. As usually happens, the mores proved here the stronger protagonist. The customs of the people concerning the means of preserving a man's honor defeated, in the end, the constitutional provision prohibiting dueling.[9]

Fundamental questions that assumed great importance in the deliberations of the convention were those concerning corporations, state debt, the eastern boundary, and taxation.

The matters of corporations and state debts were discussed at length. Gwin was the chief advocate for restricting the power of the legislature with regard to the creation of state debts, the chartering of banks, and the creation of corporations by special act. While there was unanimity on most of the general questions involved, there was much debate over the manner of expressing their purpose. As to the control of banks, and their issuance of currency, Gwin was quite specific, emulating his old friend and patron, Andrew Jackson, and drawing on his personal experience in the panic of 1837 in warning against loose banks and wildcat currency. Fearing that a loophole might be left that would make possible a "moneyed oligarchy" in California, he pleaded that: "Our country is like a blank sheet of paper, upon which we are required to write a system of fundamental laws. Let the rights of the people be guarded in every line we write, or they will apply the sponge to our work." [10] He meant, in this last, that the instrument adopted by the convention could be rejected at the polls. It is interesting to note that the native Californian members of the convention and the old residents representing the people of the settled

9 For a discussion of dueling see Browne, *op. cit.*, pp. 31, 246–256.
10 Gwin, *op. cit.*, pp. 10–11.

areas of the country, who up to this period had distrusted the motives of Gwin and had feared he would embody in the constitution provisions inimical to their interests and to their constituents, came to his support almost unanimously and henceforward gave him their entire confidence.

The issues of corporations and state debts were finally settled in conformity with the principles set forth by Gwin in his minority report and defended in his speeches. Included in the constitution were articles restricting the legislature in its power to create corporations by special act or to charter banks. The legislature was given the right, however, to make general laws under which associations might be formed for the deposit of gold and silver but without the power to issue paper for circulation as money. The term "corporations" as used in the constitution was to be "construed to include all associations and joint-stock companies, having any of the powers or privileges of corporations not possessed by individuals or partnerships." It was provided that "all corporations shall have the right to sue and shall be subject to be sued, in all courts, in like cases as natural persons"—a significant recognition at this early date that a corporation is a legal person. Another article, on state debts, restricted the legislature from creating a state debt exceeding the amount of $300,000, "except in case of war," or unless some law were passed, and approved by the people at a general election, authorizing a greater expenditure for some special purpose, if ways and means other than loans were provided for the payment of principal and interest.[11]

The most extended discussion in the convention concerned the eastern boundary.[12] The main question was whether the state being created should include within its boundaries only Alta California or all the territory acquired from Mexico by the Treaty of Guadalupe Hidalgo. The proposal which, after

[11] Cardinal Goodwin, *The Establishment of State Government in California* (pp. 177–192) treats fully the convention's action in regard to banks and corporations, using as a source Browne, *op. cit.*, pp. 108–121, 124–137.

[12] The references to and extended discussion of the subject are recorded in Browne, *op. cit.*, pp. 54, 123–124, 167–200, 417–458.

many modifications, came to be known as the "Gwin-Halleck proposal," advocated the inclusion of substantially all the territory acquired from Mexico by the treaty. The plan for a smaller state was embodied in an amendment by W. E. Shannon, proposing a boundary along the Sierra Nevada almost identical with that Riley had described in his proclamation. This line was finally adopted and still is the state boundary.

In his *History of California* (VI, 291), H. H. Bancroft begins his discussion of this subject by saying, "The boundary was more difficult to deal with, introducing the question of slavery in an unexpected phase," and continues with implications that the larger state recommended in the Gwin-Halleck proposal was intended to make slavery extension possible. In making these implications he disregards the fact that an article excluding slavery from California, irrespective of its boundaries, had already been included in the constitution. Other critics of Gwin, particularly writers who dramatize history, have insisted that his advocacy of the larger state made him an arch-villain in a Southern plot, even though he voted for California as a free state.

In the debates, the Gwin-Halleck proposal was opposed on the grounds that the large state would be too big for satisfactory representation; it would invite subdivisions that would be awkward; and it would include the twenty thousand Mormons who were unrepresented in the convention and who had already applied for a territorial government. Both Gwin and Halleck maintained that the immense territory included in their proposition could later be divided into a number of states, and thus perhaps a dozen Senators eventually would represent the Pacific Coast in Congress. There is no evidence that Gwin advocated the larger boundary with the intention of securing advantage to slaveholders by later persuading Congress to split the area horizontally, giving the lion's share to slaveholders. At one time in the convention, the committee of the whole adopted the Gwin-Halleck boundary, yet feared that this would prevent the admission of California by Congress. Substitution of the Shannon proposal, strong debate, particularly by the youthful James McHall Jones, and some manipulation by him, led finally to the adoption of the boundary of the state as we have it at the present time.

An analysis of the boundary controversy, which Theodore H. Hittell, in his *History of California* (II, 768), describes as "the most vexed and exciting of the convention," yields an important historical conclusion. Cardinal Goodwin, in his *Establishment of State Government in California*, has made a systematic study of the whole question. He shows that the debates and the nine votes taken in the convention indicate that, though there were honest differences of opinion about the boundary, the usual supposition "that the extreme eastern boundary was supported by pro-slavery men for the purpose of making California so large that a subsequent division, by an east and west line, would result in the establishment of two large states on the Pacific, one to be dedicated to freedom and the other to slavery," is not substantiated by the facts. Anyone reading the debates objectively must see that, although the members were much confused with respect to procedure, they were for the most part motivated by the desire to do what would help most in obtaining immediate admission of California to statehood. A careful and thorough study of the course of legislative action reveals clearly that no Southern slavery plot inhered in the proposition for the larger boundary. It is noteworthy that in the votes taken on the different boundary proposals the delegates from the Southern states at no time united against members from the North for the purpose of forcing the extreme eastern boundary on the convention. Goodwin's scholarly analysis of the nine votes taken on different forms of the question, in which the names of the voters are recorded, reveals that in the several tallies the voters on each side included both Northerners and Southerners. What is most conclusive is the fact that in every vote taken the majority of the Southern delegates favored the boundary for the smaller state.[13]

The subject of taxation, while somewhat controversial, did not arouse the same degree of excitement or feeling as did the preceding questions. It came up on October 5, when a delegate proposed that the following section be inserted in the constitution:

All lands liable to taxation in this State, shall be taxed in proportion to their value; and this value shall be appraised by officers elected by the qualified electors of the district, county, or town in which the lands to be taxed are situated.[14]

At once, Gwin moved, as a substitute for the proposed section, the following:

Taxation shall be equal and uniform throughout the State. All property in this State shall be taxed in proportion to its value; to be ascertained as directed by law.

Delegate Jones then moved to amend Gwin's proposal by adding to it the following:

But assessors and collectors of town, county, and State taxes, shall be elected by the qualified electors of the district, county, or town in which the property taxed for State, county, or town purposes, is situated.

Although Gwin thought his simple and direct proposal was sufficient, he soon found that it did not satisfy delegates from the settled portions of the state who had great land grants and represented holders of vast grants from Spain and Mexico. These delegates objected to any plan that would subject their real estate to taxation and the burden of supporting the state, and at the same time would permit the greater part of the population, the newcomers, who had no real estate that could be taxed, to enjoy the economic benefits of these taxes, and, because of their numbers, to control politically the government

[13] Goodwin, *op. cit.*, pp. 133–174.
[14] Browne, *op. cit.*, p. 364.

for which the older population would pay. Fearing that the delegates representing the landed interests of the territory would withdraw from the convention and thus cause great damage to it, the members effected a compromise by accepting the amendment of Jones with Gwin's proposal. This gave to the assessors and supervisors elected by the landholders themselves and by those they could influence constitutional power which guaranteed protection against oppressive taxation. Those opposed to the system acquiesced in it rather than obstruct the formation of the constitution, even though they were convinced that, whereas the system could be used to protect the great landholders, it might leave the way open for the oppression of small ones—a defect which it was impossible to avoid at the time.[15]

The constitution declared that government of the state should be divided into three separate departments—the executive, the legislative, and the judicial. It also created subdivisions of these departments and arranged their powers and duties according to the customary form of state organization.

Several provisions of the constitution, which may be grouped because all carry social implications, should be mentioned before leaving the story of constitution making. The first of these had to do with divorce. Concerning this, nothing need be said further than to note the adoption, without debate, of this brief section: "No divorce shall be granted by the Legislature." [16]

The second provision had to do with lotteries. The section introduced on this subject stated, "No lottery shall be authorized by this State, nor shall the sale of lottery tickets be allowed." Efforts were made to strike out this section on the grounds that it would deprive the state of much revenue, restrict future legislatures, and misrepresent the people who had sent delegates to the convention, not to prescribe the amusements in which the inhabitants might or might not indulge, but

[15] The discussion of this subject is recorded in Browne, *op. cit.*, pp. 364–376.

[16] *Ibid.*, p. 90.

to lay down broad and general principles of religious freedom. In support of the section it was argued that something was wrong if a state could not raise revenue without entering into a system of legalized gambling, that the well-being of society was involved, that the state should be prohibited from a practice condemned in individuals, that the convention should limit the powers of the legislature, and that this was a place to begin. The sentiment of the convention, however, was that lotteries should be prohibited, and the section was adopted.[17]

No small degree of interest was manifested in a third section, that of separate property rights for married women. The section on this subject, as finally passed after extended discussion, provided that:

All property, both real and personal, of the wife, owned or claimed by her before marriage, and that acquired afterwards by gift, devise, or descent, shall be her separate property; and laws shall be passed more clearly defining the rights of the wife, in relation as well to her separate property, as to that held in common with her husband. Laws shall also be passed providing for the registration of the wife's separate property.[18]

Against inclusion of the section it was argued that the relative rights of husband and wife were matters involving laws that could more suitably be entrusted to the action of the legislature than to be made a part of the fundamental law of the land; that nature had done what the common law had done, put women under the protection of men, and that the constitution should not experiment with that relationship; that the very principle proposed was contrary to nature and the real interest of the married state; that, according to the principle of the common law as stated by Blackstone, "By marriage, husband and wife are one in law"; that setting up two heads in one house would fill the courts and senate chambers with applications for divorces; and that, since under the common law a man came into possession not only of his wife's property but of her

[17] Browne, *op. cit.*, pp. 90–93.
[18] *Ibid.*, p. 257. The subject is discussed further on pp. 257–269.

debts, the enactment of the section providing for separate property would enable dishonest husbands to protect their property against bills of execution for debt, by fixing it as the separate property of the wives.

In support of this section it was argued that, since in California the civil law is the law of the land and under it the rights of wives are protected, failure to secure and guarantee the rights of the wife to her separate property would be "a very decided invasion upon the people of California." Henry W. Halleck in his defense of the section said that, although he was "not wedded either to the common law or the civil law, nor as yet to a woman," he did have hopes of being wedded sometime, and would, therefore, advocate including this section in the constitution as an "inducement for women of fortune to come to California" and "the very best provision for getting wives that we can introduce into the constitution." He called upon all bachelors in the convention to vote for it. Others argued for the section because it had been the law of the country; because, in this advancing age, state after state had adopted the principle; because the marriage contract is a civil contract, with the law prescribing the rights of the contracting parties, and therefore one party should not be put into the position of having to relinquish rights and property in contracting marriage; and because women should not be subject to despotic provisions of the common law but rather should have the protection of a simple law which anyone could understand. The adoption of the proposed section is evidence of the vision and liberalism of the constitution makers of California.

The last in the group of provisions having special implications is the article on education. The members of the convention were consistently liberal and forward looking in their attempts to make adequate provision for the education of California's youth. Of the four sections on this subject, the first provided for the election, every three years, of a superintendent of public instruction. The second significantly asserted in its opening statement: "The Legislature shall encourage, by all suitable means, the promotion of intellectual, scientific, moral, and agricultural improvement." The section provided for receiving the proceeds of lands given by the United States for the support of schools, as well as all estates of persons who died without leaving a will or heir, and it declared that such other means as the legislature might provide should be "inviolably appropriated to the support of common schools throughout the State." The third section required the maintenance of a school in each school district for at least three months of the year. Section four provided that "The Legislature shall take measures for the protection, improvement, or other disposition of such lands as have been, or may hereafter be reserved or granted by the United States, or any person or persons to the State for the use of a University." It also provided that "funds accruing from the rents or sale of such lands, or from any other source," for the purpose stated, should make a permanent fund, the interest of which should be applied to the support of the university "with such branches as the public convenience may demand, for the promotion of literature, the arts and sciences, as may be authorized by the terms of such grant." [19]

After the convention had settled the important questions and had passed, after a third reading, the preamble and articles of the constitution, in the night session of October 10, the convention met on Thursday, October 11, for the purpose of clearing up a number of routine matters preparatory to adjournment at the earliest possible time. On this day a resolution was passed providing that certified copies of the constitution, in English and in Spanish, be presented to the "present executive of California," and that eight thousand copies in English and two thousand copies in Spanish be ordered to be printed and circulated, together with a short address to the people of California upon the importance of the constitution and its ratification.

Earlier, a resolution had been passed providing that the

[19] Browne, *op. cit.,* pp. 202–211.

sum of one thousand dollars be paid to Caleb Lyon to superintend the engraving of "The Great Seal of the State of California." The design offered by Lyon, and which was adopted, was one which had been drawn by Major Robert S. Garnett and to which Lyon had made additions. Few persons have examined the seal to note its artistry and emblematic character. Lyon described it thus:

Around the bend of the ring are represented thirty-one stars. . . . The foreground figure represents the goddess Minerva having sprung full grown from the brain of Jupiter. . . . [emblematic of] the political birth of the State of California, without having gone through the probation of a territory. At her feet crouches a grisly bear feeding upon the clusters from a grape vine . . . A miner is engaged with his rocker and bowl at his side, illustrating the golden wealth of the Sacramento, upon whose waters are seen shipping, . . . snow-clad peaks of the Sierra Nevada make up the background, while above is the Greek motto "Eureka," (I have found [it]) applying either to the principle involved in the admission of the State, or the success of the miner at work.[20]

The question of convention expenses was taken care of in an unprecedented manner. It had been agreed that each member would be given $16 per day and $16 for each mile that he traveled, and that officers of the convention would be given additional compensation. An appropriation of $10,000 was voted, to be used by J. Ross Browne in printing and publishing "for the use of the State, 1,000 copies in English and 250 copies in Spanish, of a stenographic report of the proceedings of the Convention." On the last day of the convention a resolution was unanimously adopted granting to General Riley an annual salary of $10,000 for his term of office as governor, and to Captain Halleck as secretary of state a salary of $6,000 per year. There had been discussion of various plans for meeting the expenses of the convention and of starting the new government, which would be *sans* everything in its beginning. The problem of convention expenses was solved arbitrarily by

[20] *Ibid.*, p. 304.

Governor Riley, who had early made it known that he intended to pay them from the "civil fund," a fund that had accumulated from the collection of duties during the interregnum. When the delegates and other officers visited the governor in a body, he paid the sums that had been agreed upon. As to the expenses of the new government, Gwin had presented earlier in the convention a proposal to lay before Congress a memorial calling for the support of a state government, either by turning over to the state a part of the public domain, or by appropriating a sufficient amount from the customs collected in California and the proceeds of the sale of public lands. At the night session, the next to the last session before adjournment, Gwin again made such a proposal, and this, after slight amendment and much debate, was passed.

At a short session on Friday, October 12, two resolutions were adopted and an announcement was made. The first resolution was an expression of thanks from the convention to Robert Semple for his services as chairman. The second directed that a committee be appointed to transmit a copy of the constitution to General Riley for transmission to the President of the United States. The announcement, made by the president of the convention, was that he had received official notice from General Riley that a national salute would be fired, by his order, when the constitution adopted by the convention was signed.

The convention adjourned at an early hour until the next morning, so that the hall could be prepared for a celebration ball to be held that evening, and to allow time for the convention members to get themselves ready for it. By contributions of $25 each, the members raised the sum of $1,100 for the entertainment. The cleared hall was decorated with young pines from the forest. Three improvised chandeliers gave brilliant light for the festivities. In addition to the convention members, sixty or seventy gentlemen and an equal number of ladies were present. In the words of Bayard Taylor in his *Eldorado:*

The dark-eyed daughters of Monterey, Los Angeles and Santa Barbara mingled in pleasing contrast with the fairer bloom of the trans-Nevadian belles. The variety of feature and complexion was fully equalled by the variety of dress. In the whirl of the waltz, a plain, dark nun-like robe would be followed by pink satin and gauze; next, perhaps, a bodice of scarlet velvet with gold buttons, and then a rich figured brocade, such as one sees on the stately dames of Titian.[21]

Although the costumes of the gentlemen showed great variety, they were much less picturesque. Speaking of his own and other costumes, Taylor said, "Scarcely a single dress that was seen belonged entirely to its wearer, and I thought, if the clothes had the power to leap back respectively to their several owners, some persons would have been in a state of utter destitution." In spite of all the difficulties, the company was well-mannered and respectable, and in the words of Taylor, "Perhaps the genial, unrestrained social spirit that possessed all present would have been less had there been more uniformity of costumes." The music was spirited, the dance directed gallantly by the floor manager, Don Pablo de la Guerra, his handsome, aristocratic features and dignified manner reflecting the grave, stately courtesy which had been handed down from the old Spanish times. This gathering was symbolic of the successful mingling of American and Californian life and institutions. Men of the United States, from the North and from the South, had met with representatives of the Californians to draw up a fundamental document of law for the land, and had completed a framework of government reasonably satisfactory to all; they sealed all this by a night of festivity, participated in by the convention members, augmented by other Americans and Californians. It was an occasion of historical importance.

Morning came—Saturday, October 13, 1849. In the happiest humor the convention met to perform its last duty—the signing of the constitution. A vote of thanks was given Governor Riley for the kindness and courtesy which had marked his

[21] Taylor, *op. cit.*, p. 160.

association, private and official, with the members of the body. The address to the people of California was read and unanimously adopted. At two o'clock in the afternoon, the convention members in an excited mood gathered to finish their work. The resolution providing salaries for Riley and Halleck was passed unanimously. Also unanimously passed was a resolution "that the members of this convention will wait on Governor Riley in a body after signing the constitution." Because Chairman Semple was in feeble health, the convention, on motion of Gwin, requested that J. A. Sutter address Governor Riley on behalf of the members at that time. As a final act, the members proceeded to sign the enrolled constitution.

When the delegates began affixing their signatures, at a given signal the United States colors were run up the flagstaff in front of the government buildings, and a salute of thirty-one guns began to boom from the near-by fort. At the same time, the flags from the different headquarters and aboard the ships in the port were unfurled and run up. Sutter in excitement sprang from his seat, waved his hand round his head as if swinging a sword, and exclaimed: "Gentlemen, this is the happiest day of my life. It makes me glad to hear those cannon . . . Yes, I am glad to hear them—this is a great day for California!" As the signing of the constitution proceeded, and as the national salute was being fired, the captain of the English bark *Volunteer*, which lay in the harbor, ran a line of colors up the spar, with the American flag, which he had received from shore only that morning, flying triumphantly from the main-topmast. At the loud boom of the thirty-first gun someone shouted, "That's for California!" and the members of the convention gave three hearty cheers for the new state.[22]

On adjournment, the members proceeded in a body to Governor Riley's home. There Sutter addressed him with impressive dignity, expressing the thanks of the convention for his services to the people of California. With tears in his eyes and blunt sincerity in his voice and manner, Riley said in reply:

[22] Taylor, *op. cit.*, p. 164.

Gentlemen: I never made a speech in my life. I am a soldier—but I can *feel;* and I do feel deeply the honor you have this day conferred upon me. . . . I thank you all from my heart. . . . You have formed a constitution worthy of California. And I have no fear for California while her people choose their representatives so wisely. Gentlemen, I congratulate you upon the successful conclusion of your arduous labors; and I wish you all happiness and prosperity.

Browne in his *Debates* records that at this point the members interrupted Riley by giving three cheers for him "as Governor of California," and three more "as a gallant soldier, and worthy of his country's glory." The cheering ended, and Riley concluded with gracious words for another. He said:

I have but one thing to add, gentlemen, and that is, that my success in the affairs of California is mainly owing to the efficient aid rendered me by Captain Halleck, the Secretary of State. He has stood by me in all emergencies; to him I have always appealed when at a loss myself; and he has never failed me.[23]

The convention members indicated their approval of this recognition of Halleck's services by giving three resounding cheers for the secretary of state.

Bayard Taylor, under the inspiration of the occasion, wrote these words, sentimental to be sure, but impressive and prophetic: ". . . and were I a believer in omens, I would augur from the tranquil beauty of this evening—from the clear sky and the lovely sunset hues on the waters of the bay—more than all, from the joyous expression of every face I see—a glorious and prosperous career for the State of California." [24]

The constitution signed at this time in the primitive town by the western sea was to remain the fundamental law of California for thirty years. It did not institute a government in California which in a perfect sense derived its "just powers from the consent of the governed." It did, however, embody within its articles many of the provisions for personal freedom

[23] These ceremonies are described in Browne, *op. cit.,* pp. 476–477.
[24] Taylor, *op. cit.,* p. 168.

and individual protection that had been sought through centuries of conflict by the forebears of those who drew up the Declaration of Independence. To a surprising degree, considering all the circumstances, the makers of the constitution of California, drawn from all sections of the Union, laid aside their sectional, class, and race prejudices. All through the deliberations of the convention are found evidences of the democratizing influences of the frontier upon the men assembled. For the times, their product was a remarkably liberal constitution. By including clauses protecting the property rights of wives, providing for an elective judiciary, prohibiting slavery, and by refusing to exclude free Negroes, the convention gave promise of progressiveness and freedom. The work that the group accomplished was a magnificent illustration of the capacity for self-government possessed by the newcomers to the Pacific Coast.

III

"The Legislature of a Thousand Drinks"

> *Old Thomas Jefferson Green . . . would say, 'Well boys, let's go and take a thousand drinks' . . . and so the Legislature gained that cognomen, though there was very little dissipation among the members in general compared to some legislatures of later days . . . —*ELISHA OSCAR CROSBY, *Memoirs*

ON THE DAY before the last day of the constitutional convention, Henry A. Tefft offered the following resolution as a preliminary to ratification of the constitution:

Resolved, That certified copies of this constitution in English and Spanish, be presented to the present Executive of California, and that 8,000 copies in English, and 2,000 copies in Spanish, be ordered to be printed and circulated.[1]

On the same day, October 12, the governor issued a "Proclamation to the People of California," in which he stated:

[1] J. Ross Browne, *Report of the Debates in the Convention of California on the Formation of the State Constitution . . . 1849,* p. 462. The governor's proclamation of October 12 is in the Appendix, p. iii.

47

The time and manner of voting on this Constitution, and of holding the first general election, are clearly set forth in the Schedule; the whole subject is therefore left for your unbiased and deliberate consideration. . . . The people are now called upon to form a government for themselves, and to designate such officers as they desire to make and execute the laws.

The "Schedule," which was appended to the constitution, stated that the constitution should be "submitted to the people, for their ratification or rejection, at the general election to be held on Tuesday, the thirteenth day of November next." It also provided that the governor should direct "the Prefects of the several districts, or in case of vacancy, the Sub-Prefects, or senior Judge of first Instance, to cause such election to be held" on the day prescribed, in the respective districts.[2] On the same day there should be elected a governor, a lieutenant governor, members of the legislature, and two members of Congress. If the constitution should be ratified at the election, the legislature should assemble at the seat of government on the fifteenth day of the next December to complete the organization of that body by the election of officers ordered by the constitution, and within four days after its organization it should elect two Senators to represent California in the Congress of the United States.

As soon as the constitution had been completed and signed, this document and the proclamation which was to accompany it were dispatched posthaste by Henry W. Halleck, as secretary of state, to San Francisco, with directions that the English and Spanish versions should be printed in pamphlet form for circulation among the people. Printing was begun at once at the office of the *Alta California.* Because of the early date of the election, November 13, publication was hurried. As the documents came from the press they were sent out and distributed as rapidly as possible, most of the English copies going to the northern districts and most of the Spanish ones to the districts in the south.[3]

[2] Browne, *op. cit.*, Appendix, pp. xii–xiii.
[3] *Ibid.*, Appendix, p. xliv.

The governor, prefects, and others took the responsibility of seeing that the districts designated for election purposes were properly organized, that copies of the constitution were distributed, and that preparations were made for election day. Little work was required to convince the people of the necessity of ratifying the constitution. More difficult were the tasks of getting information to the unorganized population and setting up and putting into operation the necessary election machinery, yet they were successfully accomplished.

As an illustration of the procedure, and as an example of unexcelled zeal, the activities of Elisha O. Crosby stand out. Appointed as prefect for Sacramento by Governor Riley on the request of delegates from that district, just as the convention was breaking up, Crosby at once set out overland by way of San Jose and San Francisco. On arriving at San Francisco he found the constitution and address nearly ready. When copies were available, he took his quota and went by steamer to Sacramento. Assisted by three subprefects, whom he appointed, he established fifty-two precincts north of the Cosumnes River and east of the Sacramento. He would ride into a camp, or any place where he found enough people to warrant the establishment of a precinct, and would appoint any three who might be suggested as the proper persons to hold the election. After they had been sworn in, he would leave copies of the constitution for them to examine and to show to the people, and would leave instructions for the precincts to send their election returns to him at Sacramento. Forty-nine precincts brought in returns, which were passed on to Monterey before the board of canvassers canvassed the votes there on December 10.[4]

For the various political offices to be filled there were of course many aspirants, and candidates began active campaigning as soon as the convention adjourned. Most candidates ran for office independently. The only attempt to organize a party or to fight the battle upon the old issue of Democrat versus

[4] Elisha Oscar Crosby, *Memoirs*, pp. 52–55.

Whig was in San Francisco. There the Democrats held California's first political mass meeting, on October 25, 1849. The attendance was so large that the meeting was compelled to adjourn from the hall where it had assembled, to the public square. In a prefatory statement, the meeting resolved "That *partyism* for the sake of party merely we totally reject." The assemblage passed resolutions favoring California and the Union, and tritely declared that "we are for our country first, our country last, and our country all the time." It also appointed a nominating committee. On October 27 an adjourned meeting was held in Portsmouth Square for the purpose of receiving the report of this committee; but because of objections that the appointment of the committee was not in accordance with the time-honored usages of the Democratic party, it was suggested that a meeting should be held on the following Monday, to elect, by party vote, eleven delegates whose duty it should be to select a party ticket. It was then resolved that the candidates nominated be pledged to vote for no man for United States Senator unless he would "uphold exemption of household for debt, and would vote for the formation of a railroad to our own territory in preference to any other." No further action seems to have been taken toward making nominations.[5]

Another large meeting was held in Sacramento on October 25 to discuss the new constitution and the candidates to be voted for in November. In the midst of futile discussion concerning future meetings and nominations, a motion was carried unanimously to submit to the people, on the day of election, the whole subject of selecting candidates. Four days later a nonpartisan political meeting was held in the same city, to hear the report of delegates to the constitutional convention and to consider matters connected with the approaching election. This meeting chose a committee to nominate a legislative ticket for the district, but took no further action. Many small, informal,

[5] Proceedings of these meetings are recorded in Winfield J. Davis, *History of Political Conventions in California, 1849–1892.*

nonpartisan gatherings were held, of course, in other places, at which the constitution and candidates were discussed.

In the nomination of candidates there was not a great deal of formality. A public meeting was held at Monterey on October 30, at which a nominating committee was appointed. This committee tendered the nomination for governor to General Bennett Riley. When he declined it, they named W. Scott Sherwood to run for the office. For lieutenant governor, the committee nominated Francis J. Lippitt; and for Congressmen, Edward Gilbert and James L. Ord. Candidates who ran independently for governor were: Peter H. Burnett, John A. Sutter, W. M. Steuart, and John W. Geary. Among the independent candidates for lieutenant governor were John McDougal, Richard Roman, John B. Frisbie, A. M. Winn, and Pablo de la Guerra. There were a number of other candidates for the principal offices, some of whom had been endorsed or recommended by public meetings in different parts of the state; [6] but to a large extent the candidates carried on their campaigns independently and seem to have confined their efforts mainly to the mining regions.

Bayard Taylor, a traveler and man of letters who was roving about California at this time, gives in his *Eldorado* picturesque examples of voters and the political activities of candidates for office. In the campaign period, on his second trip to the Lower Bar of the Mokelumne, Taylor was accosted by a Dr. Gillette, whom he had met in the previous summer. Describing what took place, he says:

After the first salutations were over, he conducted me to Mr. James' tent, where I found my old comrade, Col. Lyons, about sitting down to a smoking dinner of beef, venison and tortillas. Dr. Gwin, one of the candidates for U.S. Senator, had just arrived, and was likewise the guest of Mr. James. . . .

After dinner, Mr. Morse, of New Orleans, candidate for Con-

[6] Davis, *op. cit.*, p. 5; Cardinal Goodwin, *The Establishment of State Government in California*, pp. 250–251; Bancroft, *History of California*, VI, 304–305.

gress, and Mr. Brooks, of New York, for the Assembly, made their appearance. We had a rare knot of politicians. Col. Lyons was a prominent candidate for the State Senate, and we only lacked the genial presence of Col. Steuart, and the jolly one of Capt. McDougal (who were not far off, somewhere in the diggings,) to have had all the offices represented, from the Governor downwards. After dinner, we let down the curtains of the little tent, stretched ourselves out on the blankets, lighted our cigars and went plump into a discussion of California politics. Each of the candidates had his bundle of tickets, his copies of the Constitution and his particular plans of action. As it happened there were no two candidates for the same office present, the discussion was carried on in perfect harmony and with a feeling of good-fellowship withal.[7]

It is safe to assume that political scenes similar to this were enacted again and again in the well-populated mining areas.

Of some of the voters and their reasons for choosing the candidates from the lists, nearly all of whom were entirely unknown, Taylor gives a description that is both amusing and illuminating. He says:

Names, in many instances, were made to stand for principles; accordingly, a Mr. Fair got many votes. One of the candidates, who had been on the river a few days previous, wearing a high-crowned silk hat, with narrow brim, lost about twenty votes on that account. Some went no further than to vote for those they actually knew. One who took the opposite extreme, justified himself in this wise:—"When I left home," said he, "I was determined to *go it blind*. I went it blind in coming to California, and I'm not going to stop now. I voted for the Constitution, and I've never seen the Constitution. I voted for all the candidates, and I don't know a damned one of them. I'm going it blind all through, I am."

The rainy season of 1849–50 began earlier than usual and was exceptionally severe. Election day, November 13, dawned wet and cheerless; the vote consequently was light. In many of the mining areas not more than half of the number entitled

[7] Bayard Taylor, *Eldorado*, p. 237. The quotation given below is from pp. 252–253.

to vote were at the polls; some stayed away because of indifference and lack of information, others remained in their tents because of the rain, while many could not even get to the polls because of high water or unfathomable mud. Under such conditions the first American election in California took place.

The "Schedule" had provided for careful counting of the ballots and the transmission of the returns to the secretary of state by December 10.[8] It required that a board of canvassers, consisting of the secretary of state and three other officers, should compare the election tallies and publish on that day an abstract of the results in one or more newspapers of California. It further provided that, immediately after ascertaining that the constitution had been ratified by the people, the governor should proclaim the fact and declare the ratified constitution to be the law of the land.

The canvass of the votes in this epochal election took place as scheduled on December 10. It showed that Peter H. Burnett had been elected governor by a vote of 6,783 against 3,220 for W. Scott Sherwood, his nearest competitor. John McDougal had been elected lieutenant governor, and G. W. Wright and Edward Gilbert Representatives in Congress. The most important result announced on December 10 was the ratification of the constitution by a vote of 12,061 in its favor, to 811 against.[9] Two days later, and three days before the meeting of the elected legislature, Governor Riley issued a proclamation stating that the constitution had been ratified by an almost unanimous vote of the electors and that therefore he proclaimed it to be "ordained and established as the Constitution of California."[10]

California's first legislature met at San Jose on Saturday,

[8] Browne, *op. cit.*, Appendix, p. xii.

[9] Summaries of election results are given in Bancroft, *op. cit.*, pp. 305–306; Davis, *op. cit.*, p. 5; Goodwin, *op. cit.*, pp. 252–253. Detailed results of voting on the constitution may be found in "Election Returns for 1849" (MS in California State Library archives).

[10] Browne, *op. cit.*, Appendix, p. xlvi. Governor Burnett's proclamation of December 20 and Riley's orders relinquishing his administration of civil affairs are on the same page.

December 15, 1849. On roll call, it was found that only six senators of the sixteen elected, and only fourteen of the thirty-six members of the assembly, were present to answer to their names. Because of the lack of a quorum both houses adjourned until the following Monday, when thirteen senators and thirty-two assemblymen were present. After each house had organized in accordance with constitutional provision and had sent to the governor-elect and to Governor Riley official information of what had been done, it adjourned until the next day.

On Tuesday, December 18, 1849, the assembly and senate, meeting in convention, examined the returns of the election for governor, lieutenant governor, and Congressmen. On the next day a joint committee notified the governor-elect that the two houses were organized and would proceed to the inauguration as soon as it was convenient for him, and informed Governor Riley that the legislature was ready to receive from him any communication that he might desire to make.

Riley's reply came on the following day, December 20, the inauguration day of Governor Burnett, in the form of a proclamation to the people of California. In it he said: "A new Executive having been elected and installed into office, in accordance with the provisions of the Constitution of the State, the undersigned hereby resigns his powers as Governor of California." At the same time, Riley issued military orders relinquishing his administration of civil affairs in California to the new government, and relieved Halleck from further duty as secretary of state.

At one o'clock in the afternoon of the same day, the two houses met in convention in the hall of the assembly, the president pro tempore of the senate, E. K. Chamberlain, presiding. The governor and lieutenant governor were sworn in by Kimball H. Dimmick, judge of the court of first instance of San Jose. Governor Burnett made an inaugural address, and the convention was then dissolved. When the senate assembled in its own meeting place, John McDougal, the lieutenant governor, assumed his duties as president of that body and also made an address.[11] It is doubtful whether the addresses received much attention, for the members were keenly interested and even excited over the impending election of United States Senators.

At five o'clock that afternoon, the hour appointed for the election, the two houses assembled again in convention, the lieutenant governor presiding. Seven candidates seriously considered for the Senate were: Thomas Butler King, Thomas J. Henley, John W. Geary, Robert B. Semple, Henry W. Halleck, John C. Frémont, and William M. Gwin. The glamorous Frémont received a majority of the votes cast on the first ballot, and Gwin a majority on the third. They were declared elected, and the joint convention dissolved.[12] When a drawing was made to determine which of the two elected Senators should serve the full term, Gwin was the lucky one. His term, therefore, was for six years, and Frémont's was for two. The popularity which won the election for Frémont came from his fame as a "pathfinder," his connection with the conquest of California, and his subsequent trial in Washington, in which the sympathies of the people were with him. Gwin received fewer votes than Frémont because some persons were jealous of him for political reasons, some distrusted him, and others felt that he was selfishly ambitious. His qualities of leadership had, however, won for him a great deal of approval; and the fact that he was from the South and acquainted with leaders in that section made him an important instrument for securing recognition for California by Congress.

The pueblo in which the legislature held its first sessions had been made the capital of California by the constitutional convention. The section of the constitution headed "Miscellaneous Provisions" had prescribed that "the first session of the Legislature shall be held at the Pueblo de San Jose; which

[11] A complete list of members of the first legislature and the details of its first meeting are given in Goodwin, *op. cit.*, pp. 254–260; Bancroft, *op. cit.*, pp. 309–310.

[12] California, *Journal of the Senate*, 1st sess., 1850, pp. 23–24.

place shall be the permanent seat of government, until removed by law." [13] This provision had been placed in the constitution after Charles White and James Reed, who had come to the convention to speak for the people of San Jose, had urged the suitability of that town for the capital. What San Jose actually furnished for the legislative session was a crude building, sixty feet long, forty feet wide, and two stories in height, still under construction as the legislative session began. Dissatisfaction over the incompleteness of the arrangements led to a conference of a legislative committee with a committee of San Jose citizens. After deliberation, the conference reported that the building in which the meetings were being held was the only one available. A bill was introduced on the nineteenth to remove the capital to Monterey, but, though it passed its first reading, it was laid over and the business of the session was allowed to proceed.

On December 21, the day on which he submitted, in his first written communication to the senate, the nomination of Assemblyman William Van Voorhies as secretary of state, Governor Burnett transmitted his first annual message to both houses of the legislature.[14] In this, in addition to touching on a number of miscellaneous and necessary organizational matters, he dealt at length with a series of issues which he considered so basic as to require the most careful consideration of the men who represented the people.

The first issue, one on which the governor had a settled opinion, was the question whether the legislature should proceed at once to the business of lawmaking, "or await the action of Congress upon the question of our admission into the Union." On the ground that one of the powers reserved to a state, or to the people in it, was the right to regulate the internal affairs of the state, and that the general government had no authority over such affairs, the governor maintained the right of California to proceed at once as a self-governing dominion.

[13] Browne, *op. cit.*, Appendix, p. x.
[14] California, *Journal of the Senate*, 1850, pp. 30–41.

He supported this position by citing Missouri and Michigan as commonwealths which had organized and legislated for themselves before their admission into the Union, and he claimed that California had the same rights.

With the legislature's authority to proceed with lawmaking settled in his own mind, the governor believed that the adoption of civil and criminal codes of law was of immediate importance. California, it seemed to him, was in a position to adopt the most improved and most enlightened codes of law to be found in any of the states. As far as they were applicable to conditions in California, he recommended for adoption the English common law defining crimes and misdemeanors, the English law of evidence, the English commercial law, the Louisiana civil code, and the Louisiana code of practice. His idea was to combine the best features and omit the objectionable ones of both the civil and the common law.

Governor Burnett next dwelt at length upon what he referred to as "the grave and delicate subject of revenue." His estimate was that the current expenses of the state government for the first year would exceed a half million dollars. He recommended a poll tax and a property tax, and also recommended that, because miners frequently moved from place to place, the revenue law should be so framed as to require the collector to accompany the assessor, in order to facilitate the collection of taxes and to avoid loss. Because most of the agricultural lands were in the hands of a few persons, "who suffer them to remain wild and uncultivated," the governor urged that a law for the taxation of lands held in large tracts should be passed and rigidly enforced, not only for the purpose of raising revenue but also to stimulate the owners to divide and sell some of their holdings. He anticipated that native Californians might at first object to such a system of taxation, since the Mexican government had never derived any revenue from California except that produced by a high tariff on imports. He believed, however, that they would become accustomed to the new method, which would tax the property irrespective of its owner, increase the value of their property, and do away with high duties on imports.

The governor was firmly of the opinion that Negroes should not be admitted into the state. He philosophized that "a wise legislator adapts his action to circumstances," that he "must take mankind and society as he finds them, not as he would make them," and should act accordingly. Having been brought up in a slave state, Burnett disliked the presence of free Negroes. In Oregon, in 1844, he had introduced a measure against Negroes which was finally incorporated into the constitution of that state. Now, in California, he felt that if a measure excluding black slaves was popular, the excluding of black freemen would be more so. In support of his position he argued that California's commercial and mineral attractions would bring swarms of "free people of color" to its shores; that the natural increase in population in the states east of the Rocky Mountains would tend to render the value of slave labor so small that slaves would be liberated in the slave states and contracts would be made with them to work cheaply for a number of years in California, unless they were kept out; and that if the Negroes were permitted to come in they would inevitably be consigned to a subordinate and degraded position, which would make them enemies of the society and government of the state. He therefore urged laws for the exclusion of free Negroes, holding that a state had the right to prevent immigration of any class of population considered injurious to its people.

The governor, in his message, gave briefer consideration to a number of other pressing questions. To facilitate the immediate functioning of the state in all its parts, he recommended that arrangements should at once be made for the election of all judicial and political officers provided for by the constitution; that the inconvenience and distress experienced by the inhabitants of many towns "for want of an efficient city government" be remedied as soon as possible by the passage of some general laws applicable to the organization of cities and incorporated towns; and that for convenient administration of judicial, property, and political matters, laws should at once be passed for the division of the state into counties. In concluding his first message to the legislature, the governor emphasized the vast amount of labor which that body would have to perform and the great responsibility of the task of making the new state an efficient and self-governing unit. He recommended, as means to advance and make stable its prosperity, that expenditures be confined within due bounds, and that the young state be kept out of debt and made "punctual and just in all her engagements." He predicted that California would have either a brilliant destiny "or one the most sordid and degraded," and that the state would be "marked by strong and decided characteristics." And he pledged that he would coöperate cordially with the legislature in its efforts toward achieving for the state a "brilliant destiny and irreproachable reputation."

The senate adopted a resolution that the governor's message be printed: one thousand copies in English and five hundred in Spanish for the use of the senate itself, and five hundred additional copies in English for distribution among the Senators and Representatives in Congress and presentation to the President of the United States.

In his message, the governor had called attention to the legislature's constitutional obligation to name various state officers, and to the advisability of their being named as early as possible. In joint convention, the legislature elected these officials on the following day, December 22. The next immediate responsibility of the lawmakers was to pass acts defining the duties of the constitutional officers of the state, such as the comptroller, treasurer, secretary of state, attorney general, and surveyor general. In drawing up these provisions the legislators experienced little difficulty, because they had the constitutions of older states as guides and models. More than a little trouble and controversy were involved, however, in creating and providing for the offices of state printer and state translator. A provision of the constitution that all laws and regulations should be published in Spanish as well as in English made a translator necessary. Action with respect to these offices was complicated by the touchy question, how, and for what, should public money be used? Even after the office of state printer had been created and a printer elected, some persons urged that the statutes and journals be printed in the eastern states rather than in California, on the ground that eastern printers would do the work better and at less cost. After investigation and consideration it was decided that, for reasons of public policy, the public printing should be done in the state, by state officers, and under state supervision. With modification of the laws from time to time, this practice has continued through the years without interruption.

The office of state translator was a cause of trouble even before it was created. Since, for a qualified person, the work was easy and lucrative, there was much competition for the post, and much time elapsed before one of the many candidates secured enough votes for election. Results in general were not satisfactory, and at the next session of the legislature the office was abolished. From that time the translating was done by contract. With the rapid infiltration of the English-speaking population, Californians by necessity as well as choice became more and more acquainted with the English language, and the Spanish translations finally became a useless burden. As a result, the provisions of the first constitution requiring Spanish translations, as well as the laws permitting legal proceedings in Spanish in certain parts of the state, were left out of the constitution of 1879.

At the time the governor presented his message, and the senate adopted the resolution to print numerous copies of it, California had no revenue, and the legislature had not even half a sheet of paper on which to write its first resolution; it had no inkstand, no pen, and no means of purchasing them. Members of the legislature would say, "Mr. President, we want some paper [on which] to keep the minutes," or, "We want a journal book." The lieutenant governor could only reply, "I have not got any," or facetiously say, "Mr. Sergeant-at-Arms, will you supply the senate with the necessary stationery." [15] A joint resolution, that the secretary of state, comptroller, judges of the supreme court, and other state officers should have power to procure the necessary blankbooks, stationery, and furniture for their offices, failed to pass. The weather, their accommodations, and their sore needs were enough to dampen the ardor of legislators, but they continued their work, with only three days of the Christmas holidays for recreation. Their spirits were perhaps lightened somewhat by a ball given for them in the assembly chamber on December 27 by the citizens of San Jose, to which "came the beauty and chivalry of California, at least as much of it as could get there through a drenching rain, on a Liliputian steamboat, from Benicia, and by whatever means they had from other directions." [16]

With conditions as they were at the beginning of the legislative session, finance was one of the pressing subjects to be considered. Even before it had received the governor's recommendations, the assembly, on December 20, had passed a resolution directing the committee of ways and means to study methods of raising the necessary funds for supporting the civil government of the state for a year and for liquidating the debt which would thus be incurred, and to make a report on the most practicable method. On the day the governor submitted his recommendations, the assembly authorized the same committee to inquire of General Riley whether he had any money belonging to the state which he would be willing to turn over to the state authorities. The senate, on the following day, appointed a committee for the same purpose. Also, on that day, Madison Walthall, chairman of the ways and means committee of the assembly, reported that Riley had said that he had neither money nor evidences of debt belonging to the state, but that

[15] Crosby, *op. cit.*, p. 59.
[16] Bancroft, *op. cit.*, p. 315.

he had written to the proper department at Washington for instructions concerning the several hundred thousand dollars that he had "under his control," which he thought might belong to the state, and that as soon as he received a reply he would communicate with the legislature.[17] Not only was Riley unable to get favorable action on the fund he had in hand, but, as it later turned out, these monies were never paid to California.

The first bill on finance passed by the legislature was an act authorizing the borrowing, on the faith and credit of the state, of money to pay the immediate demands on the treasury until a permanent fund could be raised for the purpose. As it was passed on January 5, after having been introduced on December 24 and subsequently amended, the bill provided that the state treasurer should receive proposals in writing, until noon of January 25, 1850, "from any and all persons to loan to this State a sum of money not exceeding two hundred thousand dollars, for a term not more than twelve nor less than six years, payable at the pleasure of the State at any time after six years." Unfortunately, sufficient care had not been exercised in drawing up the bill; and on January 26, Thomas J. Green, chairman of the senate committee on finance,[18] reported that, upon more careful examination, deficiencies had been found in it that made it a nonfunctioning measure.

Green, in conformity with an agreement made at the time of his adverse report, submitted, on January 28, a document dealing with both the subject of taxation and that of obtaining a temporary loan. Since, in regard to taxation, the constitution provided that "all property in this state shall be taxed in proportion to its value," Green maintained that the ad valorem principle here imposed would develop resources such as "no state ever witnessed," and that means of payment of the taxes

---

[17] See Goodwin, *op. cit.*, pp. 269–270. The quotation in the next paragraph is from *ibid.*, p. 271.

[18] Bancroft, *op. cit.*, p. 315, describes Green as "the irrepressible senator to whom everything was a huge joke, who had been elected in a frolic, and thought legislation a comedy."

would be easy because the new state was very rich in resources. He recommended that both the assessment and collection of taxes should be made in July, 1850, and expressed the belief that taxes might be imposed which by the end of July would produce an income of from $600,000 to $700,000.[19]

Some of the taxation recommendations drawn up by Green in consultation with the ways and means committee of the assembly were embodied in two bills brought forward by G. B. Tingley of this committee on January 30. One was a bill defining the amount of revenue to be collected to defray the expenses of the government of California for the year 1850; the other was a bill prescribing the mode of assessing and collecting public revenue. The bill defining the amount of revenue to be collected to defray the expenses of the government of the state for 1850 became a law on February 5. The amounts to be collected were: on each $100 worth of taxable property, 50 cents; and a poll tax of $5.00 on every male inhabitant of the state over twenty-one years of age and under fifty years and not legally exempt from the payment of a poll tax. The bill prescribing the mode of assessing and collecting public revenue was not passed until March 30. Under this law all real and personal property within the state was liable to taxation, except that devoted to public uses, United States property, and part of the personal property of widows and orphans, of which $1,000 of each was exempt from taxation. Chattels and money were taxed as personal property, and corporations were liable for taxation on their capital.

Green, in his report, had recommended that both the assessment and collection of taxes be made in July, 1850. In order to create a fund for the immediate necessities of the state, "to be used before the taxes could be collected at the end of July," he had recommended that bonds be issued, payable six months after date, not to exceed $300,000 in amount, and bearing an interest of 1 per cent per month. After some changes had been

[19] Green's report is summarized in Goodwin, *op. cit.*, pp. 272–273. For the bills mentioned in the next paragraph, see *ibid.*, pp. 275–277, and Bancroft, *op. cit.*, pp. 315–316.

made, the bill was passed by the senate on January 29, and by the assembly on the next day, and was signed by the governor on February 1. The bill authorized the state treasurer to issue bonds in amounts of $100, $225, $500, and $1,000, payable six months after date, bearing interest of 3 per cent per month (Green's proposal of interest of 1 per cent per month was regarded as ridiculously low when the lowest bank rate was 5 per cent per month), and having a total value of not more than $300,000.

Among other measures of a financial nature considered and passed by the first legislature was an act passed on January 31, "prescribing the mode of receiving, keeping, and paying out the public funds." [20] Another was a bill, which became law on February 12, appropriating, out of the general fund, $750,000 to pay the expenses of the government for the first half of the fiscal year ending on June 30, 1850, and $250,000 to pay some of the expenses of the half year beginning July 1. On February 20 a bill was passed "concerning the revenue, funds, expenditures and property of the state, and management thereof," which was supplemented by an explanatory act which became law on April 18. On April 4, an "Act in relation to money or accounts of this state" was passed; and on the sixteenth, another act was passed "relating to bills of exchange and promissory notes."

If the financial provisions made by this first legislature for an undeveloped area with a small population seem extravagant, it should be remembered that the rapidly changing scene was such as to fill the minds of optimistic young men with expectations of great things to come. And the rapid influx of people, combined with the apparently unbounded opportunities for wealth in the area, produced what modern economists call inflation. The financial provisions of the first legislature proved, in the end, to be not extravagant but inadequate for the needs of the government in its first year of existence.

Before lawmaking could get far on its way in what the

[20] See *Statutes of California*, 1850, pp. 69-70.

California legislature believed was already a self-governing dominion, laws had to be passed creating local units of government by dividing the state into counties and providing for the incorporation of cities and towns.[21]

Important but not spectacular, and attended with a minimum of controversy, was the passage of a series of acts dividing the state into twenty-seven counties, designating county seats or making provision for their selection, and creating the county offices to be filled. A senate committee on county boundaries, appointed early in the session, made its first report on January 4, submitting a plan for eighteen counties and naming the seats of justice in all but three. The committee thought it inadvisable to form an entire county within the mining districts, because of the unstable character of the mining population, and recommended that these districts be included within the counties most accessible to them and with which they had the greatest economic connections.

The report was discussed briefly in the senate, then returned to the committee for reconsideration. Before the committee made its second report, on January 18, a number of petitions and protests had come in, with the result that instead of eighteen counties the committee now recommended twenty-five. Of the previously reported names, Oro had been changed to Tuolumne, Benicia to Solano, Fremont to Yolo, and Redding to Shasta. The seven new counties were Coloma, Yuba (sometimes spelled Yubu), Coluse (spelled also Colusi, and now Colusa), Trinity, Marin, Mendocino, and Santa Cruz. As finally passed, with the addition of Napa and Calaveras counties, the bill divided the state into twenty-seven counties; the name Santa Clara replaced San Jose; Contra Costa, Mount Diablo; El Dorado, Coloma; and Branciforte, Santa Cruz. It designated county seats in all the counties except four. For judicial purposes, Marin and Mendocino counties were attached to Sonoma County, Colusa to Butte, and Trinity to Shasta. After the bill

[21] See Goodwin, *op. cit.*, pp. 297–305, for an account of the legislative proceedings and detailed references to the *Journals* of the legislature, 1850.

was amended by both the senate and the assembly, it was finally passed by the assembly on February 13, and by the senate on February 15, and was signed by the governor on February 18. Two bills, of April 6 and 18, respectively, changed the boundaries of several counties, and changed the name Branciforte back to Santa Cruz. On the last day of the session, April 22, the governor signed an act for organizing Marin County, with San Rafael as the county seat.

A bill that provided for holding the first county elections was shuttled back and forth between the assembly and the senate from early February until March 2, when it was finally passed and was signed by the governor. An act supplementary to it was passed on March 9. Under the act of March 2, the prefects were required to designate the requisite number of election precincts in their counties and respective districts and to give notice of county elections, which should be held on the first Monday in April for the purpose of electing the following officers: a clerk of the supreme court; a district attorney for each judicial district; and, for each county, a county judge, a county clerk, a county attorney, a surveyor, a sheriff, a recorder, an assessor, a coroner, and a treasurer. Elections might be held at any place where thirty or more voters were present. The inspectors in each county were required to meet at the county seats of their respective counties, as a board of canvassers, one week after the election. The president of the board was required to notify the successful candidates of the results of the election, after the votes were counted. By an act passed on March 3, regulating elections, county elections were to be held every two years on the day designated in the act of March 2.

The first legislature passed acts providing for the incorporation of cities and towns in general, and special acts for the incorporation of particular places. Six cities were incorporated by special acts: Sacramento on February 27; Benicia, San Diego, and San Jose, on March 27; Monterey, on March 20; and San Francisco, on April 15.

The bill that provided for the incorporation of cities in general was presented to the governor on March 16 and was signed by him on March 18.[22] Under this act, Sonoma and Los Angeles were incorporated on April 4, and Santa Barbara on April 9. It provided that any city having a population of more than two thousand might, upon application, be incorporated either by the legislature or by the court of the county in which it was situated. A community desiring incorporation should present a petition to the county court, signed by the majority of the electors in the town, setting forth the boundaries of the town and asking incorporation under the act of March 18. If satisfied that the population exceeded two thousand and that a majority of the qualified electors had signed the petition, the court would declare the town incorporated as a city. Incorporated cities were to be governed by a mayor, a recorder, a city marshal, a city attorney, an assessor, a treasurer, and a common council consisting of not more than twenty nor fewer than seven members.

A measure making possible the incorporation of any town or village with a population of two hundred or more was passed on March 27. This law provided that a town might be incorporated by the county court of the county in which the town was situated, on petition of a majority of the electors of the town. If the county courts had not yet been organized, the petition would go to the governor, who was given authority to act. A five-member board of trustees would constitute the legislative department of the town government, and would have duties and responsibilities similar to those of the city council. The act also provided for the holding of an election on the first Monday in May of each year, for the purpose of selecting members of this board and also a treasurer, an assessor, and a marshal who would serve also as tax collector. An incorporated town, like an incorporated city, could sue and be sued in all courts.

A subject of legislation, perhaps as important as any passed

[22] See Goodwin, *op. cit.*, pp. 297-305, for discussion and references.

upon by the first legislature, was that having to do with the judiciary and the system of law for California. The first of a series of laws creating the courts was the act passed on February 14, 1850, which provided for the organization of a supreme court, with a chief justice and two associate justices, determined the method of their selection, and described the court's jurisdiction and procedure. A second law, with the date of February 28, 1850, was an act to abolish courts of the second instance and third instance which had been organized upon occupation of the territory by American troops, and to provide for the supersession of courts of the first instance, together with the offices of alcaldes, prefects, subprefects, and other minor semijudicial officials, as soon as the new courts and new county offices were organized. A third act, passed on March 16, provided for the organization of district courts; it divided the state into nine judicial districts, each with a resident judge. On April 11 the legislature passed an act to organize a court of sessions in each county, which should be composed of the county judge and two justices of the peace, and on April 13, an act making provision for county clerks became law; these acts established the jurisdiction of the court and clearly defined certain procedures. The old judicial system and the old judicial offices were swept away and for all time abrogated by this series of legislative acts.[23]

More important than the organization of the courts was the choice of the system of law which should serve as the basis of the jurisprudence for these courts. Was the common law or was the civil law the most desirable basis for use in California? That was the question. Governor Burnett's recommendation, as has been noted, was for a mixed system, made up of the English common law and the Louisiana civil code and code of practice. It was a plan for engrafting some common law on the basis of Roman civil law. The system of jurisprudence used in California before its acquisition by the United States, as far

[23] For the acts creating these courts, see *Statutes of California*, 1850, pp. 57–58, 77, 93–96, 210–211; T. H. Hittell, *History of California*, II, 797.

as there was a system, was that of the civil law, the system used in Spain and Mexico. Naturally, some of the lawyers who had practiced their profession while California was Mexican territory, now a small minority of the lawyers in the area, were more familiar with the civil than with the common law and were encouraged by the governor's message. But the great majority of the people in California after 1849 had previously lived under a system of common law, and most of the members of the legal profession had practiced under it. They felt that under the hybrid system proposed by the governor, law in California would be difficult and complicated and not in harmony with other forms of American control.

Less than a week after the governor's message was received, John E. Brackett, on January 26, proposed, in the assembly, a resolution favoring the adoption of the common law and instructing the judiciary committee to report an act in conformity with this position. Discussion of the subject increased among the members of the legislature, among the people generally, and particularly among the lawyers of San Francisco, of whom there were approximately a hundred. About eighty of these lawyers petitioned the assembly on January 30 for adoption of the common law; whereas eighteen, in a petition to the Senate on February 1, prayed "the legislature to retain in its substantial elements the system of civil law" recommended by the governor, instead of the English common law as urged by the majority petition. The judiciary committee of the senate, after carefully considering this minority petition, through its chairman, Elisha O. Crosby, on February 27, made a report which is of historical importance in California's legislative history.

The report included a classic statement of the origins, history, and character of both the civil and the common law, indicating the Latin origin of the civil law and the Anglo-Saxon origin of the common law. It pointed out that English colonies all over the world clung to the common law, and that in the United States, of the three states of non-English background—Louisiana, Florida, and Texas—which formerly had been under civil-law countries, only Louisiana retained the civil law. The committee maintained that the civil law looked to quiet and repose, with somewhat strict control, rather than to the promotion of activity and progress, and that it looked to the spirit of the past, filled with memories of an antiquated order of things; whereas the common law made an independent being of a man when he became twenty-one, fostered his independence, recognized him as capable of making a contract for himself, treated him as a freeman, and gave him responsibility. The common law was thus a system through which energetic and vigorous life could express itself in progress for the future. In summarizing the character and accomplishments of the common law, the report said:

To that system the world is indebted for whatever it enjoys of free government, of political and religious liberty, of untrammelled legislation, and unbought administration of justice. To that system do we now owe the institution of trial by jury, and the privileges of the writ of Habeas Corpus, both equally unknown under the Civil Law. Under that system all the great branches of human industry—agriculture, commerce, and manufactures—enjoy equal protection and equal favor; and under that, less than under any scheme ever devised by the wisdom of man, has personal liberty been subject to the restrictions and assaults of prerogative and arbitrary power.

To its long argument for the adoption of the common law, the committee added a statement of its belief that the choice to be made on this question of law was by far the most grave and serious duty which the first legislature would be called upon to perform in laying the foundation of a system of laws.

The minority report of the lawyers of San Francisco had stated that the civil law had been and was in full force in California. The senate committee report, in denying this, pointed out that the great distance from the Mexican capital and the instability of the Mexican congress had left little power to enforce laws in California, with the result that the people of California were governed principally by local customs, which were sometimes in accordance with civil law and sometimes in contravention of it. The committee argued that the American people, finding in California little enforcement of laws and much confusion, had effected order and organization by applying the common law, the only system with which they were acquainted. They had made their bargains pursuant to it; employing its usual formalities, they had executed their contracts, deeds, and wills; under it they had solemnized marriages; and they had followed its rules in distributing property.

In their final appeal, the committee called attention to certain practical considerations. Most of the California immigrants came from that part of the Union where the common law was recognized. The large majority of the lawyers and judges of California were familiar with the common law, but though they had a general acquaintance with civil law, they did not possess and could not acquire for a long time an accurate and critical knowledge of its details. The great body of that law was to be found only in works printed in foreign languages, and these were costly and rare. On the other hand, most of the lawyers were steeped in the common law by education and practice, and they could easily procure reference books concerning it. Because of these reasons and a number of others, the committee recommended that "the Courts shall be governed in their adjudications by the English Common Law, as received and modified in the United States; in other words, by the American Common Law." [24] The senate accepted the report, and on motion of Senator Elcan Heydenfeldt, ordered that five hundred copies be printed.

After John E. Brackett introduced in the assembly, on January 26, a resolution instructing the judiciary committee to report an act substantially adopting the common law, and the senate committee, on February 27, approved it, several weeks elapsed before a bill was introduced in the assembly to provide a law embodying the sense of Brackett's resolution and that of the senate committee. On April 2, Brackett introduced in the

[24] California, *Journal of the Senate*, 1850 (App.), pp. 459–480.

assembly a bill concerning the common law; the bill was read the first time on the same day, and a second time on the following day, when it was ordered engrossed for the third reading on April 4. On that day, after Alexander P. Crittenden, as chairman of the appointed committee, reported the slight amendment desired, the bill was voted on and passed by the assembly by a vote of 17 to 6. Without dissent, the title of the bill was changed from "Bill concerning the common law," to "An Act adopting the common law." The bill was read in the senate on April 3, passed the second reading on April 6, the third on April 12, and was signed by the governor on April 13. As enacted and embodied in the California *Statutes* of 1850, it read as follows: "The Common Law of England, so far as it is not repugnant to or inconsistent with the Constitution of the United States, or the Constitution or Laws of the State of California, shall be the rule of decision in all Courts of this State." [25]

An example of deviation from the common law in the constitution of California may be seen in the sections concerning the relation of husband and wife to their property, in which it was provided that all property acquired by either spouse after marriage, except that acquired by gift, bequest, devise, or descent, was made common property, thus disregarding the old common-law rights of dower and courtesy. Of this property, the husband had management; but one-half of it, or, if he left no descendants, all of it, became solely the wife's on his death. The constitution had gone no further than to provide that the property owned by the wife before marriage, or that acquired afterward by gift, bequest, devise, or descent should be her separate property.[26]

In order to remove every encumbrance of the old laws, an act was passed abolishing all laws in force in the state, except those that had been passed by the legislature. A saving clause

[25] See *ibid.*, pp. 281, 289, 323; California, *Journal of the Assembly*, 1st sess., 1850, pp. 1111, 1123–1124, 1204–1205; *Statutes of California*, 1850, p. 219.

[26] Hittell, *op. cit.*, p. 801. Also, see *ibid.*, pp. 799–801, 806–807, for the acts discussed in the ensuing paragraphs.

provided that the act should affect no rights that had been already acquired, or contracts that had been made, or suits that were pending, and that the laws relating to *jueces del campo* (judges of the plains), the officials appointed to superintend the herding and branding of cattle, should remain until "provision is made for that office by law."

The acts considered up to this point are the more important of those passed by the first legislature and for the most part have to do with the functions of the state government. In all, 146 acts and 19 joint resolutions were passed by the two houses and signed by the governor between December 15, 1849, and April 22, 1850, the date of adjournment. Obviously, it is not possible to discuss all these measures or even to enumerate them all in a work of this kind. Among the acts which were founded on and intended to carry out the principles of the common law were: an act regulating proceedings in criminal cases; a habeas corpus act; an act concerning crimes and punishments; acts concerning wills and the settlement of the estates of deceased persons; acts concerning bills of exchange and promissory notes, conveyances, and commissioners of deeds; acts regulating proceedings in civil cases in the various courts, such as those relating to mechanics' liens, forcible entry and retainer, and possessory actions; and a statute concerning frauds.

Of the other laws passed, some were similar to those of other states yet differed from them in part. Among those bearing on the social and business relations of the people there was an act which regulated marriage. This declared marriage to be a civil contract, and it provided that no persons should join in marriage any male under the age of twenty-one, or any female under the age of eighteen years, without the consent of parent or guardian. There was an act concerning corporations, which made liberal provisions for many forms of associations and the bringing together of capital for carrying on enterprises too extensive for private undertaking; an act for the relief of debtors imprisoned on civil process; an act fixing the legal rate of interest at 10 per cent per annum but allowing large latitude if the parties agreed in writing upon a different rate; and a statute of limitations, fixing a much shorter period in which actions could be commenced than that allowed in most of the Atlantic states. Among other measures on various subjects were: an act providing for the appointment of pilots for the different ports and harbors of San Francisco; an act providing for the safekeeping of records; an act for the creation of marine hospitals; an act defining the duties of the state librarian and laying down rules for the government of a state library; an act providing for the organization of the militia; an act providing for the upkeep of roads and highways; an act for the incorporation of colleges; and an act to determine the preference of the people in regard to a permanent location for a seat of government. The act relating to the capital did not name a permanent site but left the choice to be made by election, from the towns aspiring to the honor. The result was that the seat of government was moved about, from San Jose to Vallejo, back to San Jose, to Vallejo again, then to Sacramento, back to Vallejo, and then to Benicia for a short period. Finally, in 1854, Sacramento was decided upon as the permanent capital.

Attempts were made, without success, to pass two acts having moral or social implications—one had to do with the question of gambling, the other concerned the free Negro. The raising of these questions in the legislature, like the discussion of the subjects of lotteries and the free Negro in the constitutional convention, was a reflection of the unsettled mores of a frontier. A bill to suppress gambling, which was heatedly discussed in both the assembly and the senate, was left among the unfinished business. The prejudice against free Negroes expressed in the constitutional convention carried over into the first legislature. There the question provoked considerable conflict. A bill to prevent the immigration of free Negroes and other "persons of color" into the state was passed by a vote of 18 to 7 in the assembly on April 15; but when it reached the senate and came up for its second reading, David C. Broderick of San Francisco moved that it be indefinitely postponed, and the motion was carried by a vote of 8 to 5. The voting on the question, in both the assembly and senate, clearly showed that the members from the mining districts were opposed to the coming in of free Negroes, whether the miners were from the North or from the South. Although those favoring the exclusion of the free Negro failed in their purpose, an undemocratic section was inserted in the act to regulate proceedings in civil cases, which prohibited any black or mulatto person or any Indian from giving evidence in any action to which a white person was a party in any court of the state. This unfortunate provision remained on the statute books for thirteen years.

The first legislature of California, which completed its work on April 22, 1850, often has been referred to as "the legislature of a thousand drinks." Some have attempted to make the basis for this characterization the fact that candidates for the United States Senate came to the capital early, and there, preceding and during the election, "kept *ranches*, as they were termed—that is, they kept open house. All who entered drank free, and freely. . . ." There is little ground for their contention, for Elisha O. Crosby, a member of the first senate, definitely stated the origin of the designation, in his *Memoirs:*

Old Thomas Jefferson Green was the man who gave the Legislature the name of the "Legislature of a thousand drinks." He was a man of some fortune and he had established just out of the Legislative Hall a place where he kept a supply of whiskey and every chance he got he would say, "Well boys, let's go and take a thousand drinks." That was the way he extended his invitation, always to take a thousand drinks, and so the Legislature gained that cognomen . . .[27]

Unfortunately, the phrase which came from the frolicsome Green and his roistering friends, and the statement of John A. Sutter to the effect that one-third of the members were

[27] Crosby, *op. cit.,* pp. 58–59.

good and the rest bad, and that "they appeared in the legislative halls with revolvers and bowie knives fastened to their belts, and were drinking, rioting and swearing nearly all the time," [28] make a picture almost impossible to obliterate. Certainly, Sutter's words lack authority, for, not being a member, he saw little of the great work of the legislature; and, in the light of what the legislature actually accomplished, his picture of it is a crude distortion. The testimony of Elisha Crosby and other reliable men on the ground shows that the cognomen evolved from Green's facetiousness is clearly a misrepresentation. Crosby freely admitted that there were some men who went to the legislature for lack of something else to do and spent their time in idleness, dissipation, and drink. Among the associates of Green and the lobbyist hangers-on were a few roistering fellows who played pranks. But, Crosby asserted after admitting this, "there was very little dissipation among the members in general compared to some legislatures of later days. . . . As a body the first legislature was composed of very sterling men." In conclusion, Crosby asserted that he questioned "whether few Legislatures ever met together with more patriotic feeling and applied themselves to the work of organizing a system of laws for their state with more zeal and industry than the first and second Legislatures of California." [29]

It is to be noted in making an appraisal of accomplishments that, starting with nothing, the objective of the first legislative body elected in California was to provide a series of laws that would effectively carry out the purposes of the constitution and would make California eligible for a place in the United States system of states. In carrying out these purposes it was necessary for the lawmakers to copy to some extent the statutes of other states, but in doing this they had to make choices and exercise discretion. Almost every act passed was a necessity in the situation. There was practically no legislation of a special or local character, and there were few schemes seeking private

[28] "Personal Reminiscences of General John Augustus Sutter" (MS in Bancroft Library, University of California), p. 201.

[29] Crosby, *op. cit.*, pp. 58–59.

advantage as opposed to the general welfare. Most members of the legislature were honest, indefatigable workers. They had to create in a short time an entire new code of statutes, with few resources and with few authorities to consult. Considering these limitations, their labors were most creditable.

It is doubtful whether, up to the present time, any legislature has ever done more work, relatively speaking, or more important or better work than that done by the legislative session which completed its labors and adjourned four and a half months before California was admitted into the Union. It was called together under circumstances that were novel, challenging, and important. In most matters it acted with consummate good judgment. In a region far from the seat of the national government, it discarded old institutions that were adapted neither to the habits, nor to the tastes, nor to the political philosophy of the newly arrived population. New ones were quickly constructed by the talents, understanding, and industry of a small body of young legislators. These men may not have perfected what they built, but they did lay a fair foundation of enduring quality. The adaptation of the governmental structure of the state to changing conditions is a perennial tribute to the devotion and political wisdom of the builders in California's first legislative session of nearly one hundred years ago.

IV

"Thirty-first Star"

On the 29th [October, 1850, in San Francisco] there was a formal celebration of the event, when a new star was added to the flag which floated from the mast in the centre of the plaza, and every species of amusement and parade was made to attest the satisfaction of the citizens of the first American state on the Pacific coast.—H. H. BANCROFT, *History of California*, VI, 348

TRADERS engaged in illicit commerce, followed by trappers and hunters, constituted the spearhead of United States penetration into California. Next, in the 1840's, came organized overland immigration. The restless frontiersmen who comprised this immigration were impelled by a desire for adventure and material gain and often were unconsciously driven on by the spirit of expansion energized by the concept of "Manifest Destiny." The war with Mexico, an incident in the imperialistic policy of the time, gave the United States possession of California. The news of "Gold! Gold! Gold from the American River!" brought an inrush of people to the territory and produced the economic, political, and social conditions so fully described by Owen C. Coy in his *Gold Days.*

It is not to be wondered at that even before the "gold days," Americans in the territory wished to supplant a regime they did not understand by a system which they regarded as embodying the American principles of self-government. After the population had been substantially increased by gold seekers from "the States," groups of politically conscious Americans in California came to the conclusion that, since Congress would not act for them, they should act for themselves. Conscious of the independent spirit of American frontiersmen, the United States administration decided to do what it could to act with them. An orderly procedure resulted, as we have seen, in a constitution for California.

Although some Americans in the new territory would have welcomed an independent state on the Pacific Coast as an avenue of power for personal gain, the great majority of the inhabitants of California felt sufficiently modest or dependent to want the protective aegis of the United States over them. After the constitution was completed, they believed, or at least strongly hoped, that the newly created state would be speedily admitted into the Union. With this expectation, the people ratified the constitution by an almost unanimous vote and at the first election under it chose two men to represent California in the House of Representatives. Soon afterward, the legislature elected two United States Senators; and on January 1, 1850, George W. Wright and Edward Gilbert, the elected Representatives, and William M. Gwin and John C. Frémont, the Senators-elect, left San Francisco for Washington, carrying with them certified copies of the new constitution.

By the time the Congressional delegation from California arrived in the national capital, discussion of the California question had begun in Congress. Even while the state was being organized, and a homogeneous system of institutions and polity was being created out of heterogeneous material, political leaders had begun to be concerned about the effect the addition of California would have upon the political balance then existing between the slave and the free states. After the tense Thirty-first Congress, which assembled December 3, 1849, had spent nearly three weeks in conflict over the election of a Speaker, President Taylor, in his first and only annual message,[1] conveyed information about what had been happening in California and made some recommendations. He reported that the people of California, "impelled by the necessities of their political condition," had formed a constitution and would soon apply for admission into the Union; and he recommended that, if it should be found that the constitution submitted conformed to the requirements of the Constitution of the United States, the application for admission should be favorably considered. Since the national government had waited for the people in California to act, and they had acted in good faith, the President recommended that topics of a sectional character which were producing painful apprehensions in the public mind be not introduced, lest lack of harmony delay action on the application for admission. He notified the Congress that the administration had already acted with respect to several matters: a collector of customs had been appointed for San Francisco, and arrangements had been made for determining sites for lighthouses on the coasts. In view of the mineral wealth of California and the advantages of California's position with relation to the commerce of the Pacific, the President recommended that reconnaissances be made to find a suitable route for a transcontinental railroad. He recommended also that the revenues that had been collected in California when it was under United States military authority should be expended within the territory.

The President's reference here to collections of revenue was to monies that had been collected through what was called the "war tariff" and that had accumulated in what was commonly

[1] President Taylor's annual message to Congress was dated December 4, 1850. For the sections of the message dealing with California, see *Messages and Papers of the Presidents* (Washington: Bureau of National Literature, 1913), IV, 2556–2558.

called the "civil fund." [2] The collection of this fund was at first an arbitrary act, a necessity of war; it was continued after California was ceded to the United States, until the revenue laws of the land were extended to the new territory and a collector of customs was appointed. This fund, legally or illegally, had been drawn upon to maintain the *de facto* government, to aid immigrants who had been caught in the snows of 1848–1849, and (by Governor Riley) to pay the expenses of the constitutional convention. When the revenue laws of the United States were extended over California, about $900,000 remained in this fund. Before California was admitted into the Union both General Riley and General Smith favored turning over to California a part or all of what remained of the civil fund, for use in getting the new government started; but William H. Crawford, the Secretary of War, ordered Riley to place the remainder in the United States Treasury, to be held subject to the action of Congress. Although the governor and legislature of California insistently held that the monies from duties on imported goods, collected at San Francisco and other ports before the customhouse laws of the United States were extended to California, belonged to California after its admission into the Union, and bills for return of the funds were introduced in the Senate by Senator Gwin, all efforts to secure the refund of the monies were unsuccessful. The several attempts made to have Congress appropriate $200,000 of the funds to pay the expenses of the state from the time of its organization until it was admitted into the Union also failed. The only concession made to California was the admission of the committee of finance, circumstantially forced at the end of the second session of the Thirty-first Congress, that it was proper to allow the state to deduct from the civil fund, before it was transferred to the Treasury of the United States, $175,000, the sum that had been expended in payment of the costs of the constitutional convention and the civil government, and an-

[2] For a history of the "civil fund," see Joseph Ellison, *California and the Nation, 1850–1869,* pp. 108–119.

other $100,000, the amount paid out for the relief of immigrants, since Congress had neglected to provide for California and an attempt to reclaim funds that had been already expended would be useless.

The introduction of the subject of California by President Taylor was followed by much informal discussion, around the capital, as to the implications of the question of its admission into the Union. Definite action began when, on December 31, 1849, the House of Representatives, by resolution, requested the President to communicate to Congress what had been done in California. In reply he issued a special message, on January 21, 1850, in which he stated that he had advised the people of California to form a constitution and to apply to Congress for admission into the Union, that they had formed such a constitution and would soon submit it for the approval of Congress, and that it must have the assent of Congress before it could be effective. He stated that he had not sought to influence the delegates and that he was actuated only by the desire to have the proper steps taken to avoid dissension in the United States.[3]

The next move made in Congress on the California question was on January 29, 1850, when Henry Clay brought forward a series of compromise measures in the form of eight resolutions. The first of these declared that "California, with suitable boundaries, ought, upon her application, to be admitted as one of the states of this Union, without the imposition by Congress of any restriction in respect to the exclusion or introduction of slavery within those boundaries." [4] Although Clay wished to avoid immediate debate, even requesting the members of the Senate to take time for consideration of the resolutions before discussing them, members of the body insistently raised objections to the proposals, especially to the one providing for the admission of California, and stated their opinions in no un-

[3] *Messages and Papers of the Presidents*, IV, 2564–2568.
[4] Thomas Hart Benton, *Abridgment of the Debates of Congress . . .* (16 vols., New York, 1857–1861), XVI, 386.

certain terms. For the most part, the objectors to Clay's resolutions were in accord with Jefferson Davis, who stated that he would never accept anything less than extension of the Missouri Compromise line to the Pacific Ocean, with recognition of the right of owners to hold slaves at their will in the territory south of that line. Much to Clay's displeasure, discussion of the question was renewed on February 5 and 6, and came up almost every day from then on.

The arrival in the East of the California delegation naturally created excitement in political circles. Mail steamers made trips but once a month. Consequently, news of what had transpired in California in the way of governmental organization—the installation of the governor and the lieutenant governor, the election of Congressional representatives, and the activity of self-government since the adoption of the constitution on November 13, 1849—did not reach the East until the steamer which conveyed the delegation arrived in New York harbor. The Senators- and Representatives-elect went at once to Washington to place the constitution in the hands of the proper officials. Having duly called upon the President, to whom they gave a certified copy of it, they delivered other certified copies to the Vice-President, the Speaker of the House of Representatives, the Chief Justice and Associate Justices of the United States Supreme Court, and a number of prominent members of the two houses of Congress, including Henry Clay, Daniel Webster, Thomas Hart Benton, Stephen A. Douglas, and John C. Calhoun. The members of the delegation were received with consideration by the distinguished Senators, except by Calhoun, and were given the impression that the prompt admission of California into the Union was assured.

When the delegation called upon Calhoun they found his health in so precarious a state that he could not receive them in a body. But he soon sent for Gwin, who promptly responded to the invitation. Since no one else was present at the interview between Gwin and Calhoun, it seems proper to use Gwin's own report of what took place:

The meeting of these two gentlemen was solemn and impressive in the extreme. There were but few persons in the United States who had been more intimate with Mr. Calhoun than Mr. Gwin, from their meeting in Congress until Mr. Gwin went to California. At this meeting, the last between them, they differed as widely as the poles as to the policy that should be pursued by the Congress of the United States in the admission of California. . . . Mr. Calhoun was then dying, and he soon after passed away. In words which proved to be prophetic, he depicted what would be the result of the admission of California as a state. He said it would destroy the equilibrium between the North and the South in the Senate, the only safeguard the South had against the numerical superiority of the North, and that the equilibrium once destroyed, the agitation of the slave question would become more intense and inevitably result in civil war and the destruction of the South.[5]

Shortly after the arrival of the California delegation on February 13, President Taylor, by special message, announced their presence, transmitted the constitution they had brought, and presented to Congress the formal application of the new state for admission. In the discussion which immediately followed, and through the motions presented in the Senate, the California delegation soon learned that Calhoun not only opposed the admission of California but he was spokesman for Senators and Representatives from the Southern states who intended to resist the recognition of the new state with all means at their command.

It is not possible here to describe in detail what followed the introduction of the constitutional document. Of significance were the efforts of Benton of Missouri to secure the appointment of a committee, with Clay as chairman, to consider the subject of California, and Senator Henry S. Foote's resolution to refer the message and accompanying papers to a select committee of fifteen, to be chosen by ballot. Although neither motion was acted upon at the time, they were indicative of a trend.

[5] William M. Gwin, "Memoirs," California Historical Society *Quarterly*, XIX, 15.

A vital step toward bringing the California question into the open was taken on February 28, when, after informal and floor discussion of related issues, Senator John Bell of Tennessee submitted another set of compromise resolutions.[6] Each of his nine resolutions was accompanied by arguments in its favor, and by answers to four objections to the admission of California. Bell enumerated these objections as: (1) The boundaries included in California's constitution embraced too much territory. (2) The manner in which the constitution was framed was irregular. (3) Many of the residents of California were not citizens of the United States. (4) The constitution was framed under the exercise of an improper influence on the part of the President of the United States. In answer to the first objection, Bell said that he did not consider the territory included in the boundaries to be too extensive. In answer to the second, he contended that the vote of ratification showed that the constitution was satisfactory to the people of California—which was the important consideration. He held that the third objection was unfounded, because, even though there were some foreigners and transients in California, there were many permanent inhabitants, and these were the ones who had drawn up the submitted constitution. In answer to the last objection, that the President had exercised improper influence, Bell declared that he had seen no evidence to sustain the contention, and he pointed out that the people had taken the initiative in forming the constitution before any message had come from the President expressing his opinions and policy. Although Bell's resolutions were not passed, they, like the original ones of Clay, were discussed frequently until the committee of thirteen was appointed. The resolutions of both were more or less integrated into the report of this committee.

As the discussion of the California question got under way, Clay became disturbed at the determined and growing antagonism to the admission of the state, quite apart from the

---

[6] For statement of these resolutions and their discussion, see *Congressional Globe*, 31st Cong., 1st sess., pp. 436–439.

settlement of slavery issues. The opposition to his original resolutions, and the conflicting proposals that were being presented, convinced him that California's admission might not only be seriously delayed, but might even be prevented. He sensed the possibility of civil war and a threat to the safety of the Union, and a great fear took possession of him. When the California delegation first visited him, he informed them that he was in favor of the prompt admission of California as a state of the Union, and that they could rely upon him to do his utmost to bring it about. He continued to favor admission in the face of determined opposition, but he came to see clearly that it could be effected only if the California question was linked with a number of other issues. Clay felt that he must apprise the California delegation of his changed position. Accordingly, he sent for Gwin, who had retired to New York to avoid the appearance of partisanship, and Gwin came back to Washington to talk with him.[7]

In his conversation with Gwin, Clay stated that since he had met with the delegation a number of reliable and distinguished Southern men from the lower house of Congress had waited upon him. They had informed him that members from the South, in sufficient numbers to prevent the passage of any bill, would unitedly continue to oppose the admission of California as a state unless its admission were joined with other questions of vital consequence to the South. Clay stated that for the first time in his life he was forced to believe that the Union was in jeopardy. He explained that, because of this and upon mature and deliberate reflection, he had changed the opinion he had first expressed to the delegation, that Congress should act favorably upon California's petition for admission into the Union, considering the matter as an isolated question, and he had determined to propose a compromise of all the questions on the subject of slavery which were then agitating the country. Much to the surprise of Clay, Gwin acquiesced in his views, agreeing that all these questions should be settled

[7] Gwin, *op. cit.*, pp. 16–17.

at once, and asserting that he would rather never occupy his seat in the Senate if by occupying it he would endanger the existence of the Union.

The question of California was now reaching a crucial stage. Stirred by developments which he thought carried great dangers for the South and for the nation, Calhoun, rousing himself from a mortal illness, on March 4 presented, in the Senate, his last great speech. Rising to address the chair, he explained that on account of physical weakness he was unable personally to deliver the argument he had prepared. Turning to James M. Mason of Virginia, he asked him to read the address which was his valedictory. He strongly opposed the admission of California as a free state and argued that it should be remanded back to the condition of a territory. He asserted that, in making a constitution for California without having been instructed by Congress to do so, a group in California had usurped the sovereignty of the state and had acted in defiance of the authority of Congress. What they had done, he said, was revolutionary and rebellious in its character and anarchical in its tendency. He then called attention to another phase of the question, the great increase of Northern power which had destroyed the old equilibrium between the sections. The failure of the South to keep pace with the North he attributed to the Ordinance of 1787 and to the Missouri Compromise, which had excluded slaveowners from opportunity in territory belonging to them. Also, he argued that the protective tariff and the system of internal improvements had worked to the detriment of the South. Calhoun insisted that, if the Union were to be preserved, the North must recognize the equal rights of the South in all the recently acquired territory; the North must return fugitive slaves; and the people of the North must cease their agitation of the question of slavery. He looked upon the effort to bring about the admission of California as a scheme to weaken the South and increase what he believed was the coercive power of the North. Calhoun had begun his speech by saying:

I have, Senators, believed from the first that the agitation of the subject of slavery would, if not prevented by some timely and effective measure, end in disunion. . . . The agitation has been permitted to proceed . . . until it has reached a period when it can no longer be disguised or denied that the Union is in danger.

After showing the danger as he saw it, with disunion as the only alternative left to the South if the North continued to increase its ascendancy over every power of government, he made the charge that

the responsibility of saving the Union rests on the North, and not the South. . . . If you who represent the stronger portion cannot agree to settle them [the great questions at issue] on the broad principle of justice and duty, say so; and let the States we both represent agree to separate and part in peace. If you are unwilling we should part in peace, tell us so, and we shall know what to do, when you reduce the question to submission or resistance. If you remain silent, you will compel us to infer by your acts what you intend. In that case, California will become the test question.[8]

In the emotional atmosphere which the California question had engendered and Calhoun's speech had intensified, Daniel Webster resolved to present a plea for the Union. Webster's speech, known as "The Seventh of March Speech," was an attempt to answer strongly but courteously his old and dying friend, Calhoun. As Webster began his great oration he was unaware that Calhoun, swathed in flannels, had been brought into the Senate chamber to hear him. The Senator from Massachusetts had begun a reference to the speech of the Senator from South Carolina with the words, "An honorable member, whose health does not allow him to be here today," when a Senator broke in with the information, "He is here." Whereupon Webster said, "I am very happy to hear that he is—may he long be in health and the enjoyment of it to serve his country." [9] He then proceeded with his historical and consti-

---

[8] Calhoun's speech is given in Benton, *op. cit.*, pp. 403–414.

[9] *Ibid.*, p. 420. Gwin in his "Memoirs" (pp. 15–16) says that when Webster referred to Calhoun, "Mr. Calhoun rose up . . . as a man rising from the

tutional argument, which was several times countered with brief speeches by Calhoun. When Webster moved directly to the California question, he said:

Now, as to California and New Mexico, I hold slavery to be excluded from those territories by a law, even superior to that which admits and sanctions it in Texas—I mean the law of nature—of physical geography—the law of the formation of the earth. That law settles forever, with a strength beyond all terms of human enactment, that slavery cannot exist in California or New Mexico.

After elaborating his meaning he gave voice to thoughts which brought reproach from many friends:

I look upon it, therefore, as a fixed fact . . . , that both California and New Mexico are destined to be free . . . free by the arrangement of things by the Power above us. . . . I would not take pains to re-affirm an ordinance of Nature, nor to re-enact the will of God.

He declared that California had become what it was in the order of things by forces which could not be reversed. Its people, without compulsion and on their own initiative, had drawn up a constitution; they were asking for admission of California as a state. Near the end of his speech, after stating his conception of secession and its results, Webster indicated his position on the admission by saying:

Now, sir, when the direct question of the admission of California shall be before the Senate, I propose . . . to say something upon the boundaries of California, upon the Constitution of California, and upon the expediency, under all the circumstances, of admitting her with that Constitution.[10]

In criticism of Webster's effort there were emotional outbursts. Horace Mann wrote: "Webster is a fallen star! Lucifer descending from Heaven." Whittier, in weeping words for which he afterward was sorry, wrote, in his poem "Ichabod":

---

grave, for he looked like a corpse, and said in a hollow, deep-toned voice, 'I am here! . . .'"

[10] The quotations from Webster's speech are from Benton, *op. cit.*, pp. 425–426, 434.

> All else is gone; from those great eyes
> The soul has fled;
> When faith is lost, when honor dies,
> The man is dead!

Theodore Parker compared the speech with the act of Benedict Arnold; Josiah R. Giddings of Ohio and James Russell Lowell spoke of a blow struck at freedom, and of mean and foolish treachery; and there was much similar critical comment. On the other hand, expressions of confidence and words of praise came to Webster from many places. It seems certain that his speech did much to produce a cooler temper and to break up the immediate secessionist movement. Before he spoke, six states had appointed delegates to a convention to be held at Nashville for the purpose of considering the matter of secession. By the time that the convention met in June, sentiment had been so mollified that the resolutions were harmless. As Robert C. Winthrop expressed it, Webster's speech had "knocked the Nashville convention into a cocked hat." Many students now believe that Webster's argument was a strong factor in preventing the immediate outbreak of civil war.

Many speeches were made on both sides of the issues, and one of them, that made by William H. Seward on March 11, undoubtedly nullified in some measure the moderating effects of Webster's speech. Seward advocated admitting California unconditionally and at once. To the reasons given by those who would keep her out—that she had come unbidden, that the consent of Congress to the framing of the constitution had never been asked, that she had chosen her own boundaries, and that she had formed her state government under executive influence—he answered that a recommendation from the executive that the people of California relieve themselves and him of the exercise of military authority was not improper, nor was the action the people had taken improper; the new state had manifested the right spirit and was justified in all the irregularities of its methods. He admitted that the public domain of which California was a part had been acquired by the valor and the wealth of the whole nation; yet he denied that the nation had arbitrary power over it, saying:

The Constitution regulates our stewardship; the Constitution devotes the domain to union, to justice, to defense, to welfare, and to liberty. But there is a higher law than the Constitution, which regulates our authority over the domain, and devotes it to the same noble purposes. The territory is a part—no inconsiderable part—of the common heritage of mankind, bestowed upon them by the Creator of the Universe.[11]

The government, he maintained, was bound to discharge the trust imposed by the higher law in such a way as to secure human happiness in the highest degree. To Webster's claim that the soil and climate would exclude slavery, Seward replied that these could not exclude it, for had they had such power, slavery could never have existed, as it once did exist, in states north of the 40th parallel. He thought also that it was not absurd to reënact the law of God, and held that there was no human enactment, which was just, that was not a reënactment of God's law. He denied that the Union was really in danger and must be saved by compromise. The Union existed, he said, not because men chose that it should exist, but because no other form of government could exist in our country. If it were to be dashed to atoms today, it would rise again in all its magnificent proportions tomorrow. As to slavery, he felt assured that it must give way; "that emancipation is inevitable, and is near; . . . that, whether it be peaceful or violent, depends upon the question, whether it be hastened or hindered—that all measures which fortify slavery, or extend it, tend to the consummation of violence."

The speeches of Clay, Calhoun, Webster, and Seward were made with intensity of conviction, and at times with flashes of passion, yet on the whole they were expressions of calm reasoning, considering the excitement of the times. On the other hand, the reactions to these speeches, of the press, the public,

[11] For Seward's speech see *Cong. Globe*, 31st Cong., 1st sess., XXII (App.), Pt. 1, 265.

and among the members of Congress, reflected the emotional atmosphere, as did also the excited and determined attitude of the President. At the time of his inauguration, General Taylor, according to Polk, expressed himself as thinking that California and Oregon were too distant to become members of the Union and that it would be better for them to be independent in their government; yet now he violently opposed the compromise measures and warmly advocated the admission of California as a separate measure. In answer to a committee of Southern members of Congress, who reportedly had waited on him to coerce him with threats of secession, the President expressed himself as determined to preserve the Union at any cost, and declared that, should armed action eventuate, he would block- ade Southern ports, call for volunteers, and, if necessary, pour out his blood in defense of the Union.

In this state of mind, President Taylor, through Secretary of the Treasury William M. Meredith, summoned Gwin, who had again retired to the city of New York, to an interview with him in Washington. On arriving at the capital, Gwin at once called on Secretary Meredith, who explained why the Presi- dent wished to see him. Meredith said, in effect, that the President wanted the Senators- and Representatives-elect from California to join in a communication to the two houses urging Congress to take immediate action upon the question of ad- mitting California as a state, without tying it up with any other measure of the compromise. Meredith stated also that the other members of the California delegation had agreed to the pro- posal, and that Gwin's acquiescence was all that was necessary to ensure prompt action and the seating of the California dele- gation within a week. Gwin records that the interview was an exciting one, in which he detailed the discussion he had had with Clay and expressed his concurrence with Clay's views, from which, he said, he could not retire. Gwin's subsequent interview with the President was very unpleasant, Taylor be- ing almost violent in his determination, and Gwin remaining firm in his purpose. Gwin believed that, if the mortal illness which shortly seized the President and resulted in his death had not overtaken him, civil war would have resulted at that time.[12]

On March 12, the day after Seward's "higher law" speech and not long after Gwin's interview with President Taylor, the Senators and Representatives from California, Gwin, Frémont, Wright, and Gilbert, issued in their joint names a memorial to the "Senate and House of Representatives," setting forth at length the circumstances leading to the formation and adoption of the constitution.[13] In an introductory paragraph, the delegation expressed their astonishment and regret at learning, since their arrival in Washington, of "the existence of an organized, respectable, and talented opposition to the admission of the new State which they have the distinguished honor to represent." In answering the charges and arguments of this opposition, important in numbers and ability and sectional in character, the delegation first gave a succinct history of the circumstances leading up to the making of the constitution. Next, by argument that was almost demonstration, they showed that the *de facto* government of California was insufficient for the exigencies of the country and that, while the region was in a state of uncertainty and fear, the Americans there, placing patriotism and love of law and order above other considerations, sought to secure present and future prosperity for California by a common effort to form a state government. In answer to the claim of some Senators that the government created in California had resulted from administrative dictation, the memorial declared:

That the people of that country did not adopt such form of government in obedience to dictation from the executive here, through General Riley there; but on the contrary, actually took the initiative in the movement, and only concurred in the suggestions of the *de facto* Governor as a matter of convenience, to

---

[12] Gwin, *op. cit.*, p. 17.
[13] The memorial is published in full in J. Ross Browne, *Report of the Debates in the Convention of California*, Appendix, pp. xiv–xxiii.

save time, and with a patriotic resolution to merge all minor differences of opinion in one unanimous effort to avert impending ills
and remedy existing evils.

After showing in detail that the steps in making the constitution and starting government under it were the expression
of the will of the people of California, the California delegates,
in answer to the charge that the rights and wishes of the people
of the United States had been disregarded, stated in their
memorial that:

It was not from any desire to establish a State Government in opposition to or regardless of the wishes and rights of the people of
the United States, that the people of California pursued this course.
No improper motives, no ambitious impulses, no executive influence prompted their action. They believed that their brethren
on the Atlantic appreciated their sufferings, admitted their patriotism, and would hail their action with joy. They thought that
the Congress of the United States would instantly open its doors
to their delegated representatives, and that the State would be
immediately and gladly admitted. To this impression the tone of
the public press, the dispatches of executive officers, and the
speeches of distinguished statesmen in Congress had contributed
in a very great degree; and as nothing of a contrary character had
ever reached the Pacific shores, it is not surprising that the sentiment became a general one. . . . They did not anticipate delay,
and consequently could not perceive or guard against a con-
tingency arising from such a state of things. They believed their
action to be eminently right and necessary, and sanctioned by the
approving voice of the American people.

As they came toward the end of their argument and plea,
the delegates spoke in conciliatory but forceful words:

The people of California are neither rebels, usurpers, nor
anarchists. They have not sought to sow the seeds of revolution,
that they might reap in the harvest of discord. They believe that
the principles that guided them are true—they know that the
motives which actuated them are pure and just—and they had
hoped that their action would be acceptable to every portion of

their common country. They did not expect that their admission as a State would be made the test question upon which would hang the preservation of the American Union, nor did they desire such a result; but urged by the imperative and extraordinary necessities of their country, they united in such action as they believed would secure them a government under and in conformity to the Constitution of their country.

The California Senators- and Representatives-elect, in their final plea, spoke with the independence of American citizens, seeking the recognition of their State as a self-governing dominion. Their memorial ended with these words:

This people request admission into the American Union as a State. They understand and estimate the advantages which will accrue to them from such a connection, while they trust they do not too highly compute those which will be conferred upon their brethren. They do not present themselves as suppliants, nor do they bear themselves with arrogance or presumption. They come as free American citizens—citizens by treaty, by adoption, and by birth—and ask that they may be permitted to reap the common benefits, share the common ills, and promote the common welfare, as one of the United States of America!

Whether the memorial of the California delegation markedly influenced the vote for the admission of California it is not possible to say, but in it the facts concerning California's action were stated fairly and in words that can profitably be read by Californians today. Two of the four signers were influential persons—Frémont, by reason of his glamorous reputation as a "pathfinder" and the fact that he was the husband of the brilliant Jessie Benton, the daughter of Senator Thomas H. Benton; and William Gwin, because he was a Southerner and was acquainted with many influential persons in official life, particularly in the South. Elisha O. Crosby, who, although he was a caustic critic of Gwin, greatly respected his abilities and political acumen, later said, "I believe that if we hadn't elected Gwin we would not have been admitted at that time. I have been confirmed in that opinion by the declaration of persons who were members of Congress at that time." [14]

In the weeks that followed the issuance of the memorial by the California delegates on March 12 and Calhoun's death on March 31, Senators made speeches and motions that only caused delay, until April 18. On that day, a motion, which had been submitted by Senator Foote on April 11 and 17, to send an earlier resolution of Bell to a select committee of thirteen was carried, after being modified to include the previous resolutions of both Clay and Bell. Also included in it was a statement "that the Senate does not deem it necessary, and therefore declines, to express in advance any opinion, or to give any instruction, either general or specific, for the guidance of said committee." The significant advance was that at least the committee of thirteen had been provided for, and that on the next day its members were elected. As had been carefully arranged beforehand, the committee was composed of six Democrats and seven Whigs. Clay, the chairman, and six other members were from the South, and six were from the North.

On May 8 the committee made its report and presented two bills, one of which became known as the Omnibus bill. This dealt with five topics in addition to the admission of California. The majority of the committee, with their recommendation of the admission of California, included an observation which bears marks of having stemmed from the memorial of the California delegation. This recommendation was to the effect that any "irregularity by which that state was organized without the previous authority of an act of Congress ought to be overlooked, in consideration of the omission by Congress to establish any territorial government for the people of California, and the consequent necessity which they were under to create a government for themselves best adapted to their own wants." [15] The part of the Omnibus bill which referred to California pro-

[14] Elisha O. Crosby, *Memoirs*, p. 62.

[15] Quoted in Cardinal Goodwin, *The Establishment of State Government in California*, p. 334. For the report of the committee, see *Cong. Globe*, 31st Cong., 1st sess., XXII, Pt. 1, 944.

vided that, as a free state and with boundaries as fixed by its constitution, California should at once become one of the states of the Union.

Debate on the Omnibus bill began immediately and continued at intervals until August 1. This bill, from the time of its presentation, had strong support. But complications, with attendant bitterness, continued to obstruct it, because of objections by Taylor and his followers, the insistence of Seward and the Free Soilers that the admission of California be taken up as an independent measure, and the demand of Southern extremists like Jefferson Davis and his followers that the 36° 30′ line be extended to the Pacific. There can be little doubt, however, that better feelings began to prevail in Washington after the Nashville convention adjourned without having taken steps to dissolve the Union. It seems certain, too, that the death of President Taylor, on July 9, and his succession by Millard Fillmore, who turned the influence of the administration in behalf of the compromise, did much to ease the tenseness of the situation. Notwithstanding this fact, by July 30 it was obvious that it would be impossible to get a majority of the Senate to support all the measures of the collective bill. Discussion of the Omnibus bill accordingly ceased, and dismemberment of the bill began. Piece by piece it was taken apart until all that remained of the original bill was the section entitled "An Act to establish territorial government in Utah." Although there was some indignation over the fact that sparsely settled Utah should be granted a government, while populous and prosperous California was prevented from becoming part of that Union, the rancor lessened when it became apparent "that measures which could not pass, when joined, were quite likely to pass when separated." [16]

At this point Douglas called up his bill for the admission of California (Senate Bill 169), which had been proposed by the committee on territories on March 25. This was the beginning

[16] J. B. McMaster, *A History of the People of the United States* (8 vols.; New York, 1907–1914), VIII, 40.

of the direct march to the acceptance of California. Since it had been expected that the committee of thirteen would provide a satisfactory bill for the admission of California, Douglas' bill had not been considered since April 19. His bill was discussed in the Senate and attempts were made to amend it in various ways, on August 2, August 6, August 10, and again on August 12; but on each occasion the attempts to amend it were defeated by a substantial vote. The Senate was evidently ready to pass Douglas' bill and no other. This it did on August 13, by a vote of 34 to 18.

On the next day the Senate bill was sent to the House of Representatives, where it was read twice and committed. On September 7 it came before the House for discussion. Here, too, attempts were made to delay, modify, or defeat it. A member from Kentucky moved to amend it by adding a bill organizing the territory of New Mexico. After this motion was deemed out of order by a vote overruling the Speaker, a member from Mississippi moved that the part of California below the Missouri Compromise line be cut off. This and all other efforts to hamper or modify the bill were defeated by large majorities. After being read a third time, the California bill was passed by a vote of 150 to 56. The act was approved on September 9. On the eleventh, the California delegation were sworn in, Gwin being presented in the Senate by Stephen A. Douglas in accordance with an agreement which the two men had made in front of Willard's Hotel on the day of President Taylor's inauguration.

California citizens, who felt that they were offering the United States a rich gift when, after drawing up a state constitution, they applied for admission of California into the Union, were surprised and disappointed when the first news from the East indicated that California seemed to be not only undesired as a member of the Union but could become a bone of contention that might precipitate a serious struggle. When they learned that the introduction of the California question had engendered perhaps the bitterest controversy in the nation's history, they began to be alarmed. The introduction of compromise measures mollified their feelings and offered hope, but the news of the defeat of the compromise bill, with the consequent possibility that any action by Congress for the admission of California would be postponed for an indefinite period, aroused angry feelings and threats of rebellion. Reproach for the federal government was voiced by high officials and found expression in the press. Some urged that if favorable news did not soon come by steamer, an independent government should be set up, or rather, that the existing government should continue to be independent. Conservative journals discountenanced bitter feelings but acknowledged that a critical situation would result if California were rejected.

When the fears and distrust of the people were at their height, unexpected news caused an immediate change of feeling. On the morning of October 18, the mail steamer *Oregon* entered the harbor of San Francisco bearing two flags, or banners, on each of which was inscribed, "California is a State." In an entry in his diary for the eventful Friday, Charles E. Huse tells of the reception of the news:

At 11 o'clock A.M., the "Oregon" came up the harbour, draped in flags from stem to stern, while her guns thundered out to tell the Californians, "California is admitted." This is glorious news. A salute was soon after fired on the Plaza [Portsmouth Square], and the flag, with another star of paper pinned on was run up on the lofty staff, which a Yankee climbed to reeve the halyards at the cap. A general discharge of small arms and firing of crackers, with now and then the booming of a hoarse mouthed cannon kept up till after midnight, proclaimed the joy with which the glad news was received.[17]

The town declared a holiday, and practically the entire population, in great excitement, congregated in Portsmouth Square to congratulate one another. Surprisingly soon the city

[17] The two-volume diary of Charles E. Huse is in the possession of the Santa Barbara Historical Society and is being edited by William H. Ellison for publication.

took on a festive appearance. More flags than anyone knew were in this part of the country soon decorated the shipping in the harbor and the buildings throughout the city. Guns were fired, processions formed, bands played, and at night bonfires were lit. Hubert Howe Bancroft records how the glad news was spread from San Francisco to San Jose: "Mounting his box behind six fiery mustangs lashed to highest speed, the driver of Crandall's stage cried the glad tidings all the way to San Jose, 'California is admitted!' while a ringing cheer was returned by the people as the mail flew by." [18]

The event was formally celebrated in San Francisco on October 29. Then, a new star, the thirty-first, was added to the flag which floated from the flagpole in the center of the Plaza. The citizens of the new state attested their gratification by getting up a colorful parade and other amusements. The parade was extravagantly described in the press throughout the state. After grand marshals and buglers came mounted native Californians bearing a satin banner displaying thirty-one stars on a blue satin ground and the gold-lettered inscription, "California, E. Pluribus Unum." These were followed by California Pioneers, army officers and soldiers, navy officers and marines, and representatives of foreign governments. A Chinese company in rich oriental costumes, with its own marshal, marched along carrying a blue silk banner inscribed "The China Boys." There was a float on which boys symbolizing the thirty states surrounded a young girl robed in white and wearing a breastplate bearing the inscription, "California, The Union, it must and shall be preserved." At the Plaza fitting ceremonies were held, with music, an oration, and the reading of an ode written for the occasion. This, the first Admission Day celebration, marked a milestone in the history of a self-governing dominion.

With his description of the admission celebration in San Francisco and his interpretation of the addition of the thirty-first star, Bancroft quotes in a footnote the following statement from the London *Times:*

[18] H. H. Bancroft, *History of California*, VI, 348.

Forgetting for a moment the decorative features of this exhibition, let the reader consider the extraordinary character of the facts it symbolized. Here was a community of some hundreds of thousands of souls collected from all quarters of the known world—Polynesians and Peruvians, Englishmen and Mexicans, Germans and New Englanders, Spaniards and Chinese—all organized under old Saxon institutions, and actually marching under the command of a mayor and alderman. Nor was this all, for the extemporized state had demanded and obtained its admission into the most powerful federation in the world, and was recognized as a part of the American union. A third of the time which has been consumed in erecting our house of parliament has here sufficed to create a state with a territory as large as Great Britain, a population difficult to number, and destinies which none can foresee.[19]

If the formation and admission of the State of California did not bring to realization the ideals of the Declaration of Independence, they did mark a step or two in that direction. The frontier achievement in California and the nation moved toward democracy, although it fell short of it. California's admission into the Union was a great event for the Pacific Coast and for the Union, even if that entrance, for the time being, made of the United States a divided house, for the final result was greater unity. Denial of admission into the federation at the time would have provided opportunity for setting up an independent republic facing the Pacific Ocean and the Far East, and would have changed the course of events. Whether or not destiny had a hand in making California a state in our Union, it is certain that the admission of the state was a milestone not only in the history of California but also in that of the American nation and the world.

[19] *Ibid.*, p. 350.

V

Who Owns the Land?

*The rights of sovereignty and eminent do-
main possessed by each State, carry with
them the right to all the lands . . . in the
State . . . unless the State have yielded up
that sovereign right . . . to another. The
people of California . . . formed a government of their own . . . The sovereignty, the
jurisdiction, and the right to public property
within the State, reside in this State.*—ME-
MORIAL TO CONGRESS, CALIFORNIA SENATE,
April 4, 1853

WHO OWNS the land? How may it be
acquired? To find the answer to these two questions was more
difficult in California than on any other American frontier.
From the beginning there were complications in the California
situation. From the States came a sudden influx of immigrants
indoctrinated with the concepts of "higher law" and "manifest
destiny." These Americans, sure of themselves, accustomed
to small grants of lands, "squatter's rights," and fixed boundaries, were suspicious of the native Californians, who seemed
to obstruct the way to their goal. The newcomers were disappointed and irritated to find great sections of the best lands

claimed and occupied by Mexican grantees, and the rest, except certain grants to the state made under law, held as public domain by the United States. In high political circles in California, statements were often made that the lands should be turned over to the state for distribution. American immigrants frequently asserted that these lands belonged by right to the citizens who had come a long way to occupy them, and that everything in California rightfully belonged to the citizens of the conquering nation. More than a decade passed before the land-grant claims and other phases of the California land problem were settled.

A halting investigation of the California land question was started even before immigrants in large numbers arrived and before the constitution was drawn up. As early as July, 1848, the committee on public lands reported to the United States Senate a bill to ascertain claims and titles to land in California and New Mexico, and the bill came up again for discussion in January, 1849. This provided for the appointment of several officials to act as a board of land commissioners and to present to Congress in 1851 a detailed report of all land titles. Senator Benton opposed this bill, offering as a substitute one which would simply authorize the District Court to take action against grants believed to be invalid. These bills were recommitted and put to rest, and the land question did not come up again until after California had become a state.

In the meantime, two important reports on Mexican land titles in California were made.[1] The first was that of Captain Henry W. Halleck, who had been directed by Governor Mason to collect and examine the archives that were deposited in various places in the territory. On April 13, 1849, Halleck made an accurate and comprehensive report on the situation in California and suggested a cautious policy. He pointed out

[1] Henry W. Halleck, *Report on Land Titles in California*, 31st Cong., 1st sess., Senate Ex. Doc. No. 17; and William Carey Jones, *Report on the Subject of Land Titles in California*, 31st Cong., 1st sess., Senate Ex. Doc. No. 18, are the initial sources for any study of the land question in California.

that in a large number of California land titles the boundaries were not definitely indicated, and that many grants had not been confirmed, and the papers of some had been antedated. This report, as Bancroft contends, may have magnified somewhat the prospective difficulties and may have led settlers to distrust all Mexican grants. It seems certain that it stimulated settlers who were without the means to purchase land, or who were indisposed to pay what they thought were exorbitant prices for lands which they believed belonged to the United States, to resort to force in their effort to get possession of desirable properties. Students of the period believe that the famous "squatter riots" of 1850 in Sacramento were stimulated, or at least encouraged, by Halleck's report. At that time a number of settlers, under the leadership of James Zabriskie, a young lawyer, and Dr. Charles Robinson, who later became governor of Kansas, challenged the validity of Sutter's title to the lands he claimed as Mexican grants.

The second report was that of William Carey Jones, who had been sent by the Secretary of the Interior as an agent to investigate the land question in California. Jones was familiar with the Spanish language and with legal usages. He was aided by the authorities and had the benefit of Halleck's work. His report of March 9, 1850, was clear and complete, and much more encouraging than that of Halleck. He admitted the probability that some fraudulent titles had been made since July, 1846, but he believed that there were not many of these, and that they would not be difficult to detect. His report stated that most of the land grants were held under valid titles, and that those which were not lacked only some formality or evidence of completeness that would have been perfected had political conditions not been disturbed. Jones recommended that an official survey be made of the grants, in order to clarify disputed claims. This, he thought, would be for the best interests of the United States and all Californians. The government should reserve the right to take legal steps to settle titles where this seemed necessary. This report was reassuring both to the Californians and to the officials in Washington. But many complications were to follow the two reports before satisfactory adjustments could be made.

About the time these reports were made, aggrieved settlers, in a memorial to Congress, complained that they had emigrated to the Pacific Coast under the assumption that California belonged to the United States. They complained, further, that on their arrival they found not only that they were considered trespassers on soil claimed by Mexican landowners but that they must fight in self-defense against speculators who had formed a land monopoly by appropriating to themselves all the public lands within the state. In urging Congress to legislate in favor of actual settlers, the memorialists were consciously or unconsciously attempting to rationalize their desire for the most valuable lands, since plenty of other lands were available to them. It was natural, in the complicated situation, that all who were interested in the welfare of California should urge speedy settlement of the question of Mexican land titles so that the wealth in the rich tillable land could be realized.

Scarcely had Gwin and Frémont been sworn in as Senators from California, when Frémont offered eighteen elaborately prepared bills. Among these was "A bill to provide for the ascertainment of private land claims in California, and for the adjustment and settlement of the same." [2] Although less than three weeks remained of the session, when Frémont introduced this measure, and it was very difficult for anyone, especially new Senators from a new state, to get attention on any matter at so late a date, the question was debated at some length. However, the session ended without any legislation on the subject having been passed.

Since Frémont did not take his seat in the second session of the Thirty-first Congress, Senator Gwin alone represented his state in the Senate. The first bill on which he desired action was the one which concerned California land titles. On De-

[2] See William M. Gwin, "Memoirs," *California Historical Society Quarterly*, XIX, 18.

cember 9, 1850, he moved to make that subject a special order in the Senate at an early day, urging that speedy action be taken because of the constant danger of collision between settlers and the owners of Mexican grants over what the settlers contended were public lands. Gwin's motion did not then prevail, but on December 23, when he again brought forward his proposal, he was able to get before the Senate, for discussion, Senate Bill 346, "A bill to ascertain and settle the land claims in California." [3] In making some remarks on the bill, Gwin reemphasized what by that time was well known, that much excitement and exasperation existed in California over the subject of land claims. He argued that these could be allayed only by the passage by Congress of a bill for the settlement of claims. Various amendments were offered to the bill, and it was again postponed for consideration at a later day. When the bill came before the Senate again, on December 26, Benton stated that the bill, in his opinion, was of such importance that a full Senate should be present when it was discussed. He said that at the proper time he would show that the bill, if passed, would cause the United States to violate its treaty with Mexico; it would infringe on the law of nations; and it would despoil the inhabitants of California of their lands. He therefore moved that the bill be laid over for one week and be made a special order for the day. In spite of objections by Gwin, the Senators agreed to the postponement.

When Gwin's bill on land titles came up for consideration again on January 3, 1851, Benton, as the champion of the Mexican grantees, proposed a substitute measure. In addressing the Senate in opposition to the Gwin bill and in favor of his substitute, he expressed the belief that the commission plan advocated by Gwin was equivalent in its operation to confiscation of the landed property of the Mexican landowners in violation of the treaty of 1848 and the law of nations. Benton objected strongly to the provision of the commission plan which would submit the land cases to the United States Su-

[3] Gwin, *op. cit.*, p. 22.

preme Court for final decision, stating that the litigation would be very expensive to the litigants and the delay dangerous to their interests. After describing the manner in which Spain, by generous grants of land, induced colonists to settle in California, he said:

> Now, Sir, when we have got possession of such a people as this, how strange it is to find ourselves at once arraigning every title, holding every title to be a fraud against the United States, until the parties shall prove in three different courts, and one of them the Supreme Court of the United States, that they were not frauds against the United States.[4]

His own plan, intended to effect a speedy and liberal confirmation of titles, provided for a recorder who would collect the evidence of titles to land claims and, in conjunction with the United States district attorney, would summon to a hearing all claimants the validity of whose ownership was questioned. A decision in favor of the claimant would be final.

Gwin, championing the settlers' interests, argued that the plan he proposed would not work injustice to the Californians, because their titles, if they were legal, valid, and equitable, would be confirmed. His bill, he asserted, would not, as alleged by Benton, hold a Spanish grant to be a fraud until the grantee should prove in three different courts that it was not fraudulent, since the law of prescription placed in the bill provided for the confirmation, as a matter of course, of every grant made under the government of Spain when it was shown to have been so made. In answer to Benton's remarks that "there may be a hundred thousand people there, for aught I know, who want the land of the few," Gwin said:

If from this the inference may be drawn that any portion of the people of California desire to appropriate to themselves any lands lawfully granted by the Governments of Spain and Mexico, I meet it with an unqualified contradiction. No portion of the people of California will ever countenance a violation of the rights of

[4] *Ibid.,* p. 160.

property guaranteed to any portion of the inhabitants of that country under the treaty with Mexico. All they desire is that some competent and impartial tribunal, such as is provided for in this bill, will decide what is private property, and it will be respected.[5]

A weakness in Gwin's presentation of the case for his bill was his failure to answer the practical part of Benton's argument, that the claimants would frequently lose their land in the long process of defending it.

The land act passed by the Senate on February 6, 1851, and by the House of Representatives on March 3, was substantially Gwin's bill,[6] although it had been modified slightly in the judiciary committee and by amendment. In its final form, the land act of 1851 provided for the appointment, by the President, of a board of three commissioners, which was to serve for three years from March 3, 1851, unless discontinued by the President, and was to hold sessions at places named by him. The commissioners were to appoint a secretary, skilled in Spanish and English, who should act as interpreter and keep a record of the proceedings. The President was empowered to appoint an agent "learned in the law and skilled in the Spanish and English languages," to superintend the interests of the government. To this board, every person desiring confirmation of title to lands claimed in California under Spanish or Mexican grants was required to present his claim within two years, accompanied by all supporting documentary evidence and the testimony of witnesses. The board was required to decide the case upon the evidence presented, and to certify to the United States district attorney the validity of the claim, giving the reasons for its action, within thirty days after the decision was rendered. Either party might then appeal to the District Court, and again from its decision to the Supreme Court of the United States. Each of the tribunals—the Board of Land Commissioners, the District Court, and the Supreme Court—was to be

[5] Gwin, *op. cit.*, p. 161.

[6] Gwin had proposed the bill. As spokesman for the California settlers, he had won support for its passage in an elaborate argument in its favor on January 8, 1850. See *ibid.*, pp. 157–162.

guided in its decision "by the Treaty of Guadalupe-Hidalgo, the law of nations, the laws, usages, and customs of the government from which the title is derived, the principles of equity, and the decisions of the United States Supreme Court, so far as they are applicable." The act specifically provided that all the lands of the rejected claims and claims not presented should be regarded as part of the public domain. The Surveyor General of California should survey each confirmed claim, make a plot of the land, and issue a certificate. The General Land Office would issue a patent to the land on presentation of this certificate by the owner. The patent would be conclusive only against the United States and would not affect the interests of third persons. On petition of a contesting claimant, the District Court might grant an injunction preventing the issuance of the patent until sufficient time for deciding the controversy had elapsed. Claims for town or farm lots held under grants from corporations or towns to which lands had been allotted by former governments should be presented not by the lot owners but by the municipal authorities or by the original grantees. Proof that the town had come into existence before July 7, 1846, should be accepted as conclusive evidence of the grant to the corporation, and therefore to the person who held title under the corporation.[7]

In appraising what was attempted and done, one must consider certain facts of the times. First, under the spell of the doctrine of "manifest destiny" the newly arrived settlers believed California to be their "land of promise"; many of them were convinced that Providence had led them to the land and that therefore it was theirs by right. They noisily asserted that in the conquest of California the United States had acquired not only sovereignty over the country but ownership of the land for United States settlers. They hoped that some just way could be found to keep a large portion of the California acres,

[7] The act is in United States, *Statutes at Large*, IX, 631–634. Adequate summarization of the act is given in Joseph Ellison, *California and the Nation*, pp. 13–15. See also, H. H. Bancroft, *History of California*, VI, 540–541.

now their acres by "providential act," from being withheld from them by Mexican grants, real or pretended. Their desires inevitably caused them to feel that frauds were more widespread than they actually were. In the second place, discovery of gold made a bad situation worse by greatly intensifying the interest in land. Gold hunters based their ideas of real-property values on what they knew of lands at San Francisco and Sacramento, and pictured California as a succession of gold mines and towns, with farming land here and there, worth fabulous prices per acre. Many of the newcomers were strong in the faith that, as American citizens moving with "manifest destiny," they were entitled to lands under the "higher law," as free American citizens. They were suspicious of all that was Mexican, attacked the validity of Mexican law, charged that particular titles were fraudulent, and even engaged in "squatter riots," as at Sacramento in 1850. This spirit continued to make itself felt through the whole period of litigation, exercising a potent influence in politics, on juries, and through the press.

At the time the Gwin bill was under discussion, a strong undercurrent of feeling similar to that in California existed in Congressional circles in Washington. Members of the Senate and House thought of California as a country conquered by the United States and to which Americans had gone because destiny had led them there. They gave little heed to the vast ranchos which had long been possessed by those living on them, or by their fathers. Although they were willing to concede that claims for some of these lands might be valid, they were convinced that many were fraudulent, and centered their attention on those. They believed that speculators were holding lands the settlers wanted; that the mining regions were covered by diabolically contrived titles, and that Frémont, Sutter, Vallejo, and others were in a position to seize important areas; that British subjects were preparing by nefarious schemes to secure as individuals what the Empire had failed to acquire; and that American settlers and miners were finding themselves without homes. In this kind of psychological atmosphere the land act was conceived.

Here appears a concrete expression of the purpose of Americans to be masters of what they believed to be their own in a theoretically self-governing dominion. The action taken by Congress was natural under the circumstances. It is doubtful whether any other general plan that could have been devised would have turned out to be much better than this one that came out of a rather heavily loaded emotional situation. There was, moreover, a desire for justice, and the belief that generous liberality would be shown when the exact state of things became known. It is therefore not surprising that the courts, which it was believed could decide wisely, were given so important a function in the legislative act.

The Land Commission began its sessions on January 2, 1852, in San Francisco, and held all its sessions there until it finally adjourned on March 1, 1856, except for one brief term at Los Angeles in the autumn of 1852. Instructions to the board stated that the object of the law of March 3, 1851, was to validate all *bona fide* land titles, and "to detect and forever put to rest, all fabricated, fraudulent, or simulated grants." The board received, in January, a number of petitions and notices from claimants, but made no decisions until August, when it confirmed three claims on "broad principles of equity," which the board agreed should form a guide for future action.

In applying a system of common law to a situation that had its genesis under a system of civil law, and that was further complicated by fortuitous circumstances which brought contrasting ideas of rights into strong juxtaposition, the board, as was inevitable, often moved with uncertainty and at times was swayed by political- and personal-interest pressures. In attempting to carry out broad principles of equity and to protect the claims under the treaty with Mexico, the commissioners had to inform themselves of the intricate matters of the land grants. The United States agent, on his part, had to work assiduously to master the law in its application to the cases, in order to face on equal terms the counsel of the claimants, recruited from the ablest legal talent to be had.

Under the circumstances in which they were placed, the commissioners were attacked not only because they were forced to move cautiously but also because many decisions which they made were regarded by one side or the other as invasions of its vested rights. Although some persons defended the board's policy and early decisions, many others accused its members of inefficiency, corruption, and dereliction of duty. Governor John Bigler went so far as to ask the legislature to memorialize Congress to repeal the land act of 1851 and pass another in which authority would be vested solely in the District Court. A resolution to this effect introduced in the legislature failed to pass, partly because of the belief that such a law would make for delay and would crowd the District Court with land cases. Under advice and pressure, President Pierce named a new commission in 1853, which, with some reorganization, continued to function until the board adjourned sine die on March 3, 1856.[8] Not until several decades after this were all the appealed cases settled.

Most of the 813 claims presented to the commission were confirmed; about one-third of these were settled by the board, and about two-thirds by the District Court or by the Supreme Court on appeal. Most of the cases were appealed to the District Court, either by the claimants or by the United States. This court seemed to be more favorable to the claimants than the board had been, since it overruled many more rejections than confirmations, probably because claimants strengthened their weak points by presenting additional evidence when making the appeal.[9]

An examination of several of the land-claim cases will indicate the procedures employed by the Land Commission, and both the direct and indirect results of its action. A complicated

[8] Joseph Ellison, *op. cit.*, pp. 15–16; T. H. Hittell, *History of California*, III, 695.

[9] Bancroft, *op. cit.*, p. 542; Joseph Ellison, *op. cit.*, p. 24.

case, but one in which the steps are clear, is that in which the claim of Andrés Castillero to Santa Cruz Island, one of the islands of the Santa Barbara Channel, was validated. In accordance with an order from the Mexican President directing Governor Alvarado to grant to Castillero one of the islands on the California coast, the governor conveyed Santa Cruz Island to Castillero on May 22, 1839. The land transferred was "in extent of eleven square leagues of land and no more, and has for its boundaries the water's edge." On April 13, 1852, the petition of Andrés Castillero seeking confirmation of title to the island of Santa Cruz was filed with the land commissioners. Castillero's counsel, on September 25, 1854, filed a stipulation showing when and how the grant had been made, and asserting that Castillero had been in possession of the island for some twelve years and knew of no conflicting claim. Confirmation of the grant was asked on the basis of the original papers, the records of the archives under the charge of the Surveyor General, and such other proofs as might be required.

Conflicting claims did appear, however, for at the same time counsel for James R. Bolton presented a supplementary petition in which it was set forth that, because of nonpayment of taxes on the island, the treasurer of Santa Barbara County had sold the southeastern half of it to Francisco de la Guerra for $26, the highest price offered, and that in turn this half of the island had been sold to James R. Bolton for $130 on December 30, 1850. Bolton's petition asked for confirmation to him of the undivided half of the island which he claimed he had bought.

Another claim counter to that of Castillero was that of José Antonio Aguirre, who also asked for one-half of the island, claiming that Castillero had transferred to him this half about the same day the island had been granted to him. Juan B. Alvarado, governor at the time the grant was made to Castillero, testified that Castillero had agreed that Aguirre, as remuneration for taking care of the island, should have one-half of it, and that Aguirre's ownership of half of the island was publicly accepted at the time (1839). When the Aguirre case came before the Land Commission in San Francisco in September, 1854, the commissioners adjudged that Aguirre's claim was based on oral testimony only, that there was no record of either the sale or delivery of the land, no record of the title, and no proof that Aguirre had taken care of the island. The commission, therefore, in handing down its decision on July 5, 1855, denied his claim, and Aguirre himself dismissed it on March 4, 1858. On July 3, 1855, the commission denied the claim of Bolton to one-half of the island, holding that, though Bolton had offered the deeds in evidence, he had failed to supply proof that the tax sale had been conducted under the provisions of the California statute regulating the mode of selling lands for the payment of delinquent taxes, or that the sheriff who sold the land for taxes was the sheriff at the time the sale was made, or that the treasurer who executed the deed was the real treasurer at the time of its execution.

At the time the commission denied Bolton's counterclaim, the commissioners said of Castillero's claim, "But the evidence on the part of the petitioner is sufficient in our opinion to entitle him to confirmation and a decree will be entered accordingly." The commission therefore decreed that Castillero was the owner of Santa Cruz Island which, with a shore line of at least 53 miles, embraced approximately 52,760 acres. As with most of the claims, the decision was then appealed to the United States District Court. The action of this court, filed January 14, 1857, confirmed the opinion of the commission. Some of the other claimants, as well as a few officials, were not willing to accept as final this confirmation of Castillero's claim and appealed to the United States Supreme Court. This court heard the appeal in December, 1859, and filed its decision on March 18, 1861. In reviewing the historical and legal facts in the case, the court affirmed that the evidence of Castillero's ownership had been fully substantiated, and on the basis of the law and evidence in the case it confirmed the claim of the grantee. The island was, therefore, the property of Andrés Castillero.[10]

In the Santa Cruz Island case, the grant, claim, and settlement appear to have fulfilled the requirements laid down for validation of claims. The appeals and judgments here, as in most of the cases, seem to have been made in conformance with the rules, and apparently incurred no subsequent criticism.

The Mariposas grant, however, claimed by John C. Frémont, introduced some variance in court procedure, and the courts accepted as legal what some regarded as liberalization of the rules through influential pressure. Consideration of this case brings out the problem of the "floating grant" and shows that the interpretation of the law varied with different conditions and with different persons.

On February 10, 1847, Juan B. Alvarado, through Thomas O. Larkin and upon payment of $3,000 by John C. Frémont, executed in favor of Frémont a deed to Las Mariposas—property which had been granted to Alvarado by Governor Micheltorena in 1844—in spite of the condition attached to the grant, which prohibited the grantee from selling, transferring, or mortgaging it. On January 21, 1852, Frémont filed his claim to the Mariposas grant, according to the American law, with the Land Commission appointed to adjudicate such claims. In December following, the commission confirmed the grant. Subsequently, Caleb Cushing, the Attorney General, appealed from the decision of the commissioners, to the United States District Court, holding that the concession originally made to Alvarado was null because of the uncertainty of its description, its indefinite location, and for other reasons. This court, on January 7, 1854, reversed the decision of the board on the ground that there had been no surveys, no plans, no occupation, no confirmation by the proper public authority, and no performance of any of the conditions annexed to the grant.

Colonel Frémont then appealed to the Supreme Court of the

[10] See W. H. Ellison, "History of the Santa Cruz Island Grant," *Pacific Historical Review,* VI (1937), 270–283.

United States. This body reversed the decision of the District Court, declared the claim valid, and ordered an official survey. In delivering the opinion of the court, Chief Justice Taney held that the provision against alienation attached to Alvarado's grant was void, and that though the land under the Mexican government would have been forfeited by conveyance to aliens, it by no means followed that conveyance to Frémont incurred the same penalty, since California at the time of the conveyance was held by American forces as a conquered country subject to the authority of the American government. There was, he pointed out, no principle of public law which prohibited the citizen of a conquering nation from purchasing property in the territory thus acquired, nor was there anything in the principles of our government which required him to forfeit the property purchased. The decision declared that "the purchase was perfectly consistent with the rights and duties of Colonel Frémont, as an American officer and an American citizen." [11] Accordingly, under the date of February 19, 1856, a patent confirming the grant was issued to Frémont.

The official survey of the grant ordered by the Supreme Court and carried out under the direction of the Surveyor General of the United States for California, produced results never fully explained. In locating Frémont's "floating grant," the surveyors swung the grant around, making it include the valuable Ophir, Pine Tree, and Josephine mines near the Merced River, and territory which Frémont had not previously claimed. Thus, included in Frémont's claim were mines that had long been in possession of miners who had no intimation that the surveys would include their workings. Several lives were lost in the battles which ensued. The situation was further complicated by the fact that Mexican law did not convey the gold or other minerals with a grant, and American law had not yet decided the point. Frémont eventually won

[11] See John Bigelow, *Memoirs of the Life and Public Services of John Charles Fremont* (New York, 1856), p. 386.

both the gold and the land, since in 1859 it was judicially decided that the mineral title was vested in the owner of the land.[12] The Mariposas case is noteworthy because validation of Frémont's claim eased the requirement of building on the land and occupying it within a year, a condition which neither Alvarado nor Frémont had fulfilled; the Indian danger and political disturbances were accepted as excuses for the neglect. Likewise, the validity of inchoate equitable titles was recognized, as time, the push of settlement, and influential persons had their liberalizing effect.[13]

It would seem that the course of events in California demonstrated the need for such a law as was passed, to subject the land claims of California to rigid scrutiny. Injustice to Mexican grantees under the law, which had been feared by Senator Benton, was obviated to a large extent by the overruling of numerous claims in the courts of appeal when new evidence was introduced. Some of the equity which he advocated was afforded by liberal interpretation of the law, as in the decision in Frémont's Mariposas case. In the process of applying the law, it was inevitable that some good claims should be rejected and some fraudulent ones confirmed. Approval of the old and settled grants brought little adverse comment from settlers or from organs of public opinion. But protests were voiced when it was even suspected that the United States district attorney had not made sufficient effort to defend the people against unscrupulous speculators; and when the commissioners confirmed several large claims which were commonly believed to be fraudulent the cause of the settlers naturally became more popular.

Two cases that did much to increase criticism of the board and to fortify the settlers' position were the ones known as the Bolton and Barron, or Santillan claim, and the Limantour

---

[12] 14 Cal., 279, 380.

[13] For a full statement about Frémont and the Mariposas grant, see Bigelow, *op. cit.*, pp. 379–386. See also Bancroft, *op. cit.*, pp. 544–546, 552; Frederick S. Dellenbaugh, *Frémont and '49* . . . (New York, 1914), pp. 464–465; B. C. Howard, *United States Supreme Court Reports*, VII, 564–565.

claim.[14] The Santillan claim purported to be a grant of three square leagues of land at Mission Dolores, including substantially all the land of the city and county of San Francisco south of California Street, which the claimant averred had been made on February 10, 1846, by Governor Pío Pico, to Prudencio Santillan, a priest at the Mission. The claim was confirmed by the commission in 1855, and by the United States District Court in 1857, but was declared fraudulent by the United States Supreme Court in 1860. It had long been regarded as a fraud and should have been rejected by the lower courts.

José Yves Limantour maintained that four square leagues south of what is now California Street in San Francisco had been granted to him on February 27, 1843, by Governor Micheltorena; and that Yerba Buena and Alcatraz islands, the Farallones, and one square league of land opposite Angel Island in what is now Marin County had been granted to him on December 16, 1843, by the same governor. The Land Commission confirmed these claims in 1856. James Wilson, one of the original members of the commission, as the attorney for the claimant, had prepared the case for presentation. His confidence in the validity of the claims had led him to induce many persons to purchase from him, as Limantour's attorney-in-fact, quitclaim deeds for their property. When the cases came before the United States District Court on appeal, Judge Ogden Hoffman rejected the claims on the ground that documents on which they were based were gross forgeries, characterizing the cases as being without parallel in the judicial history of the country. The decisive point in establishing the fraud was the discovery "by persevering scrutiny . . . that the seal of state, which was applied to all Mexican land grants, and the seal that was used in the Limantour grants had one important difference: the spread of the wings of the eagle on each differed from an eighth to a sixteenth of an inch, and it was demon-

[14] See Joseph Ellison, *op. cit.*, pp. 21–22; Bancroft, *op. cit.*, pp. 554–555, 558; Hittell, *op. cit.*, pp. 696–698.

strated that the seal on the Limantour grants was counterfeit." [15] These cases did much to discredit the commission and the District Court in the public mind.

There were many fraudulent claims, and because great blocks of capital were represented in them, many eminent men of the legal profession were employed in their presentation. So great was the danger of their confirmation that the government employed additional counsel to aid the United States district attorney in his efforts to prevent it. Jeremiah S. Black, United States Attorney General under President Buchanan, with the authorization of the President, selected Edwin M. Stanton as special counsel for the government in untangling the snarl of fraudulent cases pending in California at the time, particularly the Limantour cases. After his arrival in San Francisco in February, 1858, Stanton spent several months examining grants, records, and Mexican land laws, and collecting, arranging, translating, and binding the California archives. Lists of professional witnesses for the false claims, with brief biographies of nearly all the men who had been engaged in the fraudulent schemes, were carefully compiled. These were translated, collated, printed, photographed, and bound in several hundred uniform folio-sized volumes, with labels on their backs indicating their contents. These volumes were finally deposited in the office of the United States Surveyor General for California. They constitute an exceedingly interesting and valuable collection, not only as records of title, but as historical documents.

The voluminous records brought together were examined and studied by Stanton and other able men. By using them and the evidence which the archives yielded, and by comparing testimony, Black and Stanton felt able to determine with almost absolute certainty the truth or falsity of almost any claim presented. So effective and persistent were they and their aides in presenting the cases and convincing the courts, that when Black made his report to the President he stated

[15] Gwin, *op. cit.*, p. 163.

that more than two-thirds of the forged land claims, valued at "probably not less than $150,000,000," had been exposed and defeated. In the same report, he said that the investigations furnished irresistible proof that an organized system of fabricating land titles had been carried on for a long time in California by Mexican officials, and that forgery and perjury, with the making of false grants had become a trade and a business.[16] On April 22, 1858, as quoted by Hittell, he pronounced the Limantour case "the greatest in atrocity as well as in magnitude . . . the most stupendous fraud ever perpetrated since the beginning of the world." [17] Later, in reference to fraudulent grants in general, he stated that there had been found in the hands of persons who were in close correspondence with high officers of the Mexican government numbers of blank forms for grants, bearing the signatures of distinguished officials of the Californias, dated ostensibly before the Mexican War, and ready to be filled in with names and data about lands and mines belonging to the United States.

As might be expected, Attorney General Black's report to Congress was bitterly criticized by persons who were interested in the lands, either directly, as speculators, or indirectly, as attorneys for claimants whose grants were being invalidated because they were based on fraud. William Carey Jones, who was attorney for some of the claims which had been declared fraudulent, wrote a series of letters in which he sharply criticized the Attorney General's statement and theories. He denounced Black's report as "reckless and mischievous mendacity" and exposed with skill and fairness some of the blunders that were contained in it. On the other hand, there was much commendation of the energetic measures used in "giving the subject of fraudulent manufactured grants a thorough and searching ventilation," as the *Alta California* (June 27, 1860) expressed it. Theodore H. Hittell, the historian, praised highly

[16] For a discussion of these frauds, see Alston G. Field, "Attorney-General Black and the California Land Claims," *Pacific Historical Review*, IV (1935), 238–240; Hittell, *op. cit.*, pp. 698–704.
[17] Hittell, *op. cit.*, p. 699.

Stanton's unmasking of the Limantour and other frauds. Agreeing that some valid claims had been rejected as well as some fraudulent claims confirmed, and admitting that a few of the estimates made by the Attorney General may have been somewhat extravagant, Hittell declared that Black was entirely correct with reference to the character of the frauds attempted, and that great service had been done to the government and the people by exposing and defeating them.[18]

After the lapse of nearly one hundred years, if we take into account certain considerations, we are able to understand some of the difficulties faced in the administration of the California Land Act, and the sharply variant opinions respecting it. On the one hand were the grantees who had received tracts of land, some of which had never been surveyed or had only been outlined and measured with a rope or lariat or in some other indefinite way. Descriptions of these property lines were often vague and uncertain, and it was difficult to determine just what land was granted or intended to be granted. All these grantees expected as a matter of course, under the Treaty of Guadalupe Hidalgo, to be left in possession of what they considered to be their lands. Complications were increased manifold by the great number of grants which were clearly forged or which offered just grounds for suspicion. On the other hand, there were persons who believed that "manifest destiny" had brought them to this western land, and that all its acres belonged to the United States by right of conquest.

In a frontier situation such as this, the question of ownership of land was not a matter which the government could either take action upon or leave alone. The government was compelled to act. Any one of a number of plans might have served. A bill such as the one proposed by Senator Benton could have been passed, providing for an authorized record and survey, the government reserving the right to contest claims of certain classes. This would have saved claimants much of the ex-

[18] See *ibid.*, pp. 698–701.

pense involved in proving, in several courts, legal ownership of the land they claimed. Or, similarly, there might have been merit in the position of John S. Hittell, who held that:

The government should have made a list of all ranchos, the possession of which was matter of common notoriety, and mentioned in the archives; should have confirmed them summarily, then surveyed them and issued patents. The claims which were not mentioned in the archives, or had not been reduced to possession, might properly have been subjected to judicial inquiry.[19]

Much might be said also for the plan recommended by Elisha O. Crosby to Senator Gwin. Under Crosby's plan a board of registration would record claims and take evidence, turning over each case, as soon as it was completed, to the Surveyor General for prompt survey; disputed boundaries would be settled by arbitration; a survey would be made, which would be final; and a patent would be issued after an interval of one year in which interested parties could present claims or charges in the District Court. Or, the policy suggested by Henry George might have been followed: the government should confirm all the small claims after a brief examination of their titles, and the federal court should handle the large and suspicious claims. What the government actually did was to adopt the policy of the land law of 1851, sponsored by Gwin, which required proof for all claims; under this the settlements were made.

In retrospect, it is clear that the land law of 1851 caused much financial loss through litigation, and that the unsettled conditions resulting from its application held back the utilization of California's resources. On the basis of these facts, it is easy to appraise the law as being only moderately successful, or to condemn it as thoroughly bad in every respect, as many have done. Viewing the situation realistically, however, one can be sure that, whatever the system, there would have been some errors—some bad claims would have been confirmed and

[19] Quoted in Bancroft, *op. cit.*, pp. 579–580.

some good ones rejected—with resulting dissatisfaction, losses, and disappointment for many. It is certain that under the circumstances no system could have produced results entirely satisfactory or could have avoided extensive litigation. Whatever the defects of the policy that was followed, the statistics of results speak impressively. They indicate that of the 813 cases presented to the commission, embracing, as estimated by Attorney General Black, an area of 19,148 square miles, 612 claims were confirmed, 178 cases were rejected, 19 were discontinued, and 4 were left pending.[20]

The questions of the ownership of lands by missions and pueblos, and what, if anything, was done with claims for such lands require only brief attention.[21] With respect to the "mission lands"—areas which adjoined the missions and were utilized at one time or another by them—it should be pointed out that no grants of these were ever made by either the Spanish or the Mexican government. It was acknowledged, however, that the church itself had an equitable and recognized right, which became in a large sense legal at the time of secularization, to the possession of the church buildings, priests' houses, the cemeteries, and small tracts at each mission, and to ground regularly used as gardens and orchards. As for the ungranted lands adjoining the missions, Andrés Pico, governor ad interim, leased and finally granted or sold the remnants of these mission estates to private parties, who assumed obligations to aid the church and the Indians and to recognize the title of the church to the property which properly was a part of it.

When the Land Commission began its hearings, mission claims were presented to this body in three classes. First, there were the claims under Pico's sales, of which there were seventeen. The lower tribunals rejected seven of these for fraud, for lack of archive evidence, for irregularities, or because some of the claims were for church property. In 1863 the Supreme Court decided, in the cases of the mission estates of San Gabriel

---

[20] Joseph Ellison, *op. cit.*, p. 24; Bancroft, *op. cit.*, p. 575.
[21] For a fuller presentation of these topics than is possible here, see Bancroft, *op. cit.*, pp. 562–570.

and San Luis Rey, that the governor had had no right at any time to sell these lands; but by this time eight of the claims had been confirmed. In the second class were the claims of the archbishop for a square league of land at each mission and for additional lands to be held in trust for the Indians at Missions San Miguel, Santa Clara, and Santa Inez. The claims for the square league at each mission were not based on alleged grants, but claims for the "additional lands" were based on certain orders of 1844 for the distribution of lots to Indians in the process of secularization of the missions. These claims were rejected, however, because there had been no grants and no occupation of the lands to make the claims valid before the courts. A third class was the valid and equitable claim of the archbishop for the church property at each mission, including a few acres for a garden, an orchard, and a vineyard, and for the Santa Inez College rancho in Santa Barbara County and Rancho La Laguna in San Luis Obispo County, which rested on formal grants.

In the true sense of the term there were only three pueblos in California: San Jose, Los Angeles, and Branciforte. Each pueblo was entitled to four square leagues of land, the disposal of which was in the hands of the municipal authorities. Because of the rights and privileges of the pueblo institution, many towns in 1846 claimed to be pueblos. Pueblo claims were later recognized by the United States judicial authorities in the cases of San Francisco, Sonoma, Monterey, Santa Barbara, San Diego, San Jose, and Los Angeles. The pueblo of Branciforte passed out of existence soon after its founding, and no land claim stemmed from it. Claims of the towns of Sonora and Sacramento for land were rejected because no basis was presented for them.

The land belonging to pueblos was only rarely granted by the government at the time of their founding. At any time thereafter surveys could be arranged by the pueblos themselves, and these served in lieu of grants. Lands in the pueblo were then distributed to individuals by officials of the town, not by the governor, who made grants of ranchos. By the act of 1851, the very existence of a town on July 7, 1846, was to be regarded as prima-facie evidence of a land grant. It was held that the United States was bound to acknowledge and perfect the equitable and inchoate title of a pueblo, just as it had to acknowledge the titles of individuals, and that each town was entitled to the lands granted or assigned by survey, or was entitled to four square leagues if no area or bounds had been fixed. The claim for the grants would then be presented in the name of the town and not in the name of the tract owners. On the basis of this principle the claims to lots bought and occupied before 1846 were almost automatically confirmed. Sales proved to have been made by alcaldes after 1846 were valid. With the pueblos, as with individuals, there was delay in the final settlement of the claims. Most of them, however, were decided by the board and courts before 1860, though surveys and the issuing of patents continued for a decade or two more.

Assertions of individual and state independence attended the private quest for ownership of mineral lands in California and raised in another area the question of land ownership in what was tacitly assumed to be a self-governing dominion.

Immediately after the gold discovery, the opinions of individual officials differed widely on the question of the mineral lands. Governor Mason recommended either the granting of licenses which would permit the holder to work small tracts, paying rent to the government, or the sale of small tracts at public auction. Thomas Butler King opposed the sale of mineral lands but favored the licensing of American citizens to dig anywhere in California on the payment of an ounce of gold to an official to be named. President Polk recommended to Congress that the mineral lands be held for the use of the United States government, or that they be sold at a small price; his successor, President Taylor, favored dividing the gold fields into small tracts to be disposed of by sale or lease. General Persifor Smith considered all gold diggers to be trespassers, and Governor Riley was against monopolization of the gold fields by any class of people; but neither offered any clear solution of the problem.

The people of California were naturally greatly concerned about the ownership and use of the mineral lands. In the constitutional convention of 1849, the delegates from the mining districts, on the whole, favored free mining or regulation of the mines for the benefit of the state, and expressed this sentiment in resolutions addressed to Congress. Because miners and settlers of the state held sharply divided opinions on the question of mineral lands, it was extremely difficult for anyone to work out a well-ordered plan for the regulation of these lands. The two groups were pretty well united, however, against the policy of leasing or selling the gold fields, and were strongly in favor of giving such lands to the state. All this was reflected in the first legislature, which opposed the policy of leasing or selling the mineral lands, the majority of the legislators being of the opinion that American citizens should be permitted to work the mines freely, paying only a small tax for protective purposes, on the ground that California had been acquired by the Americans and they should receive the benefits of the acquisition.

The American miners, with few exceptions, were hostile to foreign miners. As a result, the first legislature passed an act prohibiting foreigners from digging gold in California unless they paid a foreign miner's license fee of twenty dollars a month. Although the California supreme court upheld the constitutionality of the law, opposition to the tax by some merchants and many lawyers, and the difficulties of collecting it, led to its repeal in 1851. After its repeal, miners, in public meetings, petitioned the legislature for laws prohibiting certain groups of foreigners from entering California or working in its mines, and threatened mob action if their request were denied. Under pressure, the legislature of 1852 passed a bill requiring foreign miners to pay a license fee of three dollars a month. In spite of protests made by persons of Latin origin against the discriminatory practices of collectors under the law, the legislature, at the next session, raised the fee to four dollars a month. The act was further amended in 1855. It should be noted in this connection that, in their efforts to have fees levied on miners they considered to be foreigners, while avoiding additional taxation for themselves, the California miners were not following the democratic practices usual to an American frontier.

The attitude and action of the federal government in the question of the mining lands after its admission of California, stated briefly, is this: Among the eighteen bills which Senator Frémont offered immediately after he was sworn in was one entitled "A bill to regulate the working of the placers and the gold mines in California, and to preserve order by granting temporary permits to actual operators to work the same in limited quantities." With some amendments, the bill passed the Senate, but in the House it was laid over until the next session. Although Frémont defended his plan in an "Address to the People of California," he found a majority of the citizenry opposed to government regulation of the mineral lands of the state he represented. They did not accept either the method or the principle of Frémont's proposal, and he did not return to Washington to back his bill in the next Congressional session.

President Fillmore, supported by his Secretary of the Interior, Alexander H. H. Stuart, urged Congress to provide for the sale of the mineral lands in small tracts, with effective safeguards against capitalistic monopoly control. In California, this plan was opposed on the ground that miners did not want title to land but only freedom to dig for gold and to move on to another mine as soon as one gave out. The legislature adopted a joint resolution opposing the policy of selling mineral lands, on the ground that it was contrary to the true interests of the state and nation. At last, becoming convinced that it would be better to have the gold fields open to all American citizens, President Fillmore, on the advice of Secretary Stuart, recommended a policy of noninterference. This policy of *laissez faire*, recommended by the President and rather generally favored in California, was the policy of the federal government with respect to California mining lands until the passage of the act of July 26, 1866.

Through all of the intervening period expressions of dissatisfaction were heard, and attempts were made to formulate a different policy, such as state ownership of the mines; but the "free use" policy continued. By 1865 there had developed in Washington a strong conviction that the time had come to abandon the policy of federal noninterference. A preliminary step was taken on July 9, 1865, when a bill for the sale of mineral lands in areas limited to forty acres was reported in the House. After some debate, the bill was recommitted. Several members of Congress then journeyed to California to gain more information on the subject. There they found opinion to be divided: the quartz miners and the agricultural and commercial interests, on the one hand, favored a policy of conferring titles in fee to the miners; the placer miners, on the other hand, opposed any change, fearing that their interests would be jeopardized.

In the next year, a bill carrying elements of the bills of both houses became law on July 26, 1866. The first section of the act provided that:

The mineral lands of the public domain, both surveyed and unsurveyed, are hereby declared to be free and open to exploration and occupation by all citizens of the United States, and those who have declared their intention to become citizens, subject to such regulations as may be prescribed by law, and subject also to the local customs or rules of miners in the several mining districts, so far as the same may not be in conflict with the laws of the United States.[22]

This law made it possible for miners to acquire title in fee simple to mineral lands of the public domain—that is, to vein mines. There was no provision in it for acquiring title to placer

---

[22] Quoted on p. 76 of Joseph Ellison, *op. cit.* Ellison's chapter iv (pp. 54–78), "The Mineral Land Question in California," is a comprehensive and authoritative presentation of the subject.

mines. This omission was rectified by an act of July 9, 1870, providing for the sale of placer mines at two dollars and a half per acre. Under the law of 1866, miners who had occupied and improved mines, or who might later occupy and improve them, could obtain their patents at a cost of five dollars per acre. The law restricted the amount and location of lands in an effort to prevent monopoly control. Articles in the public press indicated almost universal approval, and Governor Low, in his message of 1866, stated: "The apprehension of miners in regard to unwise and unfriendly legislation by Congress touching the mineral lands, has been allayed by the passage of just and generous laws which guarantee the actual possession to those on whom the prosperity of the State so largely depends." [23]

Another phase of the California land problem had to do with the State of California and the public domain. When California was ceded to the United States, all the lands within its bounds which had not previously been granted to individuals and to towns became a part of the public domain. By this time, the United States had evolved a policy of making liberal land grants to new states for internal improvements and the promotion of education, and of selling acreage to individuals on easy terms. This policy of the United States on lands, in the natural order of things, found further application and development in the new self-governing dominion which began its history as a state on September 9, 1850. In keeping with it, both President Polk and President Taylor recommended a liberal land policy in California.

In the constitutional convention there was strong frontier feeling that the public domain within the new state boundaries rightfully belonged to California. Although a resolution on the subject was rejected because of doubt over the convention's right to act on a matter belonging to the legislature, and fear that such action might affect adversely California's application for admission into the Union, the convention passed an or-

[23] California, *Journal of the Senate*, 17th sess., 1867–1868, p. 53.

dinance asking Congress for extensive lands. These were to include one section for every quarter township of public lands; seventy-two sections for the support of a university; four sections for a seat of government; five hundred thousand acres in addition to the five hundred thousand acres granted to every state under the public-land act of 1841; 5 per cent of the net proceeds of the sale of public lands within the state, and all salt springs within the state.[24]

At least ten of the eighteen bills introduced by Senator Frémont just after the admission of California had to do with land donations to the state, but the session closed without their having been considered. However, California did at once receive its five hundred thousand acres for internal improvements as provided by the general public-land act of 1841, and, under an act of September 28, 1850, which granted to public-land states the swamp and overflowed lands within their limits, it became the owner of several million more acres. In the second session of the Thirty-first Congress, Senator Gwin introduced a bill in the Senate "to provide for the survey of the public lands in California; the granting of donation privileges therein and for other purposes," but due to sectional and state opposition to what were regarded as favors to California, there was no legislation on public lands for the state in this session, except that an appropriation was made for their survey.[25]

Resentment at what was regarded in the state as Congressional neglect with respect to disposition of the public domain in California found expression in the press, in political and other meetings, in messages of the governor, and in legislative resolutions. The pressure on Congress for action, and the leadership of California's Senators, resulted in the passing of the act of March 3, 1853, providing for surveys and land offices, and in the opening of unreserved agricultural public lands to preëmption under the act of September 4, 1841.

[24] J. Ross Browne, *Report of Debates in the Convention of California*, p. 467.
[25] For details on the subject of California lands, see Joseph Ellison, *op. cit.*, 28–29, 30–34, 50–51.

Provision was made, also, for granting to the state the sixteenth and thirty-sixth sections of each township for public-school purposes, two entire townships for the use of a seminary of learning, and ten sections of land to be used as sites for public buildings.[26]

It was not easy for the federal government to satisfy all the demands of frontier communities for possessions and favors, and this was particularly true of the self-governing dominion of California. The land act of 1853 satisfied neither Governor Bigler, nor the legislature, nor the press. Arguments were advanced that California had organized an independent and sovereign state and had come into the Union with the ownership of its public lands as an attribute of sovereignty. To implement these ideas the state senate appointed a special committee to inquire into the expediency of asking Congress to concede to California all the lands within the state's limits. The report of this committee, submitted on April 4, 1853, asserted that some of the members believed that the public lands within the state were, without further action, the property of the state because of the rights of sovereignty and eminent domain possessed by each state—rights which California had not yielded up. The memorial prepared by the committee asked Congress to make acknowledgment of the sovereign dignity of California by recognizing its ownership of the public lands within its boundaries. Although it was laid on the table after being accepted, and was never taken up again, it reflected sentiment in California that was markedly strong.

Similar agitation continued throughout the first decade of California's "sovereign" existence, but with weakening force as frontier independence grew less. Governor Bigler, in his annual message in 1855, urged the legislature to memorialize Congress to relinquish the public lands to the state. Although some of the legislators supported his view, others argued that the United States had acquired California from Mexico and

[26] United States, *Statutes at Large*, X, pp. 244–248.

by acquisition possessed the lands within the territory—a sentiment different from that which had at first been generally held. Although the question of the lands continued to be discussed, and as late as 1860 assertions of the state's claim to the lands on legal and constitutional grounds were occasionally made, the people in general had by that time relinquished the earlier doctrine, partly because they wanted to avoid conflict between the state and the federal government, and also because they had become aware of their dependence upon and integral relation to the Union.

Several other aspects of the land question continued through the 'fifties to agitate the people of California. Notable among them are the disagreements and conflicts between the state and the federal government over the interpretation and application of the federal law granting 500,000 acres to each new state. California officials persisted in disregarding a provision in the act of 1841 requiring that selections by the state in such grants should be in parcels of not less than 320 acres in any one location and that they should be from surveyed lands. The Commissioner of the General Land Office protested these violations, but to no avail. The California officials defended their action as being proper in view of the fact that only a small part of the public lands in California had been surveyed. Conflict occurred also between preëmptors of those lands, who were supported by the United States Commissioner, and those who had purchased lands from the state. Up to 1864 the California supreme court upheld the claims of the state purchasers, but in that year the court reversed itself, holding that "the mode, the time, the quantity of the selection and location are fixed by the act."

In its eagerness to satisfy its people and to exercise what it regarded as its rights as a self-governing dominion, California disregarded numerous other provisions of the federal government with respect to land questions. Its attempted action on the question of the school-land grant is a notable example of this failure to comply with the federal rules. The act of March 3, 1853, granted sections numbered sixteen and thirty-six to the state for school purposes. These would not be subject to the preëmption laws; and other land, selected by the proper state authorities, might be substituted for any parts of these sections on which settlement had been made before the land had been surveyed, or from which sites had been selected for public uses. Since the grant did not restrict the selections to surveyed lands, state officers claimed the right to make selections from unsurveyed as well as from surveyed lands. Carrying out this idea, the legislature passed acts authorizing the selection of school lands from any vacant lands of the public domain in California and permitting the sale of the lands selected. Up to April 1, 1864, the state had sold many thousands of acres of unsurveyed lands. The Commissioner of the General Land Office not only refused to recognize these selections but told state authorities that the office would protect the interests of preëmptors who had taken up land in good faith. Not an acre of these lands had been patented by the United States Land Office by 1863.

The question of swamplands and their disposition was another controversial issue in California. An act of September 28, 1850, granted to public-land states all the swamp and overflowed lands within their boundaries. It provided that the Secretary of the Interior should make an accurate list of plots of such lands, transmit the list to the governors of the states concerned, and, on the request of each governor, issue a patent to these lands. The proceeds from the sale of these lands were to be used to pay the costs of levees and drains that would be used in their reclamation. The people of California were pleased with a grant which would enrich the state by several million acres of fertile land bordering its bays and rivers. Difficulties began to arise when Governor Bigler held that the field notes of the United States Surveyor General would not be acceptable to the state, and the legislature passed an act providing for the sale of swamplands. To complicate matters further, some county surveyors allocated to the state land which they designated as "swamp and overflowed" but which was not so shown in the surveys and plots of the United States surveyor. Other difficulties arose when some of the land sold by the state as swampland was later offered for sale by federal officials. For a decade after the grants of the swamplands there was much controversy between state and federal authorities over the interpretation and application of the laws. The state, in this period, sold as swamp and overflowed lands forty-three thousand acres which were claimed by the United States.

Debate between the state and the nation over the school lands and swamplands continued until the Civil War had ended and an act of Congress, approved on July 23, 1866, settled the controversial questions. Briefly stated, the act confirmed to the State of California the selections made by the state from unsurveyed portions of the public lands and which had been sold in good faith under the state laws as partial satisfaction of the several grants made to the state by the nation. It also confirmed to the state mineral lands and lands held or claimed under valid Spanish or Mexican grants. Excepted, of course, were selections that were illegal because the land had been acquired by settlers under preëmption and homestead rights prior to the passage of the act. In addition, the act required the Commissioner General, within a year after the passage of the act, to confirm to the state the swamp and overflowed lands as represented on the approved plots of townships made by the United States. The act made provision for determining what, if any, of the lands claimed by California were not on the surveyed maps. Another section of the act recognized the right of the state to select for school purposes other lands in lieu of the parts of sections sixteen and thirty-six which had been settled upon prior to the survey, or that had been reserved for public uses, or that were covered by Spanish and Mexican grants. In later years many conflicting issues grew out of these settlements.

The contest over what is referred to as the "five per cent fund" was settled at so late a date that only brief mention of it can properly be made here. The fund so designated was a

Congressional grant to the public-land states from the net proceeds from sales of public lands within the confines of these states, on the condition that no state would tax federal lands within its boundaries. It was customary for this fund to be granted to states when they were admitted into the Union, but neither the California admission act, nor the act of March 3, 1853, mentioned the five per cent fund. In California the omission was considered unfair because the state had not only been admitted into the Union on an equal footing with the other states but had surrendered to the federal government the right to tax certain land. Although governors and other officials protested against what was asserted to be discrimination, the legislature of California adopted resolutions asking Congress for the fund, and at many times bills were introduced in Congress requesting the grant, it was not until 1906, after California had suffered the catastrophe of that year, that an act became law which granted to the State of California five per cent of the cash sales of public lands in California which had been sold since the state was admitted into the Union.

The question who owned or controlled the lands of California plagued the new self-governing dominion and the federal organization of which it was a part for a decade and more after California was admitted into the Union. The state and its citizens wanted all the advantages they could obtain. Their attitude and actions were expressions of the independence and possessiveness of a strong frontier community. The United States government, for its part, wished to administer California lands with justice and due regard for a state in the federal union. Because of the many complications attending the settlement of the state, the varied opinions concerning the obligations of the government to the people, the simplicity with which many persons view complex problems, and the possessive self-interest of human beings, there was continual criticism of the federal government's action or inaction in its dealings with the California land question in the 'fifties, and many persons in the state felt that the United States had failed them.

In the nature of things, government is not a perfect machine. The persons who administer government are fallible and often biased. The data on which officials must act are incomplete, changing, and distorted. The actions of Congress, administrative officers, and the courts in dealing with the land question in California, as might be expected, were accompanied by a margin of error and injustice. It is a simple matter to point out mistakes made by Congress, the Land Commission, the courts, or the federal administration in arriving at the settlement of various phases of the land question in California. It is not quite so easy to point out what should have been done, or to show that different methods of handling might have lessened complaints or reduced injustice. In a transition which takes place in the rapid making of a state, with false conceptions of sovereignty, many persons suffer hurt and loss, while many gain. It is clear that the settlement of the land question for California was an example of trial and error, of blundering and building, by which California made great advances in its formative years.

VI

Lo! The Poor Indian

---

*Let the Red Children of the Great White
Father withdraw beyond a certain line, let
them live in amity with their white brethren,
and they should be left in peace "As long as
the rivers shall run and the grass shall grow."*
—OLIVER LA FARGE, *As Long as the Grass
Shall Grow*

IN THEIR TREATMENT of the Indians and
seizure of their lands the white men were merely putting into
practice a theory that was commonly held by Americans on the
frontier—that the people who through generations had lived
on lands had no rights in them if others who considered themselves superior wanted them. This form of Americanism found
new expression in California. There, as elsewhere on the frontier, Indians were expendable for what is called progress. California's Indian frontier differed in important respects from
other such frontiers. The history of the treatment of Indians
in California, therefore, furnishes additional data for the study
of American civilization. The facts in the California story are
not all complimentary to the white men of the state, but they
illustrate a phase of the American way.

Because of the friction resulting from the eagerness of individuals and states to secure the lands occupied by Indians, many persons came to feel, soon after 1800, that the only way to deal with the situation was to separate the Indians and the whites by persuading the former to exchange the lands they occupied for new lands somewhere in the West. The new plan, which came to be known as the "removal policy," had by 1840 resulted in the erection of an Indian frontier extending from the Red River and Texas to the Great Lakes. Many believed that beyond that frontier the United States would not expand. The Indian frontier had hardly been established when the line of division was destroyed by the annexation of Texas, the settlement of the Oregon question, the westward migration of the Mormons, and the addition of an immense area to the United States by the Treaty of Guadalupe Hidalgo. As a result of these events the United States became responsible for a large additional Indian population, and treaties which it had already made with the Indians were broken by large numbers of people in crossing the Indian country on their way to the new lands.

The natives of California, when the Spaniards began the task of civilizing them in 1769, were among the least advanced of the Indians in America. In all their territory there was almost no agricultural production, practically no culture of any kind, and little tribal organization. The native groups, of which there were many, were each held together, and separated from other groups, by language and by the topography of the country more than by political or social bonds or barriers. They numbered at the time, according to various estimates, from 150,000 to 260,000 persons.[1]

Between the founding of Mission San Diego in 1769 and the

[1] Much information about the Indians in California is contained in the *Handbook of American Indians,* ed. by F. M. Hodge, Bureau of American Ethnology, Bulletin 30 (Washington, 1907–1910); H. H. Bancroft, *Native Races* (San Francisco, 1883), I, III, IV; Stephen Powers, *Tribes of California* (Washington, 1877); and *University of California Publications in American Archaeology and Ethnology* (Berkeley: University of California Press, 1903——).

year 1823, twenty other Franciscan missions were established between San Diego and Sonoma. For a period of fifty years the missions as civilizing agencies were from certain standpoints a great success. There were times when they had in their care as many as 21,000 natives, who were taught the rudiments of Christianity and some of the arts of industry and agriculture. Then came the secularization of the missions, provided for under a *reglamento provisional* passed on August 2, 1834, and practically carried into effect by 1839, which undid the work of the faithful missionaries and scattered their protégés. Many Indians, unable to readjust themselves to their old ways of living, died. Others went into the haunts of the wild Indians, whence, joining with them, they came back from time to time to raid and steal. These raids, which resulted in much conflict between the Indians and the whites, continued even beyond the date of the American occupation.

The taking possession of California by the United States in 1846, and subsequent events in the region, particularly the discovery of gold in 1848, had important consequences for the history of Indian affairs in the United States. Indirectly, as has already been noted, American acquisition helped to break down the established Indian frontier; directly it added another Indian problem to the burdens of Indian administration. This problem was a large and somewhat difficult one, for complications resulted from the character and previous history of the Indians in California, and the Indians numbered at least 100,000 in 1846, in spite of the great losses from pestilence and recent contact with the whites.[2] Adjustment between this large body of Indians and the whites, whose numbers increased rapidly, was not made without difficulty. Here, as in practically every other part of the United States where the whites took possession of lands occupied by or in proximity to the Indians, the govern-

[2] An estimate based on statements in *Handbook of American Indians* Pt. 1, p. 190; C. Hart Merriam, "Indian population in California," in *American Anthropologist* (n.s.), VII, 594–606; letters of Indian officials in California to the Commissioner of Indian Affairs, in 32d Cong., spec. sess., Senate Ex. Doc. No. 4, pp. 62–63, 67–69, 242, 379; *Report of the Commissioner of Indian Affairs*, 1856, p. 246.

ment had a dual task. It had to guard the whites, who were pressing in upon the territory, against outrages by the Indians. On the other hand, it had to protect the Indians against the rapacity and cruelty of the white people.

The intention to fulfill this task was evidenced in two proclamations issued by the military authorities in California immediately after the Americans took possession. One of these documents proclaimed that "The California Battalion of Mounted Riflemen will be kept in the service of the Territory, and constantly on duty to prevent and punish the aggressions by the Indians or any other persons upon the property of individuals or the 'peace of the Territory," providing ostensibly for the safety of settlements against raids in which cattle and horses might be stolen and persons endangered. The other was a proclamation in the district of San Francisco, ordering the release of all Indians held to serve against their wills, but declaring that those who had chosen their own employers must abide by their contracts unless they should be given permission in writing to leave, or unless the magistrate should annul the contract. By this order, also, the Indians were prohibited from wandering about the country in an idle and dissolute manner, and any found so wandering were liable to arrest and punishment by labor on the public works, at the discretion of the magistrate. The proclamations [3] very clearly were assertions of the sovereignty of the United States over the Indians and the territory occupied by them.

General Kearny, after taking office as governor of California on March 1, 1847, tried conciliatory methods in dealing with the Indians. In addition to adopting the policy of giving presents to them as a means of maintaining peace, he, by virtue of authority vested in him as military governor of the territory,

---

[3] The "California Battalion" was made up of Frémont's men and others who enlisted under Stockton. See H. H. Bancroft, *History of California*, V, 257, 283, T. H. Hittell, *History of California*, II, 579–580. References to the battalion and to Indian defense are in the San Francisco *California Star*, January 9, 16, and 23, 1847. The second proclamation referred to was a public order of John B. Montgomery, who was in military command of the district of San Francisco. See *ibid.*, February 20, March 6, 1847.

appointed John A. Sutter subagent for the Indians on and near the Sacramento and San Joaquin rivers, and appointed Mariano G. Vallejo subagent for the Indians north of San Francisco Bay. He instructed these agents to secure information concerning the Indians in their districts, to establish local regulations with the approval of the governor, and to regard themselves as protectors of the Indians.

In spite of these efforts in their behalf, the Indians continued their depredations, and the military force proved inadequate to cope with the situation. The result was that Lieutenant William T. Sherman, through Alcalde John Burton of San Jose, authorized the shooting of Indians caught stealing horses. About this time, on November 1, 1847, a general order went into effect, directing all persons having Indians in their service to give each Indian employed by them a certificate showing his employment. Any Indian found wandering about without such a certificate was to be arrested and punished as a horsethief. Wild Indians and others not employed, who wished to visit settlements for the purposes of trade, were required to secure passes from the Indian subagent of the district. These measures bear a close resemblance to the Black Codes of the South. They made atrocities against the Indians possible and fostered harsh and discriminatory action against them. Matters were balanced to some extent, however, when, with a view to correcting the evils among Indians resulting from the nefariousness of the whites, Colonel Mason issued a proclamation on November 29, 1847, making liable to severe punishment anyone who in any manner gave or sold liquor to Indians, and providing that Indians should be held to be competent witnesses in cases of prosecution. Alcaldes and Indian subagents were directed to carry the provisions of the proclamation into effect. Vigorous action was demanded against all violators of the law, and numbers of persons were rigorously prosecuted.[4]

[4] *California Star*, September 18, 1847. Halleck to Vallejo, August 16, 1847, Lieutenant Sherman to John Burton, September 6, 1847, in 31st Cong., 1st sess., Senate Ex. Doc. No. 18, p. 358. For Mason's proclamation and its effects see *ibid.*, pp. 413, 539–542, 547–548. Vallejo, "Documentos para la historia de California" (MS in Bancroft Library, University of California), XII, 319, 324.

Until peace with Mexico was assured, the dealings of the United States with the Indians of California were on an expediential basis and were confined almost wholly to the coastal area and the area just north of San Francisco Bay. After the peace treaty was signed, reports on the Indian situation were called for, and they were made by the proper governmental authorities. Then, on December 5, 1848, the President in his message to Congress recommended the appointment of a suitable number of Indian agents for the territory.

On April 3 of the next year, the Secretary of War notified the military commander on the Pacific Coast that the proper officers for the management of Indian affairs in California had been appointed and would soon proceed to the scene of their labors. On the same day, the Secretary of State gave instructions to Thomas Butler King, who had been appointed by the President, to study conditions in California and to secure information concerning the natives there. The Commissioner of Indian Affairs, on April 7, issued a commission to John S. Wilson as Indian agent at "Salt Lake, California," and on April 14 issued one to Adam Johnston as Indian subagent on the Sacramento and San Joaquin rivers. On July 15, William Carey Jones was sent to California under instructions from the Secretary of State and the Secretary of the Interior. He was directed specifically to study land titles; in addition, he was to inquire into the nature of Indian rights as they had existed under the Spanish and Mexican governments, and the manner in which such rights had been recognized, as well as to determine from authoritative data the differences between the privileges enjoyed by the wandering tribes and those enjoyed by the tribes who had made actual settlements, and to report the general form, extent, and locality of such settlements.[5]

In the summer and fall of 1849, as tens of thousands of people

---

[5] For the recommendation of the President and the appointments made, see 30th Cong., 2d sess., House Ex. Doc. No. 76, pp. 1–5; 31st Cong., 1st sess., Senate Ex. Doc. No. 1, Pt. 1, p. 157; 31st Cong., 1st sess., Senate Ex. Doc. No. 18, pp. 9–11, 97–98, 409–410; W. C. Jones, *Report on the Subject of Land Titles in California*, p. 3.

poured into the Indian-populated areas of California, unjustly crowding the natives from their accustomed haunts, the men appointed to investigate and report on the California Indian question reached the field and took up their work. William Carey Jones, as he stated in his report of April 10, 1850, found, with respect to Indian rights to the soil under the Spanish and Mexican governments, that "in the wild or wandering tribes, the Spanish law does not recognize any title whatever to the soil"; but settled Indians, according to the Spanish colonial laws, had a right to as much land as they needed for their habitations, for tillage, and for the pasturage of their flocks.[6]

Thomas Butler King's report, dated March 22, 1850, was, on the whole, of no great significance in regard to Indian administration. Little that he said about Indians was based on firsthand information, and his figures are not reliable. King did observe correctly, however, that the number of Indians had greatly diminished since earlier days, as archaeological remains in all the valleys of the Sierra Nevada and along the foothills of that range indicated. Many of the Indians which he saw were of the lowest grade of human beings and had little inclination to work or to improve their condition. They had never had any interest in the soil, nor had the Spaniards or the American immigrants regarded them as possessing any. It was King's opinion that it might be possible to gather the Indians together and to teach them in some degree the arts of civilization.

The report of Jones on the Indians in relation to lands; King's suggestion that the arts of civilization might be taught to the Indians if they were collected in one place; the important reports of Adam Johnston, which advised the establishing of depots at various points for the distribution of supplies to Indians who were crowded out of their old homes by the rapid advance of immigrants; and the recommendation of General Riley that, as far as practicable, the Indians of California should be concentrated in districts over which the United States

[6] Jones, *op. cit.*, pp. 32–34.

should have exclusive jurisdiction—all have a bearing on what the federal government worked out as a California Indian policy. Partly as a result of these suggestions from the civil and military officials in California and partly because of a desire to act for the best interests of both Indians and whites, but with little understanding of the situation in that remote region, Congress passed, and the President approved, on September 28, 1850, "An Act to authorize the appointment of Indian agents in California." On September 30 a measure became law, appropriating $25,000 for the use of the President in making treaties with the various Indian tribes in California.[7]

Redick McKee of Virginia, George W. Barbour of Kentucky, and O. M. Wozencraft of Louisiana were appointed Indian agents, or commissioners, under the laws passed by Congress. As early as possible they set out for the field of their labors. Dr. Wozencraft reached San Francisco on December 27, 1850, Colonel McKee on December 29, and Colonel Barbour on January 8, 1851. The commissioners decided to act collectively for a time, though their instructions permitted them to work separately. John McKee, son of Redick McKee, was employed as secretary of their body.[8]

On January 14, 1851, the agents went to the capital at San Jose to consult with the governor and to secure information from the members of the legislature about Indian troubles in their respective districts. They found the governor and the legislature greatly agitated by reports of Indian depredations in various parts of the state. As a result of the excitement, the legislature passed a bill authorizing a loan, of not more than $500,000, for use in repelling invasions or suppressing insurrections. Another act provided for the payment of liberal salaries to officers and soldiers who had previously aided in

[7] For Jones's report on the Indian situation, see 31st Cong., 1st sess., House Ex. Doc. No. 59, pp. 1, 2, 6–8; for that of Johnston, see 33d Cong., spec. sess., Senate Ex. Doc. No. 4, pp. 37, 41–43, 45; for that of General Riley, see 31st Cong., 1st sess., House Ex. Doc. No. 59, pp. 56–57. For the law authorizing the appointment of Indian agents see *United States Statutes at Large . . . from December 1, 1845, to March 3, 1851* (Boston, 1851), pp. 519, 544–559.

[8] See 33d Cong., spec. sess., Senate Ex. Doc. No. 4, pp. 53–54.

putting down uprisings. Still another act authorized the governor to call out troops to defend the frontier, and provided liberally for their compensation.[9] The legislators assumed that the federal government would reimburse the state for all expenditures called for under these acts. These military provisions would have been none too great if the governor's statement that there were 100,000 warriors in the state had been true.

Early in February the commissioners set out for the Indian country in the San Joaquin Valley. Accompanied by a military escort of the United States Army, they went to Stockton, then up the San Joaquin Valley to the Mariposa River. With much effort, they induced six tribes of Indians to assemble at the commissioners' camp, and there, on March 19, they negotiated the first treaty between the United States and the California Indian tribes. The commissioners next proceeded south. On April 29 they made a formal treaty with sixteen tribes, or bands, at Camp Barbour on the upper San Joaquin River.

By the treaties concluded in each of the areas, the jurisdiction of the United States over the Indians and over lands occupied by them was jointly recognized, provisions and beef cattle were promised in abundance to the Indians on the ground that "it is *cheaper* to feed the whole flock for a *year* than to *fight* them for a week," [10] and it was agreed that all cases of dispute between Indians and white men should be adjudicated by the civil authorities. The Indians in both areas, in agreeing to the treaty provisions, relinquished all title to lands claimed by them; and in return for such relinquishment, the commissioners set aside large tracts of land for their exclusive occupancy. As soon as each treaty had been concluded, the Indians affected by it were led to the reservation set apart for them.

Although the original instructions permitted each commissioner to adopt a separate course of action, the commissioners,

[9] For the various acts passed, see *Statutes of California*, 1851, pp. 402–403, 489–491, 520–521.

[10] McKee, Barbour and Wozencraft to L. Lea, May 1, 1851, 33d Cong., spec. sess., Senate Ex. Doc. No. 4, p. 76. The activities of the commissioners described in this and ensuing paragraphs are recorded in this document.

on their arrival in California, because of their slight knowledge of the country and of their problem, had deemed it wise to act as a joint board for a time. They later, however, decided to work separately, and on May 1 drew lots to determine which area each should take.

Lots being cast . . . the northern district, or that portion of the state north of 40° or 41° of latitude, until it reaches the headwaters of the Sacramento . . . fell to R. McKee. The middle district, extending from the San Joaquin on the south to the headwaters of the Sacramento, and east of the coast range to the eastern boundary of the State, fell to O. M. Wozencraft. The southern district, extending from the San Joaquin south and west, and east to the State boundary, fell to G. W. Barbour.[11]

After the division was arranged, Wozencraft and McKee left Camp Barbour on May 3 for San Francisco. Colonel Barbour at once entered upon the duties of his district in the south; there, as rapidly as possible, he brought Indian tribes together, made treaties with them similar to the two already made, and set apart large tracts of land as Indian reservations. On May 13, on the Kings River, he negotiated a treaty with twelve tribes or bands of Indians; on May 30 he arranged one with seven tribes on the Kaweah River; on June 3 he made another with four tribes on Paint Creek; and on June 10 he concluded another with eleven bands at Tejon Pass in what is now Kern County.

From there Barbour went on to Los Angeles, where, in a letter from McKee, he received disappointing news about funds. Regretfully he abandoned his plans to visit Indian tribes on the Colorado River below Los Angeles. After crossing over into the Tulare Valley to treat with the Indians who were threatening an outbreak there, he went on to San Francisco. He found there a letter from the Indian Office advising him that only $25,000 had been appropriated for the Indian work in California and directing that as soon as this sum was expended the commissioners should confine themselves solely to their

[11] 33d Cong., spec. sess., Senate Ex. Doc. No. 4, pp. 97–98.

duties as agents. Since he was unable to proceed with treaty making, because no funds were available for it, and since things were moving along harmoniously in the valley under Adam Johnston, Barbour left San Francisco for a trip east on October 4, 1851.

Although Johnston did not consider the making of treaties an effective method of dealing with the California Indians, and he believed that a line of military posts along the valley of the San Joaquin, with an Indian agent at each one, would prove to be a better means of meeting the Indian problem, it became necessary for him, as Indian subagent, to coöperate in arranging some of the treaties and to assume responsibility for certain reservations after the treaties had been made. His work, most of which was carried on in Barbour's district, resulted in the accumulation of large claims against the United States for payment for beef and other supplies and for medical services, which he relied upon the government to pay in the future. Johnston's work for the Indians before the commissioners arrived had been commendable, and he had made valuable reports to the department. His subordination when the commissioners entered upon their duties caused him to become dissatisfied, and by the end of the summer of 1851 his position had grown almost intolerable to him. From then until his dismissal from office on January 9, 1852, his services were not noteworthy.

Wozencraft, who, with McKee, arrived in San Francisco on May 8, 1851, began immediately to make preparations for a journey into the central district, and on May 24 left San Francisco for the Indian country, after having been advised by McKee of the limited funds at his disposal. As rapidly as possible he made treaties with many tribes and, like the other agents, set apart large reservations for them. He made his first treaty on May 28, with six tribes of Indians who met at Dent and Vantine's ferry on the Stanislaus River; the next he made with ten tribes at Camp Union on the Yuba River; he concluded another on August 1 with nine tribes of Indians near Bidwell's ranch on Chico Creek. Five tribes entered into a treaty at Reading's ranch on August 16; eight tribes made a treaty at Camp Colus on September 2; and four tribes on the Cosumnes River entered into a treaty on September 18. After the treaties were made, some twelve tribes were added to those on the reservation near Chico. Wozencraft stated with characteristic exaggeration that he expected that eventually as many as 75,000 or 80,000 Indians would be included in the provisions of the six treaties. While traveling and making these compacts, he piled up heavy claims against the United States. To fulfill the stipulations contained in the several treaties, $346,138 would be needed. Wozencraft, in addition to the treaties which he made in the central district, set apart two reservations below Los Angeles early in January, 1852, in the district that had been allotted to Barbour and that Barbour, when he left for the East, had asked Wozencraft to take charge of in his absence.

Redick McKee's journey into the northern district was delayed until August 11, 1851, because funds failed to arrive from Washington. He was able to start when he did only because Collector King advanced him $5,000 on a draft against the department. The party proceeded north by way of the Russian River country, Humboldt River on the coast, Klamath River Valley, and Scott's Valley, where the journey ended. With various tribes of Indians, McKee made treaties of the same general character as those negotiated by Barbour and Wozencraft. The first one was made with eight tribes at a camp near Clear Lake on August 20; another was made with four more tribes in the same general region on August 22. On October 6, on the South Fork of the Trinity River, McKee arranged a treaty with the nations of the lower Klamath, the upper Klamath, and the Trinity rivers. On November 4, after locating a reservation site in Scott's Valley—with great difficulty because of the objections of the settlers—McKee concluded a treaty with three nations that resided severally in twenty-four, nineteen, and seven rancherias, or villages.

On December 29, the day after his return to San Francisco,

McKee made a report to Washington on his activities in the north. His services from this time to the end of his relations with the Indian Office in the early part of 1853 were less expensive to the government than his earlier efforts, but they were likewise of slight practical value. Some of the time he used, not too successfully, in defending the treaties before the legislature and in the press; but the greater part he spent in controversies with the military authorities over the way in which meat had been furnished to the Indians by the northern expedition, with Governor Bigler and the members of the legislature over the blame for difficulties between Indians and whites in the northern part of the state, and with recently appointed Superintendent Edward F. Beale over the question of their relative authority.

The chief work of Barbour, Wozencraft, and McKee was the negotiation of treaties with the Indians of California.[12] In all, they made 18 treaties, affecting 139 tribes or bands. The precise number of Indians included in these tribes is not known, but it is safe to say that there were at least 25,000. Only a fraction of this number, however, was ever taken to the reservations. These areas set apart for the Indians totaled 11,700 square miles, or 7,488,000 acres—approximately as much land as there is today in the counties of Fresno, Alameda, Sacramento, and San Diego combined, or 7½ per cent of the total area of the state.

The government of the United States, in authorizing the commissioners to make treaties with the Indians of California, had appropriated $25,000 for their use in doing so. An additional $25,000 was sent to them under date of May 25, 1851. They spent all of the $50,000, as they had a right to do. In addition, they let contracts for supplies and incurred other expenses which amounted to nearly a million dollars. It is difficult to say to what extent they were justified in doing

---

[12] The treaties made by the commissioners are in *Message of the President of the United States, Communicating Eighteen Treaties Made with Indians in California, 1851–1852,* 32d Cong., 1st sess. (Washington, 1905).

this. Certainly, they had no authorization to commit the government as they did. But they defended their action on the ground that it was necessary under the circumstances, and, with a sort of Theodore Rooseveltian philosophy, they argued that men sent to perform a certain task are not to be condemned for carrying out the order in the only way possible.

In the attitude of the State of California toward the work of the Indian commissioners and its effect on action by the United States Senate we have a clear illustration of local influence on national policy. The people of California demonstrated their determination to settle questions within the state's borders, and the United States Senate plainly showed its unwillingness to challenge the will of this commonwealth.

The sentiment in California toward the work of the commissioners, from the beginning of their labors, was divided, and grew increasingly hostile as time went on. At first, a measure of satisfaction was expressed because the treaty making of these agents brought peace on some of the frontiers. But more and more doubt was expressed that the giving over of valuable lands to uncivilized natives, and especially the restricting of the reservations so exclusively to the Indians as to prevent the digging for gold on them, had been wise. The fact that the Indians through centuries had occupied a part of the vast area of California, and had had access to all of it, was ignored, especially as the economic importance of the lands increased. By the end of 1851, public statements on the subject of the reservations, while not universally hostile to the plan, were becoming more generally so. Yet there were some thoughtful and high-minded people who believed that the Indians, as human beings, had rights which ought to be respected, and that the treaties recognized these rights. They argued that by giving the Indians lands on which to live quietly, with opportunity to be weaned from their wild habits, peace and security would result for all the people. A few such friends of the Indians supported the work of the commissioners until the treaties were rejected. But that the sentiment in California was on the whole more hostile than friendly is evident from the action of the legislature, which may be looked upon as a crystallization of the feelings of the citizens of the commonwealth.

Discussion of the treaties was begun in the legislature soon after the opening of the session of 1852. On January 16, before most of the treaties had reached Washington, the state senate adopted resolutions authorizing the appointment of a committee to prepare instructions for California's Senators in Congress with regard to the course they should follow in the Senate with respect to the treaties made with the California Indians by the United States agents. On the same day, the president of the senate named the special committee called for by the resolutions.

The majority report of the committee, presented on February 11, held that, considering the circumstances which had impelled the great wave of population to come to the state, the commissioners had committed an error in assigning sizable portions of the richest mineral and agricultural lands to the Indians, who were unable to appreciate their value, and it respectfully recommended the adoption of four resolutions, with the concurrence of the assembly. These resolutions condemned as radically wrong the policy pursued by the federal government toward the Indian tribes in the state; instructed the California Senators to oppose the confirmation of the treaties that had been made; advocated the removal of the wild Indians beyond the jurisdiction of states; and called upon the Representatives and Senators from California to procure the adoption, by the federal government, of the same course toward the Indians of California as had been pursued in other states for the past quarter of a century.

One member of the committee, J. J. Warner, who was a staunch friend of the Indians, on February 13 alone submitted a minority report. It set forth the impracticability of removing the Indians from the state and urged that faith be kept with them. Warner's report may have had some influence, for in the end the majority report and resolutions did not pass. This did not mean, however, that majority sentiment was against them, for the strong antiratification opinion in that body found its expression a little later in another set of resolutions and a memorial.

The subject of the Indian reservations came up, also, in the early sessions of the assembly. Here, too, intense hostility was shown to the policy pursued by the Indian commissioners. A committee which had been asked to consider the subject made its report on February 16, 1852. In the report it expressed unfeigned regret that many and extensive reservations of land had been set apart in various sections of the state for the exclusive use of Indians. The committee had learned that many of these included tracts of very desirable mineral and agricultural lands, on which were situated populous settlements of enterprising American citizens who had occupied the lands and had acquired rights long before the treaties had been made with the Indians. These rights, the committee asserted, had been acquired by the miner and agriculturist in good faith, upon the implied assurance that the same privileges and immunities would be extended to California immigrants as had been extended to settlers in other parts of the country. These persons had expended time and labor to establish themselves, only to be told that their lands were eligible sites for Indian reservations. The committee expressed the belief that the reservations from which the whites had been ordered were occupied by as many as 20,000 American citizens, and that their value was $100,000,000. The inclusion of these lands in reservations, it pointed out, would not only bring hardship to settlers but would also work to the disadvantage of the state by greatly reducing its taxable area. After making its ringing charges, which were partly true and partly false—a compound of hearsay, imagination, and egotistic provincialism, but tremendously appealing when being told to a popular legislative body—the committee then presented two resolutions for adoption.

These called upon the Senators and Representatives in Congress to use all proper measures: first, to prevent Congress from confirming the Indian reservations that had been made in the state; second, to insist that the same policy be adopted with regard to the Indian tribes of California that had been adopted in other new states; and third, to call strongly to the attention of Congress the great evils that would result to California, to the national government, and to the Indians from confirmation of those reservations.

Ineffectual efforts were made to hold back the tide of opposition to the treaties. Friends of the Indians called attention to the exaggerated statement of the committee's report with respect to the property and persons affected, and to its specious assertions about Indians' being moved to lands long occupied by whites, whereas the Indians had been on them for centuries—until fear of the whites had caused them to flee to the mountains. Both Wozencraft and McKee met with representatives of the legislature on several occasions to explain and defend their policy as Indian commissioners. In these interviews they tried to answer the criticisms that had been made of the reservation policy, and to point out that incalculable good would result to the United States, to the State of California, and to the Indians from a confirmation of the work of the commissioners. All this was of little avail in the face of public and legislative resentment against the treaties.

The committee on Indian affairs to which the assembly resolutions had been recommitted made its report on March 22. The spokesman for the committee stated that, after having heard again, from Mr. McKee, a full explanation of the policy of the commissioners, the committee was even more firmly of the opinion expressed in its former report, that the reservation of lands which had been made for Indians within the state would, if confirmed, prove most ruinous to the prerogatives of both the Indian and white population. Because it was considered that the interests of the state would be jeopardized by the confirmation of the treaties, the committee recommended the adoption of the resolutions. After the third reading they were passed by a vote of thirty-five to six.[13]

Opposition to the treaties in the state senate was given its final expression in connection with the adoption of a memorial to Congress on the subject of the disposal of the public domain in California. A special senate committee, in reports and a memorial on February 12, made a plea for leaving all the public domain that was suited to agriculture and grazing forever open to every actual settler, and for the government to give to each settler 160 acres of land. The committee demanded protection for the quartz miners in the form of secure title to their possessions. It objected to the proposed reservation sites because they included valuable mineral and agricultural lands which it considered unsuited to the Indians, considering their former mode of life, and because the sites also included ferries on the thoroughfares leading to the mining country. The memorial stated that, because of what was taking place in the mining country and the public feeling there, it would be impossible to prevent continued collisions between the miners and the Indians unless some amendment changed materially the plan proposed in the treaties for permanently disposing of the public domain. The memorial asked for extensive modification of the treaties. It omitted the recommendation of the earlier report for sending the natives from California, and it approved the parts that had to do with payments and arrangements for provisions. It asked for a complete change in the proposals concerning land, and suggested that missions should be established at a few convenient points, where the Indians would receive their annuities and where parcels of land could be assigned to them. The Indians should have the same hunting and grazing privileges as the whites, as well as the right to dig peacefully

[13] For details of the assembly's action, see R. McKee to L. Lea, January 31, 1852, 33d Cong., spec. sess., Senate Ex. Doc. No. 4, p. 248; McKee to Lea, March 1, 1852, *ibid.*, p. 295; McKee to President Fillmore, April 3, 1853, *ibid.*, p. 308; California, *Journal of the Assembly*, 3d sess., 1852, pp. 96, 128, 202–205, 251–253, 270.

in the mines. The Indians who lived on private lands with the consent of the owners, of whom the memorial held that there were many, should be permitted to continue in this good school of civilization. Such a plan, while obviating the contemplated disposal of a large portion of the mineral and arable lands, would promote peace and satisfy the citizens in a way the reservation plan would not be able to do. After being discussed fully in the committee of the whole on March 17 and 18, the memorial, together with resolutions addressed to the California delegation in Congress asking their approval, was adopted by a vote of nineteen to four.[14]

The original manuscripts of the eighteen treaties which aroused so much resentment in California were all received at the Indian office in Washington by February 18, 1852. By this time, officials of the Department of the Interior were aware that violent opposition toward the treaties had developed in California and that the California delegation in Congress was solidly against them. Luke Lea, the Commissioner of Indian Affairs, and Edward F. Beale, the newly appointed Superintendent of Indian Affairs for California, were in favor of ratification. The Secretary of the Interior, Stuart, in presenting the treaties, together with a mass of documents, to the President on May 22, was noncommittal. The President submitted the eighteen treaties to the Senate on June 1. On June 7 his message accompanying them was read in the Senate and, with the treaties and accompanying documents, was referred to the committee on Indian affairs. The treaties were next considered in a secret session of the Senate, and all were rejected by that body.

The reasons for the Senate's action do not, of course, appear in the records. It is quite certain that the action of the commissioners in piling up immense claims against the United States was a factor in the rejection of the treaties. More potent than this, however, was the violent opposition in California

[14] For the California senate's action on the treaties, see *Journal of the Senate*, 3d sess., 1852, pp. 44–46, 111, 195–198; (App.), pp. 575–578, 588–591, 697–600, 602–604.

to their ratification, because they removed from public and private use large areas of land containing potential wealth. The members of Congress from California felt bound by the wishes of their constituents to oppose the ratification, and they probably were not personally in favor of it, anyway. In a matter of this kind the Senate was inclined to accede to the wishes of the California members. Senator Weller of California, speaking for the California members, said:

We who represent the State of California were compelled, from a sense of duty, to vote for the rejection of the treaties, because we knew that it would be utterly impossible for the General Government to retain these Indians in the undisturbed possession of these reservations. Why there were as many as six reservations made in a single county in the State of California, and that one of the richest mining counties in the state. They [the white men] know that those reservations included mineral lands and that, just as soon as it became more profitable to dig upon the reservation than elsewhere, the White man would go there, and that the whole Army of the United States could not expel the intruders.[15]

Weller summarized his thought about the whole matter by saying, "Public policy demanded that these treaties should be rejected."

Congressman Joseph W. McCorkle, an influential member of the House of Representatives from California, said of the commissioners and their work:

The history of the Republic does not present an instance so flagrant of the usurpation and abuse of power as that exhibited in the action of the commissioners. They have not only usurped powers reserved in the Constitution to the President and Senate in making and executing treaties, but they have assumed to themselves a power expressly given to the House of Representatives, in the appropriation of money, and have absolutely, with an arrogance unheard of, drawn upon the Treasury for hundreds of thousands of dollars. The absurdity and ridiculousness of their official

[15] *Cong. Globe,* 33d Cong., 1st sess., Pt. 3, p. 2173.

action almost forbids one from characterizing and denouncing it in the terms it deserves.[16]

The words of the agitated Congressman are somewhat lacking in judgment and misrepresent the actual fact, but they are an expression of a view popular at that time; and popular views, whether true or false, are powerful in effecting or preventing legislation.

Certain it is that the United States commissioners faced an immense task which even wiser and more experienced men could not have performed with complete success. The sudden immigration into California of many thousands of acquisitive persons, who believed they had a right to search for wealth freely and to take what they could find, made it extremely difficult for United States agents to make adjustments on the gold and Indian frontiers, especially since the separation in time from the authorities in Washington made impossible the coöperation of Indian Office officials. The general idea of the treaty making had much to commend it, but an examination of the California treaties shows that they were hastily and carelessly drawn, and one must conclude that they would have been difficult to execute even under more favorable conditions. Could the treaties have been carried out, some of what are now the most populous and prosperous regions of California would have remained peopled by a few Indians whose capacity for advancement probably was exceedingly limited. Though there were some injustices in the way matters turned out, and the strong and civilized profited by the deprivations and misfortunes of the defenseless and uneducated, the judgment of history must be that the commissioners blundered and that the rejection of their work was wise under the circumstances. Certainly, the commissioners were presumptuous in assuming the right to build up the heavy obligations they did against the credit of the United States.

The claims on the federal government which grew out of the unauthorized action of the United States Indian agents in

16 *Ibid.*, App., p. 1082.

making large contracts for supplies caused some embarrassment in Washington and considerable loss to some persons, for only a few of the claims were ever paid. Actual losses were not so great as they appear on the surface, for in some of the transactions much fraud was involved. The question of the government's responsibility for these obligations was first brought up in Congress on March 26, 1852, when Representative J. W. McCorkle of California proposed the following amendment to the deficiency bill under discussion: "For paying the drafts of the Indian Commissioners of California, drawn upon the Department of the Interior, for supplies furnished, and expenses incurred in the negotiation of treaties with the various Indian tribes of California, the sum of $520,000." [17] Neither McCorkle nor anyone else knew much about these claims. After some fruitless discussion, the House decided that it could take no action at the time because the information at hand was too limited. The next step was taken on April 6, when the Senate called upon the Department of the Interior for information on the subject. The department responded by sending a statement of claims amounting to nearly $800,000. The question came up again several times before the end of the session, but no actual action was taken on it.

Most of the claims were never paid—some because of prejudice against them, others because of evidence of fraud. One claim which was allowed was that of John C. Frémont for $183,825. A bill providing for the payment of this, with interest from June 1, 1851, was approved by the President on July 29, 1854. A claim of Wozencraft for reimbursement of $7,000 which he had expended in the course of his duties was paid in July, 1856. In 1860, Samuel J. Hensley was paid $96,375 for beef furnished to the Indians. Payment of other claims, although discussed from time to time, was never made. The whole question was finally disposed of in 1871, without further adjustment. [18]

---

[17] *Cong. Globe,* 32d Cong., 1st sess., Pt. 3, pp. 880–890, 2104.
[18] For further information about Frémont's claim, see 32d Cong., 1st

On March 3, 1852, an act creating a California Indian superintendency became law. On the following day, Edward F. Beale was appointed to the newly created office. Appropriations were made to meet the expenses of the superintendency, and an additional $100,000 was appropriated for use in efforts to preserve peace with the Indians who had been dispossessed of their lands, until arrangements could be made for their resettlement.

After reporting his arrival in San Francisco on September 16, Beale at once made a tour into one part of his territory. From what he saw and heard he became convinced that some definite Indian policy was immediately necessary for California. On October 29 he reported to the Indian Office that he was maturing a plan which was "recommended alike by its practicability, humanity, and economy," [19] and that he would be prepared to develop it fully after his projected visit to the southern part of the state. In brief outline at this time, Beale proposed a system of "military posts," to be established on reservations where the Indians would be invited to assemble. Sites for reservations should be selected with a view to easy removal of the Indians if increase of white population should make it necessary. Each reservation should contain its military establishment, with "the expenses of the troops to be borne by the surplus of Indian labor." The agent should live at the post and should adopt a system of discipline and instruction. Beale at once set out on his southern trip, and began examining locations where he might place Indians if his plan received

---

sess., Senate Ex. Doc. No. 61, pp. 2–26; 33d Cong., 1st sess., Senate Misc. Doc. No. 59, pp. 1–4; *U.S. Statutes*, 33d Cong., 1st sess., Private Acts, p. 80. For Wozencraft's claim, see *ibid.*, 34th Cong., 1st sess., Private Acts, p. 31. For Hensley's claim, see *Senate Reports*, 36th Cong., 1st sess., Vol. I, No. 3, pp. 1–16; *U.S. Statutes*, 36th Cong., 1st sess., Private Acts, p. 15. For the conclusion of the matter, see *Report of the Commissioner of Indian Affairs*, 1871, pp. 17, 18, 153, 154.

[19] E. F. Beale to L. Lea, October 29, 1852, 33d Cong., spec. sess., Senate Ex. Doc. No. 4, pp. 374–375. For the creation of the superintendency, see *Cong. Globe*, 32d Cong., 1st sess., Pt. 1, pp. 501, 663–664; *U.S. Statutes*, 32d Cong., 1st sess., pp. 2–3. For further details of Beale's plan see Beale to Lea, November 22, 1852, 33d Cong., spec. sess., Senate Ex. Doc. No. 4, pp. 378–380.

the approval of the Indian Office; he even went so far as to establish an experimental farm on the San Joaquin River.

A little later, Beale set forth the plan in greater detail. In this elaboration he made it clear that he proposed to care for the Indians somewhat after the manner of the missions of Spanish days, but without the religious emphasis, and that he expected his plan to succeed because the method used by the missionaries had been found satisfactory. He estimated the number of Indians in California to be from 75,000 to 100,000, and thought that an appropriation of $500,000 should be made to start the new system. General Ethan A. Hitchcock expressed himself officially as being heartily in favor of the proposal and asserted that the choice of the government lay between accepting Beale's plan and letting the Indians be rapidly exterminated or driven from the state.

While officials at Washington were groping blindly for some wise Indian policy for California, Beale's earlier suggestions were received. In response to an order of December 3, Beale went to Washington and reported the distressing condition of the natives of California and the need for prompt action in their behalf on the part of Congress. He vigorously presented his plan for small reservations where the Indians could be protected and taught to work. He proposed that, by simple agreement between them and the government, they should be persuaded to go on the reservations, but that no treaties should be made. The result was that Congress gave authorization for the creation of five military reservations in California, not to exceed 25,000 acres each, and appropriated $250,000 to defray the expenses of maintaining the Indians in California and removing them to the reservations.[20] On April 13, 1853, Beale was ordered to return west by the most expeditious route, in order to put the new plan into operation.

Immediately after his arrival in Los Angeles on August 22, Beale began the execution of his plan by going to Tejon Pass,

[20] 32d Cong., 2d sess., Senate Ex. Doc. No. 57, pp. 1–18; *Cong. Globe*, 32d Cong., 2d sess., pp. 1085–1086; *U.S. Statutes*, 32d Cong., 2d sess., p. 38.

where he held a conference with some Indians and explained to them the purposes of the government concerning them. He also conferred with some army officers, who had traveled much in the state, concerning the best place for a reservation. As a result of the discussion, he decided to establish a reservation in the Tejon region.[21]

As Beale passed northward through the valley, still working on the plan for his first reservation, he visited the experimental farm which he had started the previous year on the San Joaquin River. The progress which had been made by the wild Indians who had been placed on this farm reassured him in regard to the possibilities of his proposed reservation at Tejon.

A problem now arose in connection with the Tejon plan, because part of the land desired was covered by a Spanish land grant, and the law under which Beale was working gave no authority for the purchase of lands for Indian purposes. Beale asked the opinion of the California Congressional delegation about the wisdom of proceeding. Being advised that, subject to the approval of Congress, he should make such conditional arrangements as he considered indispensable to the successful operation of the law, he went ahead with his plan, even though the Commissioner of Indian Affairs advised postponement of the enterprise until there should be further action by the national legislature.

The Tejon reservation started out well. By February, 1854, the Indians gathered there had under cultivation some 2,500 acres of land. Later in the year, a company of men who paid a visit to the reservation reported that 3,265 acres of land were under cultivation, and more than 400 Indians were working in the fields. The visitors described what they had seen as a remarkable achievement. Their statements were concurred in by the editor of the *Pacific* (June 30, 1854), and were corroborated by the testimony of Captain P. E. Conner, in the

[21] Beale to G. W. Manypenny, September 30, 1853, 33d Cong., 1st sess., Senate Ex. Doc. No. 1, pp. 469–470, 478–479. For Beale's report of progress, February 8, 1854, see *Report of the Commissioner of Indian Affairs*, 1854, pp. 298–299.

Stockton *Republican,* July 1, 1854, who said that he saw on the reservation a great grain crop valued at a large sum, and Indians working at their various occupations with the utmost cheerfulness.

But further progress of the reservation system under Beale was rudely checked by reason of political developments and his own failure properly to attend to certain business matters. Unfortunately, Beale had neglected to use care and promptness in dealing with the department, to such an extent that a large part of the appropriation of $250,000 remained unaccounted for in the spring of 1854. This arrearage was reported on May 1, 1854, while the question of the amount to be appropriated for Indian affairs in California was under consideration in Congress. The result was that when the measure providing for funds for Indian service in California was passed, the appropriation for the development of the reservation system was cut down to $125,000, and the number of reservations which might have been created was reduced from five to three.[22] Before the final action on the measure, Beale was removed from office and another person was appointed in his place.

Beale's successor was Thomas J. Henley, an able man and a successful politician. After receiving his instructions, dated June 2, 1854, he entered upon his official duties on July 15. Going first to Tejon, he took possession and began supervision of the public property there. Although it seemed to him that Beale had somewhat overstated the degree of prosperity, he found that things were in most respects as represented. Henley was convinced by what he saw that the military reservation system was the only wise method of dealing with the Indians, and he planned to develop the establishment at Tejon along the lines on which it had been begun. He spent more than a month getting things in order so that they could be properly managed by the assistants whom he would leave in charge.

---

[22] *Cong. Globe,* 33d Cong., 1st sess., Pt. 2, pp. 1027–1028, 1041–1051; *ibid.,* Pt. 3, pp. 1895, 1945.

From Tejon, Henley went north over the emigrant road, examining the country and studying the Indians as he proceeded. From the San Joaquin Valley he continued farther north, intending to spend the remainder of the year among the hundreds of small tribes of Indians in the northern part of the state. Before the end of September he had established the Nome Lacke reservation in Colusa County, which later became one of the more permanent and useful of the reservations. He selected a site for a miltary post on the reserve and put a subagent in charge. The natives began at once to assemble and to prepare winter quarters.

Henley's reports to the department,[23] full of details of the work at Tejon and Nome Lacke, were optimistic concerning the progress and promise of the reservation system. Indeed, they made it appear that the organization and development were so satisfactory at Tejon that expenditures there would hardly be needed after the year 1854–1855. While seeking to impress the department with the results achieved, Henley recommended modification of the law under which he was working, so as to permit the establishment of five reservations instead of three, and asked for an appropriation of $200,000 for the two additional establishments. In accordance with his wishes, the law was modified to increase the number of reservations, and an appropriation of $150,000 was made. With this added appropriation, the total sum provided for Indian affairs in California for the year 1855–1856 was $360,300.

Up to September, 1856, four permanent reservations had been established. These were the Tejon, the Nome Lacke, the Klamath on the Klamath River, and the Mendocino on the shores of the Pacific. In addition, temporary reserves or farms

[23] For reports and correspondence about the reservations see T. J. Henley to Manypenny, August 28, 1854, in *Report of the Commissioner of Indian Affairs,* 1854, pp. 300–307; Manypenny to R. McClelland, November 25, 1854, in *ibid.,* pp. 15–16; Henley to Manypenny, December 18, 1854, 33d Cong., 2d sess., Senate Ex. Doc. No. 42, pp. 3–4; Manypenny to R. McClelland, January 31, 1855, *ibid.,* Doc. No. 41, p. 2; *Report of the Commissioner of Indian Affairs,* 1856, pp. 236–268; 34th Cong., 3d sess., House Ex. Doc. No. 76, pp. 138–145.

had been established on the Fresno and Kings rivers, and at Nome Cult Valley in the Coast Range. Henley's report indicated a flourishing state of affairs at practically all locations; but, unfortunately for his credibility, his glowing accounts of progress were contradicted by the reports of army officers to whom General W. W. Mackall addressed an inquiry in August, 1856. These reports indicate that Henley grossly exaggerated the prosperity and development of the reserves, and that they were improperly managed.

Although differences of opinion had developed in California with reference to the success of the Indian administration, the federal government continued for two years more to make large appropriations for the maintenance and development of the system of military reservations, relying upon the accuracy of the reports of Henley and his agents. But in 1858, just at the time when Henley was gathering from his agents their statements of progress, Godard Bailey was given instructions as a special agent to visit the reservations. He was ordered to acquaint himself with their history and actual conditions, in order that he might furnish the Indian Office with the data upon which to base an intelligent estimation of the practical working system, and of its value as applied to the Indians of the state.

Bailey visited several of the reserves, and in his report he discussed in some detail the conditions of each one. His communication, which in no sense took the form of an attack upon Henley or his agents, stated that the plan devised by Beale for collecting the Indians on farms and thereon supporting them by their own labor had proved a lamentable failure. He characterized the reservations as simply government almshouses, where an inconsiderable number of Indians were insufficiently fed and scantily clothed, at an expense wholly disproportionate to the benefit conferred. His report declared that there was nothing in the system, as practiced, that looked to the permanent improvement of the Indian, or that tended in any way to his moral, intellectual, or social elevation.[24]

[24] G. Bailey to C. E. Mix, November 4, 1858, *Report of the Commissioner of Indian Affairs*, 1858, pp. 298–305.

When the California Indian question came before Congress in 1859, no move was made to abolish the reservations, but the appropriation for the removal and subsistence of Indians was cut down to $50,000, and that for incidental expenses of the superintendency to $7,500.[25]

With the reduced appropriation, James Y. McDuffie, who succeeded Henley as superintendent, undertook to continue the system that Beale had established. His reports indicated that all the reservations with the exception of Klamath were in a dilapidated state. Under these conditions, the Commissioner of Indian Affairs recommended the repeal of all laws authorizing the appointment of a superintendent and agents in California, the abandonment of the system in use, and the substitution of some other plan. The scheme which he proposed was to divide the state into two districts, with a superintending agent in each, a supervisor to lead and direct the Indians in their labors, and only such mechanics and laborers as might be necessary to keep tools in repair. Tools should be supplied to the Indians in the southern part of the state who worked on lands. Reservations might be provided for the dispossessed Indians of the valleys, but the Indians who should settle on them were to be given to understand that they would not be fed and clothed at government expense. Based on these suggestions, after much discussion, a bill providing a new method of administering Indian affairs in California became a law on June 19, 1860.[26]

Under this law the Secretary of the Interior divided the state into a northern and a southern district. The northern district included all that part of California north of the southern boundary of the counties of Marin, Sonoma, Solano, Sacramento, and El Dorado, to the eastern boundary of the state; the southern district included the rest of the state.[27] Two superintending agents were appointed, and a modified, less expensive, but no more effective system of administration for

[25] *U.S. Statutes*, 35th Cong., 2d sess., p. 400.
[26] *Ibid.*, 36th Cong., 1st sess., p. 57.
[27] *Report of the Commissioner of Indian Affairs*, 1860, pp. 20–21.

dealing with the natives was instituted. It consisted of placing the Indians on small reservations, after making simple agreements with them but no treaties. This practice of establishing small reservations, begun in California in 1853, was rapidly extended over the West. California thus made a distinct contribution to America's Indian policy.

The United States spent nearly two million dollars in Indian administration in California between 1850 and 1860—and spent an equal amount as a result of Indian disorders. Yet one should not berate the nation for neglect. The federal government did not neglect the Indian problem in California—it failed to understand it. There was no lack of zeal, but there was a lack of knowledge, which made the government unable to handle the conditions resulting from the abnormal frontier developments in the state. In the self-governing dominion of California in the decade of the 'fifties, the people who came into the state and the government of the state forced the removal of the Indians from the lands which they and their ancestors had occupied for centuries. The federal government placed the surviving bands on small and valueless tracts, where they were given some protection and help. What more could have been done at this time of westward expansion, it is difficult to say.

VII

The Movement for State Division, 1849–1860

> The revenue laws are as . . . just . . . as
> can be made under the existing constitution;
> and no relief can be looked for until the
> State is divided, and the mining counties and
> the agricultural counties are separated and
> placed under different government. . . .
> —COMMITTEE REPORT, CALIFORNIA SENATE,
> January 28, 1853

BETWEEN the calling of the constitu-
tional convention in 1849 and the meeting of the legislature
in 1860 various efforts were made to divide California by a line
running east and west. Many writers on the history of California have obscured the real significance of the division
movement by making it an incident in the national slavery
controversy. Further investigation, however, reveals that the
slavery issue was merely incidental in the efforts to divide
the state, and that the struggle for the adjustment of local
interests in a newly formed frontier was the dominant factor.
Contemporary with the division movement, particularly in its
later stages, were attempts to crystallize sentiment for the
launching of a Pacific Republic.

The migration of population westward in the United States had been attended by conflicts of classes, nationalities, and developing sections. The movement for the division of California in the first decade of the state's history, a form of sectionalism, was a part of this struggle, yet it had phases peculiar to itself. Into this region, settled by Spaniards and Mexicans, had come a sudden influx of a great new non-Spanish population whose interests and traditions were distinctly different from those of the old. This new aggregation was so powerful that the older instead of the newer community was forced to struggle for equality and justice and for continuance of its way of life. Before the discovery of gold, the interest of Californians was predominantly, almost exclusively, pastoral and agricultural. The province was held in great estates by a sparse population that subsisted easily by raising stock and grain. By far the greater number of the people lived in the southern district. But with the discovery of gold the centers of population shifted to the Sierra, where the dominant interest was in the mines, and where at this time the lands were not owned but occupied at will and later were leased. In the summer of 1848, it is estimated, there were in California about 7,500 Spanish Californians, 6,500 Americans, and a negligible number of foreigners. By the end of 1849 the population had increased to more than 100,000, most of whom were newcomers seeking gold.[1] The sparse population of the southern part of California was for the most part still made up of Spanish Californians, satisfied with old conditions and glad to be left free to enjoy their landed estates. The two sections, therefore, were widely divergent—one an old, Mexican, sparsely settled, landowning community, the other a new and numerous mining people, who leased their lands.

The spirit of sectionalism in California began to manifest itself in the convention that gathered in Monterey on September 3, 1849, for the purpose of forming a constitution for California. It became evident immediately that the people of

[1] H. H. Bancroft, *History of California*, VI, 71, n.

southern California did not desire to have their fortunes linked in civil government with the territory farther north. They were distrustful of the newcomers, who formed a majority of the voting population; and in the preliminary discussion of September 5 the delegates from the southern section made their sentiments known to the convention. At that time, the question arose whether the constitution to be formed should be for a state or for a territorial government. The delegates from northern and central California took it for granted that the purpose of the convention was to form a constitution for a state government, but José Antonio Carrillo, a native Californian from a southern district, expressed the opinion that the formation of a state government would be contrary to the interest of his constituents. He proposed that, since a majority of the convention appeared to be in favor of this form of government, the country should be divided by running a line east and west from San Luis Obispo, and that all north of that line should have a state government, and all south of it a territorial government.[2] When the vote was taken on the question of a state or a territorial government, twenty-eight voted for, and eight against, the formation of a state constitution. The eight who opposed it were the six from the extreme southern districts who were present and voting, a delegate from Monterey, and one representing the San Jose district.

The reason that the delegates from the southern districts wanted their section to have territorial status was brought out in the debates on the representation of districts and on taxation. The native landholding class felt that the representation should be on a basis that would take into consideration the permanence of their interests and the transitoriness of those of the inhabitants of the San Joaquin and Sacramento valleys. They saw the difference between a settled, landholding class and a transient population, and believed that injustice could easily be done to the permanent class.[3] The issue was made even clearer

[2] J. Ross Browne, *Report of the Debates in the Convention of California on the Formation of the State Constitution,* pp. 21–22.

[3] *Ibid.,* pp. 400–416.

when the subject of taxation was being discussed. The arguments revealed that the people in the south [4] had been apprehensive from the first that a state government would bear heavily upon them, and that they therefore wanted a territorial government, under which taxation would not be a burden. So great was the dissatisfaction of the southern delegates over what they believed were prospects of oppressive taxation that for a time it was feared that they would leave the convention and thus break it up.

The southern delegates, however, remained and joined the convention in its work. They were influenced to do this by a compromise on the question of taxation which incorporated in the constitution a provision giving constitutional power to local assessors of the counties, and to the boards of supervisors elected by the landholders themselves, this being a guarantee against their being taxed oppressively.[5] But it is evident that there was much dissatisfaction in the south, for in the early part of 1850 a group of citizens there protested against the plan to seek admission of California into the Union and began to formulate plans for bisecting the state. On February 10, 1850, a meeting was held in Los Angeles in that interest, and on March 3 another, and larger one, was held there. The main objective of this second meeting was to get signatures for a petition opposing the admission of California with its proposed boundaries, and attempting, in effect, to make a territory of the southern part. The petition, addressed to the Congress of the United States, was signed by most of the citizens of Los Angeles. A letter containing the resolutions passed at this meeting was sent to San Luis Obispo, San Diego, and Santa Barbara.[6]

For a decade the people of southern California continued

---

[4] The terms "north" and "south" (not capitalized) when used in this chapter refer to northern and southern California, respectively; capitalized they refer to national sectional divisions.

[5] Browne, *op. cit.*, p. 446; William M. Gwin, "Memoirs," California Historical Society *Quarterly*, XIX, pp. 13–14.

[6] See Valentin Cota, "Documentos para la historia de California" (MS, Bancroft Library), pp. 25–36; Benjamin Hayes, Scrapbooks, "Constitutional Law," p. 5; Santa Barbara Archives (MSS in Bancroft Library), pp. 229–230.

strongly to urge the division. Among the reasons they gave for this position were two that harmonized more closely with American principles than the proponents realized. The first was that the expenses of a state government would necessarily bear heavily upon landholders, even to working their ruin. The second was that the thinly populated south would be under the complete control, in political matters, of the northern part of the state, which had many material advantages and large transient populations; this, and the great distance from the northern to the southern end of California would not only put a burden upon the south, but would also be an inconvenience to its people. For these and other reasons the southern Californians petitioned Congress to separate their part of the state from the northern area by a line running eastward from the Pacific Ocean just north of the district of San Luis Obispo, and to make of the region south of this line a territory to be known as the Territory of Southern California.

The efforts made in Congress to divide the area before considering the subject of admission of California into the Union are part of the history of the state-division movement. An expression of an intention to divide it came early in the Congressional discussion of the petition for admission. One of the chief spokesmen for division was Senator Henry S. Foote, who advocated extension of the Missouri Compromise line—latitude 36° 30′—to the Pacific and the admission of all of California north of that line. Foote submitted a proposal to this effect in the Senate several times. On August 1, as an amendment to an earlier amendment, he suggested that California be divided by a line running along latitude 36° 30′, and that the Territory of Colorado be formed from the southern part thus cut off. This amendment lost by the vote of 23 ayes and 33 noes. In expectation that the bill for the admission of California might soon pass, on August 6, Senator Hopkins L. Turney offered an amendment which provided that when the inhabitants of California, in assembled convention, should establish as a southern boundary a line not farther south than latitude 36° 30′, the State of California might be admitted into the Union, on the proclamation of the President. Senator Foote then proposed an additional section, which provided that, as soon as practicable after the passage of the act admitting it as a state, California should ascertain by vote the feeling of its people on the question of modifying the boundaries of the state so as to make the line 36° 30', or some other line fixed by them, its southern boundary. It further provided that, when the people should declare for such a modification of boundaries by a majority vote, the portion cut off should at once become the Territory of Colorado. On August 10, Senator Turney again made an attempt to restrict the state to the portion falling above the line 36° 30'.[7]

But none of the proposals looking to division carried, and the bill admitting the state with boundaries as indicated in its constitution passed the Senate on August 13, the vote being 34 ayes and 18 noes.

On September 7, the bill from the Senate came up in the House, where its passage was strenuously resisted. Opposition to the admission of the part of California south of the Missouri Compromise line was particularly strong. On this, the last day of the bill's consideration, Jacob Thompson of Mississippi, who earlier in the session had spoken in favor of making the southern boundary of the state latitude 36° 30', made a final speech of opposition to admission of the state with the boundaries proposed in its constitution. In his last plea he said, "the adoption of a territorial government for South California is demanded by the people of that country. The whole south asks for the division as an act of justice. Every consideration of sound policy demands this division."[8] But the bill, after several dilatory motions and votes, passed the House by a vote of 156 ayes to 56 noes.

After the admission of California, especially in the first three

---

[7] *Cong. Globe*, 31st Cong., 1st sess., XXII, Pt. 1, pp. 367, 967; *ibid.*, App. II, 485, 1510–1511, 1519–1522.
[8] Samuel H. Willey, *The Transition Period of California*, p. 158.

years of its statehood, objection to a state government, and particularly to the union of the northern and southern sections under a single government, continued to find expression in California in persistent efforts by the southern area to bring about partition.

Before the state was admitted into the Union, the sentiments of the south had been communicated to Senator Foote by Agoston Haraszthy, a prominent citizen of southern California. After its admission, Haraszthy set forth in a communication to the press a summary of grievances of the south on which the plea for division was based. Among these were the diversity of interests of the northern and the southern counties; the inequitable burden of taxation borne by the south; the unfair representation in government; the undue favoring of the mining areas; and the failure to consider the interests of southern California in the making of the laws. Others pointed out also that in proportion to its means, the southern section was the most heavily taxed portion of the state, and yet in the disposition of the general offices neither party deemed the south worth conciliating, even by a nomination. In short, the people of southern California were treated as stepchildren, and they protested. Their objection to statehood sprang naturally from their belief that they were regarded more as a conquered province than as a part of a free and independent state, and most of them believed that separation of the southern from the northern part of California was the only remedy for the ills suffered.[9]

The feelings of the people of the south found expression in action. By August, 1851, their plans had taken definite form. In Los Angeles County, all the candidates for the legislature pledged themselves to use their efforts to obtain a division of the state.[10] The San Francisco *Daily Alta California*, which

[9] *Cong. Globe*, 31st Cong., 1st sess., Pt. 1, p. 967; San Francisco *Daily Herald*, August 8, 16, 1851; San Francisco *Daily Alta California*, August 2, 19, September 25, 1851; Los Angeles *Star*, September 23, 1851; San Diego *Herald*, September 4, 1851.
[10] Los Angeles *Star*, August 23, 1851.

up to that time had opposed every action toward division, in its issue of August 9, 1851, admitted that the movement to divide the state had gathered force, and told of the plans that were being made for a convention to meet at Los Angeles, Santa Barbara, or Monterey to discuss the proposal. Because of the distance between the various sections, it was difficult to secure unified action in regard to the time and place for a general convention, but a series of local meetings, in which similar resolutions were adopted, indicated rather clearly that a concerted and serious movement for division was being launched.

The first in this series of meetings was held by a committee of citizens of San Diego on August 30. The meeting chose Santa Barbara as the place it recommended for holding the convention, and the third Monday of October as the date. The San Diego meeting not only endorsed the plan to hold a convention but adopted resolutions giving specific reasons for the desired division. These emphasized the great area included in California and the utter impossibility for any legislature, however wise and patriotic, to enact laws adapted to the wants and necessities of a people so widely differing in their circumstances and pursuits. At a public meeting in Los Angeles on September 12, presided over by the mayor, division was urged, plans for the convention were made, and resolutions were adopted similar to those passed at San Diego. An attempt was then made to hold the convention at Monterey, as had been at first proposed. Owing to a misunderstanding about time and place, a full representation was not there in October, but the delegates who were present issued an address in favor of state division. As reasons for their position, they stated that the laws passed by the legislature had not been lawfully promulgated; that in operation the laws had been unjust and oppressive to a portion of the state; that disparity in taxation existed; and that as long as the state remained so large the government would be oppressive to some of the people.[11]

[11] For the meetings mentioned in this and the next paragraph see *Daily Alta California*, September 12, October 29, 1851; San Francisco *Daily Herald*,

It was finally agreed that another convention should assemble at Santa Barbara on the third Monday of October, as had been suggested in the San Diego meeting. Thirty-one delegates attended the meeting, all the southern counties being represented. The four days of the convention sessions were taken up with discussion of what the people of the southern part of the state were seeking, and with formulation of reasons for their demands. Resolutions, reported from a committee, charged that the government which had been erected gave security and happiness to one section of the state through the sacrifices of the other section, and that while the favored section, under the government provided, had increased in all the elements which constitute the greatness of a state, the other had garnered only bitter experiences. These resolutions urged the dissolution of a political union which, they stated, was antagonistic to the various interests which society had built up and was also "in contradiction to the eternal ordinances of nature, who herself had marked with an unerring hand the natural bounds between the great gold regions of the northern and internal sections of the state and the rich and agricultural valleys of the south." The general unanimity of the convention and the frank, full statement, in the resolutions, of the existing conditions made the people in the northern part of California recognize the movement for division as an important issue. Questions had been presented that must be met by the legislature—questions which might prove to be among the more important to come before that body at its next session.

At the time this division movement was getting under way in California, discussion of its significance appeared in some Eastern papers. Since in some quarters of the East people were actively trying to secure more territory for slavery, such as Cuba and certain provinces of Mexico, some Eastern newspapers alleged that California was to be divided for this purpose. Some averred that plans were afoot to induce a revolt in the province

September 11, 17, October 12, 26, 28, 1851; Los Angeles *Star*, September 13, 1851.

of Sonora, or in Lower California, with the idea of linking one of these provinces with the southern portion of California, in order to form a new slave state on the Pacific Coast. In California, however, there was no indication that the division movement there was connected in any way with the slavery question. Moreover, the persons who favored division of the state looked with disfavor on the acquisition of Lower California.[12] Although it was recognized by many on the Pacific Coast that to divide California might open up the discussion of the slavery question, no reference to slavery and its extension was made in any of the various meetings or in the conventions held in the state in 1851.

In the years 1852 and 1853, the movement for state division came up frequently in the legislature and became a potent factor in the attempts to effect the calling of a convention for the purpose of revising the entire state constitution. Members of the legal profession, at the time the question was agitated in 1851, had asserted that a general convention of the people of the whole state would be necessary before separation could take place. At such a convention, boundaries could be established and attention could be given to other questions more or less connected with the proposed division.

Governor McDougal, in his message to the legislature at the beginning of the session of 1852, called attention to the unsatisfactory condition of relations between the northern and southern counties. After showing by facts and figures the disparity in the tax burden and in the representation of the two areas, he pointed out that the statements in the constitution that "all laws of a general nature shall have a uniform operation," and that "taxation shall be equal and uniform throughout the state," were true only in a legal sense. The southern counties, he stated, mostly by grants in the possession of individuals, paid a heavy tax upon every acre of land, which at best yielded but a moderate dividend on the valuation. The mining counties,

[12] *Daily Alta California*, September 2, 1851; *ibid.*, November 25, 1851; San Francisco *Herald*, September 25, 1851; Los Angeles *Star*, September 23, 25, 1851.

exceedingly prolific in the returns they made to their occupants, being almost entirely the property of the federal government, paid comparatively nothing into the state treasury. As a result of this situation, he declared, many citizens of the southern counties had been forced to alienate portions of their land and to sacrifice segments of their stock to meet what they considered an unjust burden. The worst thing of all was that the cords of amity between the sections were being broken. The constitution, he pointed out, prevented the legislature from remedying the evil. For this reason he recommended the calling of a convention to revise the constitution; this body could discuss all inconveniences arising from the state charter, and could make plans to remedy them.[13]

Accordingly, on February 3, 1852, a joint resolution providing for the calling of a convention to revise the constitution was introduced in the assembly. It was referred to a special committee, which, in a majority report on February 11, reiterated some of the facts of the governor's message, and, viewing the situation as a whole, approved heartily the complaints which had come from the south. The report recommended that a convention be called which should have power either to reduce greatly the limits of the state or to assign to the legislature power to rectify inequalities. The minority report from the committee, though it attempted to vindicate some of the things of which the south complained, recognized that the people of the southern part of the state had just grounds for objecting to their disproportionate taxation and unequal representation.[14]

The questions of the proposed constitutional convention and state division were heatedly discussed in some quarters outside the legislature. The *Daily Alta California* (February 7, 19, 20, 1852) bitterly denounced the whole plan. It charged

---

[13] California, *Journal of the Senate*, 1852, pp. 12–13.

[14] California, *Journal of the Assembly*, 1852, pp. 134, 166–168, 170–174. For further details of the controversy over the proposed constitutional convention, see *ibid.*, 1853, pp. 61, 258, 317, and Appendix, Doc. 26, p. 5; *Journal of the Senate*, 1853, pp. 258, 295, 297, 301, 305, 352, and Appendix, Doc. 16, pp. 1–9, 9–16, 26–29.

that the movement had been started by slavery propagandists and had been seconded by less influential men and by miserable, speculating politicians whose purpose was, and had been from the beginning, to divide the state in order that slavery might be permitted in part of the area. The paper asserted that the assembling of a convention to change the constitution would be the signal for opening, upon the soil of California, a hateful and baneful discussion of slavery, a subject which had nearly severed the Union. It further charged that the principal advocates of the impracticable and deceitful scheme for the division of the state were persons known to favor the establishment of slavery upon the Pacific Coast.

In repudiation of these charges, the Los Angeles *Star* of February 7, 1852, speaking for the citizens of southern California, explained that the sole motive of the south was to obtain a territorial government, and said:

> The resolutions of the Santa Barbara Convention, express at this time, as they did at the period of their promulgation, the views and feelings of Southern California, and if the Senators and Representatives from the Southern counties are guided by them in their measures to consummate a Division of the State, they will but second the views of their constituents.

On February 14, this same newspaper said that the people of the south greatly resented the introduction of the slavery question into the discussion, for it pushed the real issues into the background.

The assembly, on March 2, passed the bill providing for the election of delegates to a constitutional convention by a vote of 51 to 7. The bill came up in the senate several times, but failed of passage in that body.

On January 13, 1853, a bill entitled "An Act recommending to the electors to vote for or against calling a constitutional convention" was introduced in the assembly. The measure was referred to a special committee, was reported back to the assembly, and on March 24 passed that body by a vote of 46 to 12.

In the proceedings and report of the special committee there is little to indicate a connection of the bill with a purpose to divide the state, except that it was recognized that a convention and division were both unanimously supported by members from the south. The report of the committee, however, pointed out defects in the constitution and called attention to the dissatisfaction of southern Californians over the disparity in taxation of the two sections.

In the senate, there was much discussion of the proposed measure, and the purposes of those advocating a convention were more clearly brought out. On January 26, reports were presented by the select committee to which had been referred that part of the governor's message that was concerned with changes in the constitution. The majority report was against the calling of a constitutional convention, mainly on the ground that an effort to divide the state would be made should a convention be called. It pointed out that division of California at some future time was a probability and was even desirable, but that the majority of the committee opposed immediate division because, in making a division, it would be necessary for the southern part of the state to become a territory, in which the population, free from taxation, would have no inducement to diminish their estates, and development consequently would be slow. Besides, the falling back of a part of California into "a state of pupilage" under a territorial government, would diminish the dignity of the Pacific Coast in the estimation of the world.

The first minority report, in discussing the disparity in the taxation burdens, pointed out that the same inequality existed between the agricultural and the mining counties throughout the state, and that southern California did not suffer more than the other agricultural regions. Figures given in support of this contention showed that the fifteen agricultural counties mentioned, with a smaller population than the eight mining counties listed, paid $1.65 more per person than the mining counties. The report admitted that this was unjust, but at the same time it opposed both a convention and state division, believing that these would not remedy the evils. Both this report and that of the majority were laid upon the table.

Another section of the committee also presented a minority report, and the senate discussion centered about this and the bill submitted with it, providing for a constitutional convention. The lengthy report emphasized the inability of one state government to operate satisfactorily over so large an area as that included in California, and called attention to the unjust operation of the revenue laws, which caused a disproportionate share of the burden of the state government to be borne by the commercial, agricultural, and grazing counties, while the mining counties enjoyed the controlling representation in the halls of the legislature. As additional reasons for division, the report held that a larger representation in Congress from the Pacific Coast was a practical necessity, and that, since in 1841 Congress had passed a law giving to each state of the Union five hundred thousand acres of the public lands if that much was embraced within its borders, division of the state would result in a greater allotment of government land in the area. It even suggested that three states were desirable.

In answer to assertions that difficulties were likely to arise over the slavery question, the second minority report made a forceful statement. It emphatically declared that the advocates of a convention—men from all sections of the state—would at no time favor the engrafting of a slavery clause on a new constitution; they were all opposed to agitation of this discord-provoking subject. It also asserted that the friends and advocates of a convention and division of the state disclaimed all sectional feeling and did not wish even to discuss the subject of slavery.

Public opinion, as indicated by the newspapers, seemed to be as divided on the subject as was the legislature. The *Daily Alta California* (January 28, May 27, 1853), which the preceding year had bitterly fought any suggestion of division, now admitted that good reasons existed for dividing the state, but insinuated that there were still persons who had sinister purposes in advocating it. The Stockton *Journal*, of February 15, 1853, charged that a scheme had been devised to elect to the legislature representatives originally from the southern states or who had Southern proclivities, and implied that there were men who were working evil designs. The position of the Sacramento *Union* was rather surprising. The issue of February 2, 1853 said: "A division of the state into two or more states is a political necessity which will be recognized by all parties sooner or later." And in a subsequent issue (May 14) this paper asserted that it looked upon the effusions of those who professed to believe that there was any real danger of the introduction of slavery into any part of the state as the production of an imagination so diseased upon the subject of slavery as to be unable to view the matter through any medium that was not distorted. The religious press of the state was for the most part opposed to division, fearing the possible introduction of slavery.

The discussion of the convention bill of 1853 in the senate, before the final vote on April 6, was mainly of constitutional questions. There were occasional charges that conventionists had motives they dared not divulge, but the slavery question did not once come to the fore. The vote on the measure showed 16 ayes to 10 noes. Lacking the necessary two-thirds majority, the bill was lost. An analysis of the votes on the constitutional question in the two legislatures reveals that in both the senate and the assembly all the delegates from the southern counties were in favor of holding a convention, while the vote of the northern delegates was divided. The agricultural counties both north and south, but not the mining counties, demanded a convention.[15] How many of the majority of legislators voting for a convention favored state division, or even wanted to give the people an opportunity to vote on the question, is not known.

In the year 1854 the question of state division did not in

[15] See San Diego *Herald*, June 10, 1854; *Daily Statesman*, November 23, 1854; Sacramento *Union*, November 24, 1854.

any form become a vital issue in the legislature. The subject continued to be agitated in the press of southern California and received some attention elsewhere, giving opportunity for the occasional reiteration of the pertinacious charge that there was in the state a party which advocated division with the view of introducing slavery into southern California.

The state-division question did, however, come squarely before the legislature on February 27, 1855, when Jefferson Hunt of San Bernardino introduced in the assembly a bill for creating a new state out of California.[16] This new state would be called "Columbia" and would embrace the territory included in the counties of Santa Cruz, Santa Clara, San Joaquin, Calaveras, Amador, Tuolumne, Stanislaus, Mariposa, Tulare, Monterey, Santa Barbara, San Luis Obispo, Los Angeles, San Bernardino, San Diego, and the islands off the coast of these counties. On April 4, the committee to which the bill was referred reported as a substitute for the original bill an act which provided for enlarging California by changing part of its eastern boundary, and for dividing the territory included within the enlarged bounds into a southern, a central, and a northern state, to be known respectively as "Colorado," "California," and "Shasta." [17]

On April 17, arguments were made for the bill on the grounds that the state was too extensive for one government; that the representation in Congress was too small for so large a territory; and that its inequities of taxation and representation resulting from dissimilarities of the northern and southern areas could be rectified only by a division of the great territory into two or more states. In the debate, little direct opposition to the proposal was shown, but there were grave differences of opinion as to its constitutionality. After much argument, the bill was recommitted to the select committee with instructions to draw up an address to the people of California on the subject.

[16] California *Journal of the Assembly*, 1855, p. 359.
[17] See J. M. Guinn, "How California Escaped Division," Historical Society of Southern California *Annual Publications*, 1905, p. 226; Hayes, "Constitutional Law," p. 17.

In the address the committee incorporated the proposed act and set forth elaborate reasons for the proposal.[18]

The legislative session of 1855 came to an end before the subject of state division could get a fair hearing in the senate. It was expected that a division measure would pass both houses the next year; but the political situation in 1856, with the Democratic party divided, the Know-Nothings in power, the contest on for filling the vacancy in the United States Senate, and other pressing political issues demanding attention, left little place for the question of state division. The only interest shown in it was in connection with a bill introduced on February 26, by Senator John D. Cosby of Trinity and Klamath counties, providing for the creation of three states out of California. The bill, after twice being read, was referred to the judiciary committee. This committee considered it and on March 22 recommended its passage, but apparently nothing more was done about it.

A bill was passed by the legislature of 1857 for submitting to the people the question of calling a constitutional convention to revise the entire constitution of the state. The reasons given for making fundamental changes in the constitution were to some extent the same as those urged for division. Matters connected with the judiciary and taxation were prominent among them. Had there been a convention, it seems likely that state division would have been among the questions considered. The vote on the proposed convention was very close, but the measure was defeated.

The movement for segregation of the southern counties reached its climax on the eve of the Civil War. On April 13, 1858, Andrés Pico, the assemblyman from the district embracing Los Angeles, San Bernardino, and San Diego counties, introduced in the legislature resolutions which were important in that they were the prelude to the action taken by the legislature the following year. These resolutions were in effect a

[18] For what is briefly summarized here, see Hayes, *op. cit.*, p. 47; Sacramento *Union*, April 18, 1855; California, *Journal of the Assembly*, 1855, p. 693.

request to the legislature to pass an act setting off as a territory the part of California lying south of 35° 45′ north latitude. The reasons given for the request were the differences in climate, soil, and productions of the south and the north; the dissimilarity of the people in language, manners, customs, and interests; and the geographical separation of the two sections.[19] The resolutions were withdrawn by friends of the measure who thought that discussion of them would retard the business of the session, which was near its end.

It was no surprise when, on February 5, 1859, Andrés Pico again introduced in the assembly resolutions looking toward the separation of the southern part of the state from the northern part and the erection of the southern part into a territory. The preamble to the resolutions stated reasons for the proposed division. It set forth that the boundaries of the state enclosed an area too large and diversified for one state. Because uniform legislation for all parts of the state was unjust and ruinous to the south, it demanded that the untoward union be dissolved. The district which the resolution proposed should be dropped from California and organized as the Territory of Colorado, with the consent of the Congress of the United States, was the area comprising the counties of San Luis Obispo, Santa Barbara, Los Angeles, San Bernardino, and San Diego and the islands lying off their shores. The resolutions made provision for adjustment with the State of California, and asked the Congress of the United States to provide for immediate organization. At the request of Pico, the whole matter was referred to a special committee.

While the measure for the formation of the Territory of Colorado was under consideration in the legislature, a bill was introduced in the assembly, on February 17, entitled "An Act to authorize the citizens of the State of California residing north of the fortieth degree of north latitude to withdraw from the State of California and organize a separate government." The

[19] California, *Journal of the Assembly*, 1858, pp. 564, 565. For the resolutions introduced by Pico on February 5, 1859, see *ibid.*, 1859, p. 230; Sacramento *Union*, February 5, 1859; Los Angeles *Star*, February 19, 1859.

bill was referred to the special committee on the Colorado Territory.[20] The committee, after considering the bill, made a report recommending that the matter be referred to the delegations from the counties included in the territory which it was proposed to withdraw: Siskiyou, Del Norte, Klamath, Humboldt, Trinity, Shasta, Plumas, and Tehama. Nothing further was done about the bill. Many felt, at the time, that it had been proposed by northern members to offset or checkmate the demand of the southern delegates for a separate government for their constituents. Some considered it a sly satire on the southern movement, which its proponents did not expect or desire to become a law—like the bill, later introduced, to form below the Tehachapi a state called "South Cafeteria."

The special committee on the Territory of Colorado submitted its reports on March 2. The majority report expressed the belief that the inhabitants of the southern part of the state had good and valid reasons for desiring the separation requested, and that state consent to it was expedient under the conditions, restrictions, and qualifications provided in a bill which they had instructed their chairman to introduce as substitute for the resolutions under consideration. The committee endorsed the expediency of the measure but, deeming it wise to leave the matter of the constitutionality of the question open, expressed no opinion on the subject. A minority of the committee submitted another report, holding that the proposed separation could be effected only by an amendment to the constitution or by action of a constitutional convention, and that the people of the state would have to pass upon the changes proposed. This report recommended postponement of the whole matter.[21]

The proposed act,[22] submitted with the majority report of the special committee, described in detail the desired boundaries

---

[20] Sacramento *Union*, February 18, 1859. See also Hayes, *op. cit.*, p. 57.

[21] California, *Journal of the Assembly*, 1859, pp. 341, 342, 350–352.

[22] The act is in *Statutes of California*, 1859, pp. 310–311. For committee reports and action by the legislature, see California, *Journal of the Assembly*, 1859, pp. 230, 474; *Journal of the Senate*, 1859, p. 744.

of the new Territory of Colorado, which included "the counties of San Luis Obispo, Santa Barbara, Los Angeles, San Diego, San Bernardino, and a part of Buena Vista." (Buena Vista County was created in 1855 from part of Tulare County and was the forerunner of Kern County.) The act directed the governor, in his proclamation for the next general election, to instruct the voters in this area to vote for or against such segregation, and it provided that if two-thirds of the votes cast should be for the proposed changes, the division should take place, subject to the consent of Congress. The majority report of the special committee set forth clearly the basic reasons for the proposed division. These were shown to be economic and political: a disproportionate burden of taxation on the south, and too little political representation. In the legislature doubts were expressed concerning the constitutionality of the division measure, and there was substantial opposition to it, although no serious difference arose over the suitability of the separation, or the sincerity of the south's desire for it. Throughout the state it was beginning to be acknowledged that the southern section's cause was just, and that the harsh words about pestilential politicians and political fortune hunters who had taken advantage of the weakness of the southern native citizens, which some of the northern newspapers continued to print, misrepresented the character and purposes of the southern Californians and disregarded the legitimacy of their claims.[23]

On March 25 the assembly passed the act by a vote of 33 to 25. The senate passed it on April 14 by a vote of 15 to 12, and the governor approved it on April 19. All the southern California delegates from the territory affected by the proposed segregation voted for the measure. The legislators from the northern counties divided: in the senate 11 voted for and 12 against it, and in the assembly 27 expressed approval and 24 disapproval.

[23] See Sacramento *Union*, February 5, 8, March 16, 1859; *Southern Vineyard*, February 18, April 22, 1859; Los Angeles *Star*, February 19, 1859.

The election on the above measure took place at the appointed time. The returns from the election, tabulated by counties, were as follows:

	For	Against
Los Angeles	1,407	441
San Bernardino	421	29
San Diego	207	24
Santa Barbara	395	51
San Luis Obispo	10	283
Tulare	17	...
	2,457	828

These figures show that the measure carried by substantially more than the two-thirds required.[24]

On January 11, 1860, the legislature in joint session elected Governor Milton S. Latham United States Senator to fill the vacancy caused by the death of Senator David C. Broderick. On January 12, Latham, as governor, sent to the legislature a communication relative to the six southern counties which had voted in favor of segregation.[25] In the message he stated that, in compliance with the act authorizing the six southern counties to vote upon the question of separation from the rest of the state, he had transmitted to the President of the United States a certified copy of the act and a statement of the vote, and had sent with them a paper embodying his own views on the question. In this paper Latham reviewed the background for the legislative act, the results of the election under it, and his reasons for considering the act valid, though it had never been submitted to the people of the whole state. He held that Article 4, Section 3, of the federal Constitution contained all the requirements for a division of the state, and that if the people in a severed portion preferred to be organized under a territorial

[24] Sacramento *Union*, September 29, 1859. The Tulare listed is the part of the county which became Buena Vista and later Kern County.

[25] California, *Journal of the Assembly*, 1860, pp. 125–132. For the action taken by the legislature, see *ibid.*, pp. 155, 228–233, 412–413; *Journal of the Senate*, 1860, p. 415.

government, nothing in the Constitution prevented such organization.

In the assembly, the communication of the governor was referred to the committee on federal relations. On January 14, Daniel Rogers, of San Francisco, introduced in the assembly a concurrent resolution relating to the "formation of a Territorial Government by the six southern counties of this State." It instructed the Senators and Representatives of the state and its people in Congress to oppose the execution of the act authorizing the separation. This resolution was also referred to the committee on federal relations.

The majority report, presented on January 26, asserted its agreement with Governor Latham's opinion that "the act of the California legislature is valid," and that the federal Constitution, which is superior to those of individual states, does not require any action by the people in case of a relinquishment of a part of a territory by a state to the federal government. The report declared that the resolution introduced by Rogers had been brought forward and proposed without any demonstration in its favor on the part of the people "to compel by instructions the Senators and Representatives of the state and people in Congress, to oppose the execution of their deliberate and solemn act of legislation, incorporated in the statutes of this state." The committee, convinced of the impropriety of the mode proposed for defeating the objects of the law, reported unfavorably on the resolution.

The minority report, presented also on January 26, attempted to prove that the proposed mode of separation was illegal and unconstitutional. It contended that the statement in the constitution that "all political powers are inherent in the people—government is instituted for the protection, security, and benefit of the people" would not be worth a farthing if it could be destroyed by Congress in the manner proposed whenever a legislature could be found complaisant enough to sanction such a proceeding. It contended, further, that if a division should be made it would have to be effected in the same way as the constitution was adopted—by consent of all concerned—and in a manner giving all a voice, a procedure not followed in making a mere enactment. The report also expressed fear that, because of the present feeling that had grown out of the Kansas trouble, division of the state would invite another conflict. The minority, therefore, would prevent the separation on the ground of its illegality and for reasons of public policy.

On March 1, the assembly approved the majority report of the committee on federal relations by a vote of 37 ayes to 26 noes. In the senate a committee took up the questions involved in the governor's recommendation and reported favorably a bill approving the separation of the southern counties of California in accordance with their vote; but no further action seems to have been taken.

The California division question was not taken up in Washington. The issues which culminated in the Civil War began now to monopolize the attention of the country. Secession and approaching civil conflict left no place for the question of state division; the matter therefore rested until after the war and Reconstruction.

As has already been stated, writers on California history quite generally have attributed the movement to divide the state, in the decade under discussion, to the influence of slavery propagandists whose purpose, from the beginning, was to secure a part of California for slavery.[26] Josiah Royce, in his *California*, asserted that William M. Gwin, with other Southerners in the constitutional convention, worked on a deep-laid scheme to effect a division of California so that part of the area would be available to slaveholders. Similarly, J. M. Guinn, a historian of southern California, said that the scheme of Gwin and his Southern associates was to make a state of California so large that it would be unacceptable to the members of Congress from the South; then, by cutting it in two on a line running

---

[26] Josiah Royce, *California from the Conquest to the Second Vigilance Committee in San Francisco*, pp. 261–269; J. M. Guinn, *History of California and . . . Its Southern Coast Counties* (Los Angeles, 1907), I, 164.

from east to west at 36° 31′ north latitude, part of California could be brought into the Union as a slave state. Others have made similar statements about the constitutional convention.

Many writers also have tried to attach the slavery motive to the division movement that arose after California was admitted as a state. Guinn boldly made the assertion that the question of slavery was then again agitated with the confident hope of cutting off enough territory from the southern part to make a new and slave state. Tuthill, in his *History of California*, makes the statement: "As early as 1852, the Chivalry had unsuccessfully attempted a convention with the secret purpose of dividing the State and erecting the southern half into Slave Territory." The article on "California" in the *Encyclopædia Britannica*, Eleventh Edition, says: "The Gwin party hoped to divide California into two states and hand the southern part over to slavery"; and John Carr, in his *Pioneer Days in California*, asserts that, "From the adoption of the state constitution in 1849 and 1861, the southern wing of that party [Democratic] did everything in their power to divide the State, their purpose being to make a Slave State out of the southern portion of it." [27] Perhaps the climax of statements of like tenor, without supporting evidence, in connection with the division question was that of Hubert Howe Bancroft, who said that slavery advocates who had always maintained their right to carry slaves into any territory had fixed upon state division as a means of consummating their purpose of bringing slave property to the Pacific Coast.

A study of the history of the state-division movement, however, reveals that the proslavery motive had not the preponderance that these writers have attributed to it. In the first place, their statements concerning the purposes of slavery advocates in the constitutional convention are incorrect. In his *Establishment of State Government in California* (chap. vii) by an

---

[27] Guinn, *op. cit.*, p. 204; Franklin Tuthill, *The History of California* (San Francisco, 1866), p. 576; John Carr, *Pioneer Days in California* (Eureka, 1891), p. 346.

analysis of votes taken in the constitutional convention on the crucial question of the eastern boundary, Goodwin has shown conclusively the baselessness of the repeated assertions concerning the alignment of Northern and Southern men, and of slavery and antislavery forces, with reference to the boundary question. He demonstrated that the often made charge that Southerners were manipulating and working in that convention to secure conditions for the extension of slavery is not substantiated by a study of the debates and votes.

In assigning causes for the state-division movement carried on throughout the decade, the writers referred to seem to have used as the principal basis of their reasoning what they supposed was a deep-laid plan of slavery propagandists in the constitutional convention. Throughout the period of agitation for division, it is true, charges were brought that back of the movement was a purpose to make slave territory out of a part of California; but beyond inferences, charges, and innuendo, there is scant evidence to support the claim of many writers that conspiracy in favor of slavery was fundamental in the division movement. To hold, as one writer has done, that the ostensible purpose was *kept concealed through a decade*,[28] is to attribute too much to prejudice. The history of the division movement shows that the obvious differences in the character of the people and the country, north and south, the feeling that injustice was done to a section and a class, the desire of the native Californians for a separate territorial government, the developing life of the western frontier seeking a larger representation in Congress, and the continued problem of a great and diverse population, were all factors that manifested themselves in clear and definite form. Now and then, slavery discussion became an incident in the movement, but at no time did the slavery propaganda appear as a determining factor. On the basis of the evidence it is more nearly correct to say that slavery discussion was occasionally injected into the movement to divide the state, than to say that the division movement grew out of plans for the extension of slavery.

[28] Guinn, *op. cit.*, p. 204.

VIII

Judge Lynch in the Mother Lode Country and in San Francisco

> *No man who loves America, no man who really cares for her fame and honor and character, or who is truly loyal to her institutions, can justify mob action while the courts of justice are open.*—Woodrow Wilson, July 26, 1918

Much has been written about the struggle for order in the California of the 'fifties. Sanction and praise have usually been given to what was done, and apologetic and patriotic approval to the methods of doing it. Additions to American history can hardly be made by restating in a brief chapter of a book the frequently repeated essential facts about California lynch law and vigilance committee days. However, the retelling of this story after a century brings out clearly the fact that it was difficult for the assertive and independent young communities making up frontier California to accept the limitations imposed by membership in a state of the federal union. Evident also is the fact that certain California groups, in order to establish the pattern which they wanted to maintain or to enforce the rules which they wished to be observed, or to wreak the vengeance they felt was deserved and exemplary, frequently disregarded the protective practices of Anglo-Saxon justice, flouted common or civil law, condemned persons to death without adequate proof, and threatened to destroy those who pleaded for or tried to carry on established procedures. A frank scrutiny of the halting, blundering, and at times primitive and cruel steps by which the American Californians began their attempts to administer justice cannot fail to give a salutary impression of juridical progress. A representation of phases of California justice of one hundred years ago is therefore in order.

Important changes occurred in California between the date of American occupation and the summer of 1849. On July 31, 1846, when the twenty-seven-year-old Mormon elder, Samuel Brannan, sailed through the Golden Gate on the ship *Brooklyn*, with some three hundred Mormons, San Francisco was a strange and crude little town (called Yerba Buena) where only a few weeks earlier the Stars and Stripes had replaced the Mexican emblem. When, about May 12, 1848, businessman Sam Brannan rushed down the dirt street of San Francisco, which was still hardly more than a village, crying, "Gold! Gold! Gold on the American River!" little did he realize how amazing would be the results of the discovery he announced. Electrified by the news of gold in California, Americans turned their eyes toward the west. By the spring of 1849, tens of thousands of persons were on the way to California, some traveling by land, some by sea. Most of them were from the United States, but many were from more distant parts of the world. A great many overland travelers stopped when their trail reached the gold region, while hordes of others came through the Golden Gate and then went on to rivers and foothills where the gold was reputed to be. Myriads of crude, unorganized towns sprang up in the Mother Lode country. At the Golden Gate, the rush of '49 turned San Francisco into a bustling, rapidly growing town of flimsy structures, with many races and types of people, most of whom were young men.

On any frontier, before institutional organization is effected, rules must be evolved if order is to be preserved. These must be enforced by organized community action, or their administration becomes one of caprice or of mob rule expressed through lynch law. As formal law takes the place of informal local rules, legal organization and procedure provide the basis for orderly society. In the transitional phase from rules to law, community assistance may be given to officials in administering justice under the sanction of the legally constituted authorities. Because, in California, the new frontier appeared suddenly and changed rapidly,[1] rules were not quickly agreed upon in individual communities, and law tardily became effective. In the transition from temporary local rules to law, and the implementing of the codes enacted, community assistance was notably absent. Punishments were often administered by uncontrollable groups—that is, by lynch law—in large communities as well as in small, even after more formal law was established, or were inflicted by well-organized extralegal groups, acting vengefully and unlawfully. Notable among these groups was the vigilance committee of San Francisco.

In California, as was quite natural, there were forces which operated against order. In the first year of mining practically no crime or disorder occurred, but coincident with the population inrush of '49 there was a sudden outburst of ruffianism and crime. This upsurge of primitiveness may be attributed to several causes. First, along with the fine American youth bent on adventure, came men from the dregs of society of our eastern states, and criminals from many other lands, who were irked by the restraints of civilized life and journeyed to California for sinister purposes. Second, some of those who came

---

[1] Under the circumstances, "it is difficult to see . . . how preventive and reformatory measures could have been adopted," as Mary Floyd Williams says in her *History of the San Francisco Committee of Vigilance of 1851*, p. 78. Unfortunately, the recognition of this fact has led many to condone the atrocities of mob action by the miners.

with laudable purposes slipped into viciousness in the new and undisciplined life, or from disillusionment became reckless. A third factor was the presence of bad characters from Mexico, Chile, Australia, and other places, who disregarded peace, honesty, and order. These added to the troubles in the mines and in San Francisco. Americans who had a brutal and hearty contempt for foreigners charged them with many more crimes than they committed, and at times treated them with an inhumanity that now seems disgraceful.

With the baffling forces at work and the absence for a time of an effective system of control, uniform administration of justice was impossible in the rapidly changing California of the early gold days. This admission, however, does not blot from the record of those days the crimes committed by Americans in venting their race hatred, or the lawlessness of the Americans, or their inhuman cruelty in the name of justice; nor does it excuse their failure to support, or their will to disregard, agencies of order that were set up.

The story could and should have been a better one. In the caravans which made their way across the plains, rules or codes were set up, under which, in an orderly and judicious manner accused persons were punished or acquitted.[2] Had these methods been applied in California, the evolution of order on the gold frontier could have been a creditable performance instead of being spotted, as it was, with revolting mob acts. Also, universal respect for and support of the earliest officers of the law, such as alcaldes, who were chosen to be the chief officers in many camps in the winter of 1849–50, would have canceled much that was abhorrent. Many officers were treated with respect and supported in their decisions; in numerous camps they were able to give a goodly measure of security to life and property, and to protect personal rights. California's record could easily have been an enviable one in the administration of justice; but here the spontaneous and vengeful pun-

[2] The system of justice as administered on the plains is explained in T. H. Hittell, *History of California*, III, pp. 232–243.

ishments by mobs and vigilance committees, so often unjust and ill-advised, mar greatly an otherwise inspiring picture of California's past.

As an introduction to the sordid story of lynch law [3] as it was administered in the mining country, here, in brief, are early examples of mob action in which drink and race hatred played prominent parts. A deserting sailor, in the latter part of 1848, went to the mining region near the Calaveras River, where he was captured while stealing some bags of gold from a drinking shop. An improvised jury and judge tried him and sentenced him to be hanged. But when some protest was made against this punishment, he was tied to a tree, his head was sheared, his ears were cut off, and he was flogged with one hundred lashes and kicked from camp. In January, 1849, at what is now Placerville, four men unable to speak English were tried for attempted robbery and larceny and each was sentenced to be beaten. After they were thus punished, charges of earlier robbery and murder were made against them. In a new trial, the two hundred miners of the camp, as a jury, sentenced the men to be hanged. Lieutenant E. Gould Buffum pleaded for the men and was threatened with hanging if he did not desist. The crowd, crazed by drink and hatred for the foreigners, hanged the men to the same tree to which they had been tied while being flogged. A little later, in Nevada County, a crowd gave fifty lashes to a man accused of stealing money, while the guilty man looked on; and in the same county a drunken crowd hanged an innocent man on the charge that he had been a horse-thief.[4]

[3] Properly speaking, the term "lynch law" applied to the kind of law administered in summary manner by irresponsible groups in places where regular courts existed and in opposition to them. In time, all irregular proceedings, where there was or was not law, came to be called "lynch law" after the name of a supposed Judge Lynch, possibly a Virginian named Lynch, who was said to have taken the punishment of a thief into his own hands. See Hittell, *op. cit.*, pp. 142–143.

[4] For elaboration of the foregoing cases, see *ibid.*, pp. 272–274. Hittell's story of the mines and miners in this volume, pp. 33–271, and of lynch law in the mines, pp. 272–309, is comprehensive and penetrating. Although less detailed and picturesque than the presentation in H. H. Bancroft's *Popular Tribunals*, it is written with greater strength and understanding.

Besides cases such as these in which drunken revelry and race hatred were involved, there were crude attempts at justice which had some constructive results. On the last Sunday in May, 1849, a drunken row at Ford's Bar on the Middle Fork of the American River was checked when a man of commanding mien seized a musket and threatened to use it on any man who started the fight again. Some rules were then drawn up, this man was elected alcalde, and another was chosen sheriff to enforce the rules. The new arrangement was put to the test the next day, and soon it was used in other cases. Recognition of the officials did not eliminate coarseness and cruelty in the communities, but it did reduce the degree of brutality and made for greater justice. Another instance of constructive action was at Rough and Ready in Nevada County. That mining camp, aroused by a succession of crimes, in April, 1850, held a mass meeting which named a group of men as a committee of vigilance and safety to take charge of administering justice in the community. Although unable to prevent all lynch law, the committee ruled equitably, called juries, settled disputes, and punished persons convicted of crime.

With auspicious beginnings, early organization, and able leaders, the Tuolumne River mining country might have remained free from spontaneous justice and lynch law, but it did not. The first settlement in the vicinity of the Tuolumne River was made early in the summer of 1848. In the following year, the rich gold yield of the famous dry diggings called Sonoranian Camp (and also Sonorian Camp, before its name was shortened to Sonora) kept the rush moving to the area, until by the end of the year the camp's population had increased to five thousand. On Sunday, when the miners from surrounding flats and gulches came in to buy provisions, get mail, or visit saloons and gambling places, the numbers reached ten thousand. The early population was, in general, rough, but among the motley crowd were men strong in intellect and in character. In spite of the excesses and irregularities characteristic of a mining town, a system of law and order crystal-lized there, in the form of a town organization that was put into effect in the autumn of 1849, before California had a statute providing for the incorporation of towns. In February, 1850, Sonora was made the seat of justice, and on June 1, 1850, the court of sessions held its first term there.

With town and judicial organization effected under pro-visions of the adopted constitution, orderly self-government without the vengeful procedures of mob action and lynch law should have resulted. It might have done so had not the sudden inrush of a heterogeneous population, lured by the fantastic reports about gold, produced social and psychological frontier conditions that interfered markedly with such realization. When Americans found foreigners in their way, race hatred was engendered. The coming in of sharp lawyers, whose presentation of legal technicalities confounded judges who had had little or no legal training, aroused the rebellious spirit of the older miners, who felt that lawyers, laws, and judges, delaying administration of justice, invited more crime. Hos-tility to the courts developed because the justice they meted out did not satisfy the advocates of Judge Lynch methods. This antagonistic temper among the men resulted in a curious mix-ture of legal and extralegal action in Sonora and other towns of Tuolumne County. Criminal excesses, accompanied by law-less attempts to mete out justice through disorderly methods, left in the region a deplorable record.

Early in July, 1850, four Americans heard that a murder had been committed at Green Flat Diggings, about eight miles from Sonora. On going to the place, they came upon a Mexican and three Mexican Indians burning a tent and the bodies of two men, after the custom of burning the bodies of the dead in the country from which they had come. The Americans placed the four in custody and brought them to Sonora, where they were at once taken before Richard C. Barry, the justice of the peace, for a hearing. A crowd collected in front of the justice's office, carrying ropes with nooses tied in them, took the prisoners from the court authorities, put a rope round the neck of each, led them to a hill near the town, tried them in a hurried lynch-law fashion, judged them guilty, and promptly sentenced them to die. As the rope of the first victim, the Mexican, was being passed over a limb of a tree, court officers courageously stirred up some excitement in the crowd, rescued the prisoners, carried them back to town, and placed them in the jail. When the case was called for trial, the discharge of a gun accidentally dropped by a guard in the courtroom caused much tumult and the postponement of the trial until the next day. An evening of drunkenness and rioting followed, and in the morning most of the rioters from other places went off to their own camps. Sonora was left in comparative quiet on the day of the trial. It then developed that not only was the evidence insufficient to convict the prisoners, but the hostility against them was in large part the result of prejudice against foreigners. That the accused was not killed by an unreasoning mob acting as Judge Lynch was clearly due to fortuitous circumstances.

Another example of confusion in ideas of justice and administration is the armed conflict that took place in February, 1851, between a man named Joshua Holden, who was cultivating a piece of ground known as Holden's Garden, and some miners who were organized into a group known as the Washington Company. Nothing was done in adjudication of the difficulty, because the persons involved lacked confidence in the court and regular means of prosecution. Another was the case of A. J. Fuller, who in a quarrel with his partner, Tyndal Newby, shot and killed him. The light sentence imposed by the District Court confirmed the miners in their opinion that lawyers controlled the courts. About the same time, when John Thornley, who had killed George Palmer, was acquitted in a court trial, further bitter feeling was aroused against the courts. This reaction, coupled with race hatred, found expression in June, 1851, after two of the three Mexicans accused of murdering Captain George W. Snow had been captured. Completely ignoring the District Court, thus repudiating its kind of justice, a mob took possession of both men and, after they were convicted by a lynch-law court, hanged them. Soon after this, a man well known to be of bad character, who had robbed a store at Campo Seco and a few days later in Sonora had beaten a man over the head with a pistol, was taken by a mob from the jail where the sheriff had placed him, and was tried by lynch law for the robbery of the store, sentenced to death, and hanged in defiance of the sheriff who tried to protect him.

Finally, the extremes in action, the divided counsels, and the general confusion, resulted in the organization of a vigilance committee at Sonora in June, 1851. This illegal body, led and controlled by respected citizens, undertook through extra-legal processes to be a mediating agency between the extremes of mob action and the alleged neglect and inefficiency of the courts. Threats and cruel punishments, some inflicted in an orderly manner, may to some extent have prevented other crimes and perhaps stimulated the courts to greater efficiency, and in this manner served to reduce the number of lynch-law punishments.

So deeply rooted was the spirit of independence and mob action in sections of the Mother Lode country that the brutality of lynch law continued for several years after courts had begun to function. In Tuolumne County, along with legal progress, the mob spirit manifested itself violently in various places until 1855. A climactic and almost the final expression of the disgraceful lynch-law practices in that region was the hanging of John S. Barclay. On October 15, 1855, Barclay shot and killed a man named John H. Smith, who while intoxicated had forced Barclay's wife Martha into a chair after she had used violent language toward him in a quarrel over a broken pitcher. Barclay was at once arrested and put in jail. James W. Coffroth, a state senator-elect, excitedly addressed the mob milling around the jail and urged prompt action in wreaking vengeance upon the murderer of a man who he asserted had been his dear friend. After breaking down the iron doors of the jail, the mob seized Barclay and took him to a high spot, where he was tried before a jury that had been chosen by acclamation. Coffroth was the prosecutor, and John Oxley, who had been elected to the state assembly, was named defense counsel. Witnesses for the prisoner who were in the crowd were not allowed to reach the stand. When Oxley tried to speak, his words were drowned by mixed cries and curses from the mob. The sheriff, in trying to reach the prisoner, was struck on the head with the butt of a pistol and was otherwise beaten. The jury quickly rendered a verdict of "guilty." The prisoner was taken to a spot under a flume and a rope was placed round his neck. Executioners standing on the flume above him dropped and drew him up several times to break his grip on the rope. The rope tightened. He hung in mid-air, strangling, struggling, choking, while in the light of torches and the bonfire, the delirious crowd let itself go in a wild orgy. The disgraceful character of this occasion, the absence of humanity and fairness, the ill repute acquired by Columbia, and the heroic conduct of John Oxley and Sheriff Stewart, "together with the improvements which had gone forward in the administration of justice by the regular courts," may, as Hittell affirmed, have "combined to create a reaction against lynch law." [5] Although later there were isolated cases of mob action, from this time on, in this section law and order were in the ascendancy.

Although no other part of the state's mining area has so many examples of both good and bad in the evolution of order as has Tuolumne County, the same general pattern, but on a smaller scale, was present in all other areas. Every town and camp had its virtuous and its vicious men, and presented opportunities for the expression of character, good and bad. In a general sense, all mining camps had like problems of order to meet, and lynch law was not peculiar to any one of them. The punishments administered were as capricious as the weather or human moods.

[5] With these words, Hittell, *op. cit.*, p. 304, concludes his long account (pp. 281–304) of the struggle for order in the Tuolumne region.

For instance, a Swede called "Little John," a waiter in the Empire House at Rich Bar on the North Fork of the Feather River, who in October, 1851, stole four hundred dollars from his employer, was tried, convicted, flogged with thirty-nine lashes, and driven from the neighborhood. Yet, two men, arrested at Rich Bar in the fall of 1851 on suspicion of having stolen eighteen hundred dollars from their partners, received far different treatment. After being tried and acquitted, because none of the gold was found on them or could be traced to them, they went to Marysville. When one of them returned in December, he was detected retrieving gold he had buried, and was at once seized and charged with theft. Although, with the understanding that he would not be brought to trial, he gave up six hundred dollars which his companions in the crime had left him, a Rich Bar mob seized him, sentenced and hanged him, within the space of a few hours. Also, in 1851, four men who had murdered a man named McDonald, the proprietor of the Slate Creek House near Pine Grove in Sierra County, paid with their lives after the killing became known. When the body of the dead man was discovered, three of the men—including the cook at the Slate Creek House—were seized, the fourth having been killed in resisting, and were convicted, sentenced, and strung up within half an hour.[6]

The cases just cited were not as cruel and revolting as were many which could be presented. They serve to illustrate, however, that in mob action the punishments inflicted often do not fit the crime, and they are examples of the unlawful and capricious methods used in meting out punishment even after regular channels for administering justice were functioning. An illustration that goes far beyond these in showing the potential blindness, hatred, and cruelty inherent in such procedures is the lynching of a woman at Downieville on July 5, 1851. This is revolting, not only because of the brutal treatment of a woman, but because the lynching was due as much to the fact that she was not a citizen of the United States as it was to her

[6] Hittell, *op. cit.*, pp. 305–307.

guilt. Tragically enough, it followed a Fourth of July celebration; in fact, it stemmed from the celebration.

There was a great crowd in Downieville on this Independence Day. Much drinking and carousing accompanied and followed the program, one of the features of which was an address by John B. Weller. Late in the evening, one of the revelers, Jack Cannon, with a few companions, staggered by a house where a young Spanish American woman lived with a Mexican man. The man and woman were apparently sleeping. In some manner, Cannon fell, breaking through a door. His companions pulled him out and threw back a light article that Cannon had picked up. The next morning, as he and one of his companions of the night before passed the house again, Cannon told the man with him that he intended to apologize to the woman for what had happened the previous night. When they went to the door, the woman's paramour met Cannon in an angry mood; the woman also was angry when she appeared a moment later. As the three conversed in Spanish, the woman grew more excited. Suddenly she drew a knife and fatally stabbed Cannon. Because Cannon's companion did not understand Spanish, he was unable to testify whether or not Cannon had used insulting language to the woman, as both she and her paramour asserted.

The news of the murder of an American by a "foreigner" spread like wildfire. Although there were legal provisions for the administration of justice in this region, an illegal lynch-law court was at once organized. The woman and her man were brought before this court, while an excited crowd clamored for quick action. Friends of the dead man testified that what had happened the night before was the result of a drunken accident and a frail door. The two accused persons claimed that the woman's rage at the night incident and Cannon's abuse of her at her door justified the stabbing. Persons attempting to protest against popular violence or the hanging of a woman with child were threatened and roughly handled. The woman was quickly adjudged guilty and sentenced to be hanged. An hour later she was taken to what was known as the Jersey Bridge, for execution. At the improvised gallows she stated briefly that she had no defense except her anger at Cannon, and declared that she would do the same thing again if she were spared and the same insults were offered her. She then bade good-by in Spanish to her friends. The noose was adjusted, and her hands were tied behind her. Men with axes cut the ropes holding the plank on which she stood, and she dropped to her death.[7] Thus did a popular American tribunal emphasize for an American crowd the questionable right of a dominant self-governing race to act as it chooses to act on Independence Day and the day after it.

The methods of adjudication and punishment used by mobs in the mining region consistently show the depths of degradation to which Americanism drops when the lowest passions of men have no legal or social restraints. Dark as the picture was, the effect of these outbursts of popular fury may have been indirectly good, as Josiah Royce philosophically maintained. The people finally saw the fearful effects of their own irresponsible freedom. Continuing Royce's thought and paraphrasing his words: Out of such a realization, the people began to move gradually from the free and adventurous prospecting life, with its degradation, its transient glory, and its inevitable brutality, to commonplace industries of the later mining days; to the formation of governments of a more stable sort; and to the development of a society with families, churches, schools, and local interests, in which lynch law could not hold a respected place but was bound to excite in the minds of sensible men an active dread of its disorderly atrocities. Quoting Royce directly:

The lesson of the whole matter is . . . that the moral elasticity of our people is so great, their social vitality so marvelous, that a community of Americans could sin as fearfully as, in the early

[7] For a detailed account of this tragic expression of mob violence engendered by drink and race hatred, see Josiah Royce, *California*, pp. 368–374. See also Hittell, *op. cit.*, pp. 307–309.

years, the mining community did sin, and could yet live to purify itself within so short a time, not by a revolution, but by a simple progress from social foolishness to social steadfastness.[8]

The evolution of social order in the small frontier town that later became the sizable city of San Francisco in many respects followed the same pattern as that of the mining camps and towns of California. In San Francisco, as in the Mother Lode country, there were "foreigners," there were criminals, and there was crime. At times, in both San Francisco and the mining regions, minority groups attempted to effect order by unlawful means through popular tribunals, with disregard and defiance of the lawfully constituted authorities. In the mining areas, lynch law often prevailed. In San Francisco, no unruly mobs attempted disciplinary action, though the groups that took matters into their own hands were nonetheless lawless and forced such support from the populace that attempts to suppress them might have resulted in civil war and many casualties. In certain mining communities lynch-law proceedings were an assertion of self-government by groups whose defiance of authority was for the most part local, whereas the extralegal action in San Francisco was an assertion of self-government by some of its citizens in defiance of the constituted authorities of that city, of the state, and of the nation.

For the first few years after California had become a part of the United States, San Francisco was, as it has been described, a mushroom town. Its population increased from a little more than 800 in 1848 to some 2,000 by February, 1849, and to 5,000 by July, 1849; and after that date it continued to increase and change rapidly. In those early years it was a crude, picturesque, and bustling city. The population was made up mostly of young men and varied in character. There were a few adventurous women of an old profession, and there was a sprinkling of races from many parts of the world, but "Yankees"—persons from "the States"—predominated. The monetary inflation was prodigious, and there was considerable

[8] Josiah Royce, *op. cit.*, pp. 375-376.

drinking and reckless gambling. From this fertile ground for lawlessness sprang much crime, with consequent great problems of law enforcement.

The earliest temporary popular tribunal for dealing with crime in San Francisco was organized in the summer of 1849. Its formation was the immediate result of an orgy of crime started and participated in by an organization first called "the Hounds," which later adopted the name "San Francisco Society of Regulators." This band was made up mainly of men from the New York Volunteers, who had been recruited in New York by Jonathan D. Stevenson, a Tammany Hall leader, to aid in the conquest of California. The company arrived on the coast after California had been conquered. Numbers of those who went to the mines after their term of enlistment had expired soon drifted back from the mines into San Francisco. The gang had a sort of military discipline, and its members asserted that their object was to promote order. Alcalde Thaddeus M. Leavenworth is said to have occasionally employed some of them to assist in carrying out the ends of justice. Whatever the original intentions of the band were, its members became irresponsible and lawless. They sometimes paraded the streets with music and banners, and now and then supplied their commissary by making raids on stores and restaurants, insolently telling the proprietors to "charge it to the Hounds." [9] They took advantage of the antialien feeling prevalent in the town to attack persons not of American origin, particularly those who lived in the poverty-stricken area known as "Little Chile."

On Sunday, July 14, 1849, after more than a month of outrages, the so-called regulation by the Regulators, or Hounds, reached its climax in an especially violent attack upon the Chilean quarters, in which the Chilenos were beaten, robbed, shot, and chased from their homes. By recklessness and violence too barbarous even for the frontier town of San

---

[9] For a summarized but adequate statement about the origin and activities of the Hounds, see Williams, *op. cit.,* pp. 105–106. H. H. Bancroft, *Popular Tribunals,* I, 76–102, gives a more extensive and picturesque account.

Francisco, the Regulators sealed their own doom. Their vicious and lawless conduct awoke the more respectable citizens to the need for immediate action in suppressing this criminal band. In a hastily called meeting on the Plaza (Portsmouth Square) on Monday afternoon, while the Hounds were resting in their tent from the exertions of the previous day and night, a subscription was taken up to aid the sufferers, an organization was formed, and officers were chosen to assemble a force to arrest the malefactors. Two hundred and thirty citizens were enrolled for immediate service. On hearing of the meeting and organization, the Hounds at first assumed a threatening attitude, but when they learned of the strength and determination of the officers and organized companies, they were frightened and at once began to scatter.[10] They were too late in doing so, for before evening some nineteen of them had been taken. With their leader, Samuel Roberts, they were placed on board a schooner in the harbor.

After the prisoners were securely locked in an improvised prison on the United States vessel *Warren*, the assembled citizens organized a court, naming Alcalde Leavenworth as chief judge, with James C. Ward and Dr. William M. Gwin [11] as associates. A grand jury was called, the prisoners were regularly indicted, attorneys were appointed to prosecute them before the improvised court, and other attorneys were appointed to act for the defendants. In the trials, which occupied a number of days, the cases were handled according to legal form: witnesses were called on each side, and a summation was made by both prosecution and defense. Eight or nine of the men were convicted. What to do with them was a puzzling

[10] Stanton A. Coblentz, in his popular but reliable work, *Villains and Vigilantes*, pp. 35–39, makes these dramatic episodes live. A no less vivid account is that of Hall McAllister, who acted as a prosecuting attorney in the case, which is given in Williams, *op. cit.*, pp. 106–107.

[11] Gwin landed at San Francisco on the day after the riot of the Hounds. "As he walked to the Plaza, he saw a crowd collected, and went up as a spectator to ascertain what was its object. . . . Most unexpectedly to himself, he was called upon" to sit as one of the court. William M. Gwin, "Memoirs," *California Historical Society Quarterly*, XIX, 4, 167–168.

question. Some favored hanging them; others recommended whipping them upon the public square; while still others advocated simple banishment with the understanding that if they returned they would be executed. Since jails and jailers were for the most part lacking, the argument of Dr. Gwin in favor of banishment prevailed, and the convicted men were put on board naval vessels.

Some writers have characterized the affair of the Hounds as typical of the short and easy methods of the early "golden" days. This, however, is not strictly correct. The case was handled in an orderly way from beginning to end. The "Law and Order party," as the citizens' organization was called, did invade the province of the alcalde, but, instead of replacing that officer with one of their own, the group appointed two associate judges to assist him. In what was in effect an extralegal tribunal, by using a grand jury, a trial jury made up of men of solid reputation, and counsel for prosecution and defense, they recognized the safeguards of justice. The 230 volunteer constables were organized from the start in ordered companies under the authority of officers. They conducted the search for the criminals in an orderly manner, and they were ready to protect the court in its conduct of the trials. In the methods they used they did not do violence to American judicial procedures. Similar care by the mining camps and the continuance of the methods in San Francisco would have obviated the later atrocities of lynch law and certain tragic actions in the extralegal proceedings of the vigilance committees.

Writers on the period just preceding the vigilance uprising of 1851 agree that improvement of conditions in San Francisco resulting from the punishment of the Hounds was of short duration. Certain it is that crime increased prodigiously from the latter part of 1849 through 1850 and into 1851. This rapid increase may be attributed principally to the quick augmentation and shifting of population in a land in which the inducement of adventure brought together many criminally inclined

persons and gave them outlet for their criminal instincts; to
the flooding of San Francisco with a backwash from the
mines—disappointed and demoralized men made desperate by
hardships, drunkenness, and gambling; and to the influx of
distinctly criminal classes from English penal colonies. The
fear and hatred felt by the people from "the States" for the
Mexicans, Chilenos, and other "foreigners" from Latin
America, even though they were not markedly addicted to
crime, have an indirect causal relation to certain forms of
criminal activity.

Although offences against the law increased at a rapid rate
after the affair of the Hounds, the citizens of San Francisco
left proceedings against criminals in the hands of the legally
constituted authorities until 1851. Dissatisfaction with the alleged failure of law-enforcing agencies was present, however,
and even in 1850 some indignation meetings were held to protest against asserted criminal mismanagement by local officials.
As might be expected, charges of laxity and corruption were
directed against law-enforcement agencies and the courts. Frequently, assertions were made that offenders looked upon
criminal prosecution as a farce, and upon the courts as protection against popular vengeance. While the criminal conditions
of 1850 and 1851 were, in a measure, tolerated, even though
there were some mutterings of discontent, the necessity of
doing something to check increasing crime began to be discussed in the latter part of 1850. Some advocated the appointment of a committee of regulators to safeguard the public.
Others favored the use of volunteer police to serve in prosecuting and punishing criminals. Unfortunately, the talk was
of independent action, not of coöperation with constituted
authorities.

Before any well-ordered plan for dealing with increasing
crime had taken form, an incident occurred on the night of
February 19, 1851, that caused human emotions to rise suddenly to a psychological bursting point. The incident was the
attack on C. J. Jansen, a merchant on Montgomery Street.

After knocking him senseless with a slung shot, his assailants beat him on the head and left him for dead, while they robbed his safe of nearly two thousand dollars. This assault on a prominent merchant at a business hour in the heart of town naturally pushed popular indignation to unreasoning heights. The *Alta California*, usually a conservative paper, on February 2 1, and again two days later, gave editorial expression to the excitement, and at the same time increased it by declaring that no one was secure, even in his own dwelling, and that when criminals were arrested in San Francisco, they were never punished but were set free to reënact their outrages—a condition which the *Alta* blamed on the lawyers who defended the criminals. While claiming to deprecate lynch law, the editorial actually insisted that the outraged public should be defended either by legal means or by methods beyond the law.[12]

Within twenty-four hours of the assault, the police had arrested two men as suspects. One of these was supposed to be James Stuart, a Sydney convict who had murdered in cold blood Charles Moore, sometimes called "Sheriff" Moore, of Foster's Bar in Yuba County, and had escaped from jail in Sacramento some two months before the Jansen robbery. The arrested man protested his innocence and claimed, correctly, that he had had nothing to do with the murder of Moore or the robbing of Jansen, and that he was not James Stuart but a respectable British subject, Thomas Berdue. The second man arrested was Robert Windred, also an Australian, and he, too, protested his innocence. Berdue did bear a resemblance to the notorious Stuart; and officers of the law and men who had worked with Stuart testified that he was the escaped murderer. In the excitement, credence was not given to the statement of other persons that the accused prisoner was not James Stuart and was not responsible for Stuart's crimes.

[12] Royce, *op. cit.*, pp. 408–409, quotes extensively the indignation expressed by the *Alta California* at this time. After quoting an inflammatory passage from the *Alta* editorial, Coblentz, *op. cit.*, says, "A plea like this, furiously emotional yet based on well known facts, could hardly fail of its effect."

The infuriated crowd which had gathered about the building containing the supposed criminals repeatedly cried out, "Hang them! Lynch them!" before the men were taken to the victim for identification. On Friday, February 21, the still-dazed Jansen claimed to recognize the two accused men as his assailants; he was positive in his identification of the one called Stuart and had only a faint doubt about the other man. When the news of identification became known in the street, an angry crowd tried to take the prisoners from the officers, presumably to lynch them, as the men were being carried back to the station house; but the crime was thwarted by the revolvers of the guard.[13] As it finally turned out, in spite of Jansen's identification of them, the two men had not taken part in the assault on Jansen and the robbery of his store, and the man thought to be Stuart was, as he claimed, Thomas Berdue.

However, on Saturday, February 22, the innocent prisoners were brought into the court of the city hall, at the corner of Kearny and Pacific streets. They tried to establish an alibi, but their witnesses made an unfavorable impression. When the court adjourned, another effort was made to seize the prisoners and lynch them. Mayor John W. Geary, fearing such an attempt, had secretly stationed a military company, the Washington Guards, in an adjoining room. They cleared the courtroom and lodged the prisoners in the jail, out of danger. For their action the guards were hooted and hissed by the disorganized crowd. On the same day, contempt for constituted authorities and vengeful feelings against the prisoners were intensified by the careless comment of some newspapers that an outraged public would appeal to lynch law soon, unless certain things were done, and by a handbill, circulated on that afternoon and evening, addressed to the citizens of San Francisco. This sheet asserted that "law, it appears, is but a nonentity to be scoffed at," and that redress against crimes could be had only "through the never failing remedy so admirably laid down

[13] Coblentz, *op. cit.*, p. 53, vividly describes the excitement before and after Jansen's supposed identification of the prisoners. See also Williams, *op. cit.*, p. 172.

in the code of Judge Lynch," and suggested that "each man be his own executioner." The paper ended with a call for "those who would rid the city of its robbers and murderers" to assemble on Sunday, at two o'clock, on the Plaza.[14]

By dusk of Saturday evening, February 22, several thousand people were assembled around the city hall, some urging violence, others counseling against ill-advised action of any kind. After a number of speeches had been made, the assemblage appointed a committee of fourteen citizens to consider the situation, consult with the authorities, and help the police guard the prisoners overnight. The committee meeting held that night was a stormy one. When someone proposed that the accused be tried in the ordinary way, Sam Brannan, whom Royce characterizes as "the lion-hearted, a man always in love with shedding the blood of the wicked," begged his fellow members to take the chance given them by fortune and at once try the prisoners themselves. Brannan is said to have stated baldly the self-governing doctrine of lynch law, in these words: "We are the mayor, and the recorder, the hang man, and the laws!" He and three others were in favor of immediate execution, and in their report said that "the prisoners, Stuart and Wildred [Windred] are both deserving of immediate punishment, as there is no question of their guiltiness of crime." [15]

The next day, Sunday, February 23, was one of colorful drama. Its events furnish material for a lesson in crowd psychology. In the morning, an estimated six to eight thousand persons assembled in the Plaza. The majority and minority reports drawn up by the committee the previous evening were presented, the minority report of Brannan and those of like mind being distributed as a handbill. Mayor Geary and other officials addressed the people, the mayor urging them to disperse and promising that the prisoners would be tried at once

[14] This handbill was published in the *Alta California*, February 23, 1851; its text is printed in Williams, *op. cit.*, p. 453.

[15] See Royce, *op. cit.*, pp. 409–410; Hittell, *op. cit.*, p. 315; *Alta California*, February 23 and 24, 1851.

and would be promptly punished if their guilt should be established. Because of the dangerous temper of the assemblage, he even suggested that the prisoners should be tried before a court made up of the regular judge and a jury of twelve citizens selected by the assembly, and that the verdict of this court should be final. In this tense situation, which was pregnant with possibilities, twenty-seven-year-old William T. Coleman, a merchant of the city, who instinctively "had a horror of a mob and its wild and hasty excesses," [16] made his way to a railing of the crowded balcony of the city hall, where he caught the ear of the multitude with a proposal for a people's court, before which the prisoners should at once be tried. If convicted after a fair trial they would be hanged, he said. The crowd approved his proposal. A court was immediately organized, with three judges and a jury of twelve citizens. D. O. Shattuck and Hall McAllister, lawyers, were named as counsel for the defense, and by popular demand, Coleman was chosen prosecuting attorney.

It was a strange trial that got under way that Sunday afternoon. An eager, impatient mass of men stood around the building. Inside the hall was a dense crowd. The prisoners were not present. Witnesses gave uncertain and doubtful testimony against the men. The crowd outside grew so clamorous that Coleman felt called upon to appeal to them several times from the balcony. Judge Shattuck could do little to defend the prisoners in the face of interruptions from persons inside demanding their death. He did beg the jury to remember the terrible responsibility of the whole proceeding: the prisoners were being tried while they were not present, and they had none of the safeguards of Anglo-Saxon and American justice to protect them.

Far into the night, with its chilly winds, the crowd remained

---

[16] Before his appearance at this time, Coleman was not well known; his suggestion for the extralegal trial of the two accused men brought him to the attention of the public and made him a marked man. The confidence he inspired made him the trusted leader in the vigilance committees. He became wealthy later and was always respected.

massed outside waiting for the verdict. Three of the jurors respected the fact that the prisoners had not appeared before them, and that Jansen's testimony was of doubtful validity. When the jury returned to the courtroom and announced its disagreement, the mob outside broke in the windows, crowded in at the doors, and rushed for the jurors, shouting "Hang them, too!" The jurymen drew their revolvers and retired into the jury room until the excitement subsided. In the meantime an indignation meeting was held in the street; Coleman endeavored to persuade the people to disperse, while Brannan, who was for hanging the prisoners anyway, urged them on. More-conservative leaders finally quieted the crowd by insisting that the sovereign people had referred the case to the jury, and that they must abide by the decision. About midnight the crowd at last was induced to break up and go home.[17]

Fate often plays strange tricks with the destinies of men. So it was with Berdue and Windred. After being concealed for several days after the so-called trial, they were handed over to the regularly constituted authorities. About the middle of March they were tried and were convicted on flimsy and false evidence and because of popular pressure. Windred was sentenced to ten years' imprisonment, Berdue to fourteen. Remanded to prison, Windred soon made his escape, helped by Samuel Whittaker, who, with the actual Stuart, had assaulted Jansen and robbed his store. Resolving to lift the weight of injustice from Windred, Whittaker, who later became a victim of the vigilance committee, secretly sent to Windred a key that would unlock the jail. Windred escaped and hid at Mission Dolores until he and his wife were smuggled aboard a vessel that sailed for Australia on May 5, the day after San Francisco's fifth great fire. Berdue was sent to Marysville to stand trial for the murder of "Sheriff" Moore. He was even

[17] Based on original sources, the narrative of the strange trial is presented in Royce, *op. cit.*, pp. 411–416. A succinct account of the trial, corresponding in its detail with that given by Royce, written by juror G. E. Schenk, is given in Williams, *op. cit.*, pp. 174–175. For more about Berdue and Windred see *ibid.*, pp. 175–176, 257, 303, 311–312.

more unlucky there than he had been in San Francisco. In spite of conflicting evidence, he was pronounced guilty on July 4.

The Berdue-Windred trial and the accompanying events had immediate social results, both good and bad, for San Francisco. The mass of the citizens could not know how serious a crime might have resulted from the hasty methods used. Many persons who valued peace, life, and property, felt disturbed. Vengeance-hungry citizens were disappointed. Undeterred in their actions, the criminal part of the population continued to loot, burn, destroy, and kill, with what appeared to be greater confidence and carelessness. In the face of continued crime, and in their unsettled emotional state, citizens discussed among themselves the need for some sort of action and what the action should be. Purposes were strengthened and plans began to take form after San Francisco was devastated by fire on May 4, 1851, exactly one year to the day after the fire of the preceding year. Public imagination attributed the fires to a gang of incendiaries, who set fire to buildings for purposes of plunder. Leading citizens, on May 17, in collaboration with the city authorities, started a voluntary patrol to assist the police in guarding the various districts of the city. The patrol was a regular police organization, authorized by a city ordinance, sworn into office by the mayor, and directed by the city marshal. This effort at crime control was good and in order, but it was short-lived. The concatenation of events which preceded and followed it gave rise to an assertive, lynch-law emotionalism, which put an end to the planned coöperation with and support of the city authorities and found expression through an extralegal vigilance committee.

The formation of this unlawful body resulted from conditions which had led to the organization of the patrol, and from newspaper publicity given to the many subsequent crimes, and repeated references in the press to the fearful menace of arson. Veiled advocacy of lynch law in one leading newspaper and the proposal for the formation of a public-safety committee in another, which followed the arrest of Benjamin Lewis in connection with a small fire on June 2, helped bring to a focus the idea of a protective organization. A group of interested persons assembled in Sam Brannan's building on the evening of June 9 and put into form plans for the first Committee of Vigilance. At this meeting a constitution or pact was drawn up, and Tuesday evening, June 10, the constitution [18] was signed and plans for the illegal body were perfected.

In the pact it was agreed that the name of the organization should be "Committee of Vigilance"; that in a room selected for deliberations of the committee one or more members should be on duty day and night to receive reports of violence done to persons or property; and that, if in the judgment of a member or members on duty in the committee room, the act or acts presented justified action, the committee should at once be assembled for the taking of such action as a majority of those present should determine. A decision thus reached would bind all the members to defend and sustain each other in carrying out the will of the committee at the hazard of their lives. This extralegal and closely knit body was set up with studied assumption of local sovereignty in an area of government. Its members not only sealed in writing a pledge to maintain peace and order and to sustain the laws when in their judgment they were properly administered, but they also made it clear, in the second article of their constitution, that they were determined to proceed as if they were a body of constituted authority. Here was no coöperative group working under and with the mayor and police as the volunteer patrol had planned to do. This body considered itself the law and government whenever a majority of the members present, however small the number might be, decided a course of action for the committee.

Scarcely had the constitution of the committee been signed by some one hundred members on Tuesday evening, June 10,

[18] The complete text of the constitution is printed in Williams, *op. cit.,* pp. 205–206.

when an opportunity came to test its character. Early that evening, John Jenkins, a Sydney Valley resident of evil reputation, entered the store of George W. Virgin at Long Wharf and made off with a portable safe. He was detected, pursued, and captured as he tried to escape in a small boat. On the insistence of several vigilantes who were helping to guard the prisoner, he was taken to the room of the committee. A small group was still lingering in the room when the defiant Jenkins was brought in about ten o'clock. They decided at once to assemble the committee. In response to the agreed upon signal, the ringing of Monumental Engine Company's bell, some eighty members appeared, while an excited crowd gathered outside. After hasty consultation, an immediate trial took place. The verdict was "guilty."

The question of penalty occasioned some discussion. Finally, on the grounds that Jenkins had been proved to be a vicious and dangerous man, that he was rebellious and had boasted that he would be rescued, that rumors were in circulation that criminal gangs were preparing to rescue him, and that the young politician, David Broderick, was organizing opposition to the illegal methods of the extralegal body, it was decided to execute the prisoner at once. Sam Brannan, standing on a sandbank, made a vehement speech to the people outside, and a majority of the crowd indicated their approval of the committee's illegal course. About two o'clock in the morning, a clergyman's prayer for the condemned man was cut short by a committeeman's order, and Jenkins was taken to Portsmouth Square, where a thousand people were assembled. A block had been rigged on the flagpole, for the hanging, but a cry of protest prevented that desecration. Jenkins, with a noose round his neck, was then dragged to the adobe that had been the Mexican customhouse, where he was brutally pulled up to the block. There, relays of men kept his body hanging for several hours, until dawn.[19]

[19] The story of these gruesome proceedings is given with thoroughness in Williams, *op. cit.*, pp. 209–214. Coblentz, *op. cit.*, pp. 209–214, presents the revolting affair more dramatically.

The immediate aftermath of this crude administration of "justice" by an illegal body is important. The regularly con- stituted authorities were forced to act. Edward Gallagher, the coroner, took charge of the murdered man's body, impaneled a coroner's jury, and held an inquest. At this inquiry, carried on through parts of three days, it was difficult to get names of those who had taken part in the night's events. Witnesses naturally declined to answer questions which might implicate them, and were reluctant to identify any of the participants. Members of the police force testified only that they had at- tempted to rescue the illegally held victim and had been repulsed. Fearing self-constituted authorities as much as they did robbers and thugs, they dared not name persons or tell what they had seen. A few names were given by Hall McAllis- ter, who testified that he did not assist in the trial, and did not sympathize with those who held the rope; and by David Brod- erick, who identified several participants and told of his efforts to prevent the committee from carrying out its purposes. Sam Brannan, who admitted to the jury the existence of the com- mittee and its part in the trial and lynching of the victim, refused to give the names of participants, on the ground that threats had been made against their lives. On the afternoon of June 13, in an atmosphere of tension, the jury returned a verdict finding the death of Jenkins to have been "by strangu- lation" resulting from "his being suspended by the neck with a rope . . . at the hands of, and in pursuance of a precon- ceived action on the part of an association of citizens, styling themselves a Committee of Vigilance, of whom the following members are implicated by direct testimony," [20] and listed the names of nine persons.

This action did not disturb the confident vigilantes. Em- boldened by evidences of community support, as the trial had proceeded, the committee had approved publication in the press on the morning of June 13, over the signatures of the

[20] The verdict in full and the nine names are given in Williams, *op. cit.*, p. 216.

first 180 members, of an official announcement of the organization and purposes of the Committee of Vigilance and a
statement acknowledging equal responsibility of each of the
signers for the hanging of Jenkins. On the day after the coroner's jury issued its verdict, the committee defiantly published
a resolution characterizing the verdict as invidious and stating
that the names of the nine members had been "unnecessarily
picked," since all members of the committee were equally
implicated and were equally responsible. The newspapers not
only generally approved the unlawful actions of the extralegal
body but pointed out in a popular way the absurdity of a mass
trial of citizens of high standing, some of whom were among
the "leading merchants of San Francisco." There is no doubt
that the committee had considerable moral support in the community, and that the voices of opposition to it were few, and
usually timid. Almost the only active opposition was that of
David C. Broderick and a group led by him, who, because they
did "not think the people should take the law into their own
hands," opposed the vigilantes.[21] The committee and its supporters attempted to intimidate these and other opponents of
the committee's lawlessness by referring to them as "officials, politicians, and lawyers, with whose business it interfered."

On June 10, 1851, the night of Jenkins' arrest, an executive
committee composed of twenty members had been created.
This became at once, and continued to be, the vigilance committee's center of administration. Meeting almost every day, it
took up matters for first consideration, outlined work, examined prisoners, prepared reports, and made recommendations for the general committee. This general committee, which
ultimately enrolled 707 members, met once or twice a week to
review the work of the executive committee. The impetuous
Sam Brannan acted as president of the general and executive
bodies for about a month, then he resigned because of violent
differences with other officers. Selim E. Woodworth, who

<hr/>

21 *Ibid.*, pp. 217–220 and n. 31.

had resigned from the United States Navy in 1849 to become a member of the state senate, was elected general president. Stephen Payran, a professional copyist from Philadelphia, who had been in California three years, became president of the executive committee and served from about July 4, 1851, to November 12, 1851. Isaac Bluxome, Jr.,[22] who, after his arrival in San Francisco in June, 1849, had engaged in the commission business and had been burned out in three successive fires, was secretary of the executive committee throughout the life of the Committee of Vigilance, including the reorganized body in 1856. There was a chief of police with numerous deputy officers, a sergeant-at-arms, a general treasurer, and numbers of minor committees. On June 17, 1851, the committee headquarters were moved from Brannan's building to the second story of a frame building on the west side of Battery Street, between Clay and Pine.

In the short space of a week, a closely knit and independent organization having revolutionary potentialities had been formed in San Francisco and had begun to function.

From June 14 to the unexpected apprehension on July 7 of the actual James Stuart, for whose crimes Thomas Berdue nearly lost his life, the committee acted determinedly and methodically to rid San Francisco of what it denominated as "criminal classes." Its earliest and most strenuous efforts were directed against supposed criminals among Australian ex-convicts. Suspects were quickly investigated and were ordered to leave town as soon as transportation could be secured. Vessels that came in from Australia were boarded and searched for convicts, revenue officers having agreed to assist the committee in this matter. Persons adjudged to be criminals were sent away or were pursued and ordered to leave the city. The committee's efforts did rid San Francisco of some of its bad characters, and committee officials exercised salutary control in connection with the disastrous fire of June 22 and other

[22] Brief biographical sketches of Brannan, Woodworth, Payran, Isaac Bluxome, Jr., Coleman, and others are given in Williams, *op. cit.*, pp. 190–204.

happenings which afforded opportunities for lynch-law action. But San Francisco continued to have criminals, and the criminals continued to have their armed forces, though perhaps on a smaller scale than before.

While carrying on some work that may have been beneficial, and coöperating with the sheriff by raising money to complete work on the new jail, the committee made a fundamental break with civil guarantees of the state and the nation in its proclamation and in its search of homes without authorization from the legally constituted authorities. The first search of this kind was made on the night of June 22, when ten or twelve friends of Felix Argenti, an Italian banker who was one of the vigilantes, forcibly entered the home of a man named Peter Metcalf and made a thorough search among the personal effects of Metcalf's wife and daughter, for valuables Argenti claimed were secreted there. This violation of constitutional principles led to a suit by Metcalf against Argenti and others for $25,000 damages, and was a cause of dissension in the committee for some time. Nevertheless, in an address on July 5, the committee not only called upon all good citizens to assist it by giving any information within their power, but notified everyone that it claimed the right to enter any premises where it had good reason to believe suspicious characters or stolen property could be found. Some members of the committee disapproved of this repudiation of civil rights. But in spite of this, and disregarding an open letter from Mayor C. J. Brenham to the citizens of San Francisco condemning the search of homes "without any accountability"—a procedure which he said was known only under inquisitorial governments—and Judge Alexander Campbell's charge to the grand jury referring to the unreasonable and unauthorized searches,[23] the committee continued its revolutionary action of unlawfully invading private premises.

With the arrest on July 1, 1851, of a suspicious character skulking in the underbrush of the sand hills near what is now

[23] Both quoted in part in *ibid.*, p. 244.

the corner of Powell and California streets, the vigilance committee found that it had in its hands the daring and notorious robber and murderer, James Stuart. Thomas Berdue, who had been falsely identified as Stuart, was lying in jail at Marysville, under trial for the murder of Sheriff Moore. Stuart was now positively recognized by several San Franciscans, and by four men sent from Marysville on request of the San Francisco authorities. Convinced that he could no longer hide his identity and his crimes, he decided to make a full confession. He evidently reckoned that by giving a complete history of his lawless past and incriminating his associates in crime he could place himself in an advantageous bargaining position. In a full night before the executive committee, this English-born criminal, with a prison record in Australia and other lands, seemed to take pleasure in recounting his successes in many robberies and brutal attacks. But he did not mention the murder of Charles Moore, for which Berdue was being held to account. Without emotion, he told of striking the blow that rendered Jansen unconscious, and of his and his accomplices' intention to set fire to the city again if innocent Windred and Berdue were executed.

The committee, which a little earlier had almost hanged Berdue as Stuart in the Jansen case, sent a messenger to Marysville to report the real Stuart's apprehension. A stay of execution was reluctantly allowed, Berdue having already been sentenced to death, and he was a little later given his liberty. Thus, by mere chance, an innocent man was saved from being murdered by an unlawful body of his fellows. Berdue was never recompensed for his suffering and losses. Near the end of August, the charge of robbery against him was vacated by Judge Campbell, after some of the vigilantes had presented evidence that Stuart had assumed the guilt of the attack on Jansen. Recognizing Berdue's sorry plight, Jansen offered to return the money taken from him at the time of his capture. At the suggestion of Judge Campbell, a subscription was taken up, and on September 16 Berdue acknowledged the receipt of

$302 from Isaac Bluxome, Jr., who was acting for the vigilance committee.

The reorganization of the Committee of Vigilance, which took place at the time of the arrest of Stuart, climaxed differences that had been present from the first. In some of the changes of personnel, such as the replacement of the impetuous Brannan by the better balanced and more orderly Stephen Payran as president of the executive committee, a trend toward conservatism in action was shown. These new officers, however, believed as passionately as did Brannan in the sovereignty of the committee, and in the committee's right to act without restriction from any authority but itself. This was shown when Frank M. Pixley, the city attorney, got out a writ of habeas corpus summoning officials of the committee to produce the captive Stuart in court. In reply, members of the committee, on July 9, made affidavit in the California supreme court that not only did they not have Stuart in their possession, but that they never had had such custody over him as would have enabled them to comply with the court's order.

Further defiance of the court and disregard of legal authority occurred after Pixley secured the issuance of another warrant directing Sheriff John C. Hays to bring James Stuart into court on the next day. When the sheriff went to the headquarters of the committee, he was allowed to inspect them; but he did not find Stuart there or anywhere in the city, though he made a diligent search. This defiance by vigilance committee members of long-established constitutional processes expressed the self-governing theory and assertiveness of vigilantism. A few days later the committee retained another prisoner for whose release a writ had been served. Because, at this point, some committee members questioned the advisability of disregarding a legal provision so time-honored as the writ, a subcommittee was appointed to examine the question and make a report of its conclusions to the general committee. The subcommittee unqualifiedly defended the questioned action and asserted that, "if the vigilance committee be the people," it was through the committee that the people might "obtain justice and freedom from the ills which oppress and ruin our community." [24]

On Friday morning, July 11, the tapping of the bell of the Monumental Engine Company was heard again. The city understood that the Committee of Vigilance was being called to try Stuart. His confession was read. Some witnesses gave their testimony. Stuart was adjudged guilty as charged. By unanimous vote he was sentenced to immediate death by hanging. Colonel Jonathan D. Stevenson was delegated to address the assembled crowd, state the facts of the case, and ask if the people approved what had been done. The mob voiced its approval with a loud shout. About three o'clock the manacled and guarded prisoner was brought out into the street, where the committee members, about four hundred in number, formed into platoons, ten abreast, and with Stuart in the center proceeded along Battery Street to Market and to the Market Street Wharf. The prisoner walked erect to the derrick upon the pier that had been selected as the place of execution. The hangman placed his rope about Stuart's neck, and with a jerk hoisted him off his feet and to his death, while the crowd quietly watched.

The public authorities again took notice of an unlawful execution. The coroner gained possession of the body and impaneled a jury. The verdict they brought in was practically identical with that in the case of Jenkins. The mayor of the city, Charles J. Brenham, addressed another open letter to the citizens of San Francisco, in which he pointed out once more the insurrectionary tendencies of the Committee of Vigilance and appealed to the people to withdraw from its ranks and to aid the authorities in enforcing laws. Judge Campbell, of the court of sessions, on the day after the execution, called into court a grand jury he had impaneled earlier in the month. He declared to them that the people must decide whether or not

---

[24] The defensive report of the subcommittee is quoted in part in Williams, *op. cit.*, p. 267.

they were willing to throw away the safeguards of society and to place life and property at the mercy of a secret organization. He charged that the execution was murder, and called upon the jury to bring the guilty to justice. The governor of the state issued a proclamation, in which he pointed out the dangers to free government, and to liberty and order, of such extralegal organizations as vigilance committees which act outside the law, though he conceded that associations could properly be organized for the purpose of aiding the officers of the law in the execution of their duties of detecting, arresting, and punishing criminals.

Such condemnation of the Committee of Vigilance and its work, by the mayor, a judge, and the governor,[25] still failed to diminish the zeal of the vigilantes in their acts of lawlessness. Stuart had named about twenty-five participants or accomplices in robberies, and the committee began pursuing them on the day of Stuart's execution. Among those most eagerly sought were two leaders in the Stuart gang, Robert McKenzie and Samuel Whittaker. Parties sent into the Mother Lode country to search for them were assisted by vigilance groups of interior cities. McKenzie was discovered in Sacramento, where J. G. Schultz, a member of the San Francisco committee, caused him to be arrested on July 29. By August 1 he was safely held in the San Francisco headquarters.

Whittaker evaded capture for more than a week longer. This thirty-year-old English former convict, who had committed many robberies, including the robbery of Jansen, was recognized and taken into custody in Santa Barbara on August 8, by Sheriff V. W. Hearne. With his prisoner, Sheriff Hearne embarked at once for San Francisco, where he intended to deliver his captive to the local police. There, vigilantes kidnapped Whittaker and took him to committee headquarters while Hearne was looking for Sheriff Hays of San Francisco. This turn of events abruptly terminated Hearne's efforts at

[25] For the proclamation of Mayor Brenham, see Williams, *op. cit.*, p. 463; for an extract of the charge of Judge Campbell, see *ibid.*, pp. 464–465; for the proclamation of Governor McDougal, see *ibid.*, pp. 467–469.

coöperation in this case with the legal law-enforcement officers. The vigilance committee reimbursed him for the expenses of his trip to San Francisco.

The examination of McKenzie and Whittaker failed to reveal that either was a murderer, but the executive committee held that the self-confessed robbers were guilty of various heinous crimes, and without further ado sentenced them to be hanged on August 20. At this point, and in connection with this sentence, direct conflict occurred between the Committee of Vigilance and the regularly constituted authorities.[26]

When Governor McDougal, on August 19, learned that the committee planned to execute McKenzie and Whittaker on the following day, he hastened to San Francisco. There, he and Mayor Brenham at once secured from Judge Myron Norton a warrant for immediate seizure of the prisoners. The sheriff was then awakened and directed to serve the warrant with no delay. Accompanied by the mayor and the governor, Sheriff Hays and his deputy, John Caperton, went to the rooms of the vigilantes soon after midnight, where, on finding Payran asleep and the chief of police out, the sheriff and his deputy, familiar with the rooms and methods of admission, pushed past the guard at the door, seized the prisoners, and brought them out, meeting with but little resistance and no violence.

Events now moved rapidly. The next morning at eight o'clock an excited meeting of the committee took place. There were proposals for retaliation and immediate recapture of the prisoners. The usually calm Payran presented a fiery resolution, which called upon the committee to decide whether to call the city to action, in order to show who had the supremacy, or to acknowledge defeat and release all prisoners. In the end, it was resolved to execute Whittaker and McKenzie as soon as they could be recaptured.

The governor, on the same day, issued a proclamation [27] in which he stated that an armed and organized body of the citi-

---

[26] For the full story of what took place, see Williams, *op. cit.*, pp. 291–304.
[27] A copy of this proclamation is in the Bancroft Library. A photograph of the proclamation is given in *ibid.*, opp. p. 298.

zens of San Francisco County had, in defiance of the constitution and laws of the state, assumed the powers of the courts of criminal jurisdiction and had proceeded to pass and carry into effect extrajudicial sentences of death. He therefore called upon all good citizens of the county to unite for the purpose of sustaining public law and tranquility, to aid the public officers in the discharge of their duty, and to discountenance attempts to set up extralegal control in place of responsible government.

From the morning of Thursday, August 21, for several days the Committee of Vigilance appeared to be defeated and the constituted authorities to be in charge. In the meantime, however, a scheme was being worked out for retaking the two prisoners and dealing with them by extralegal authority. The committee scheduled the seizure for Sunday, August 24, as divine services were ending in the jail. The vigilantes placed a few guards in the church; and Captain John W. Cartwright's guard of thirty, in three divisions, waited near the front and rear entrances of the jail. About half past two, just as the religious service ended, at a given signal, the vigilantes overpowered the jail guards, Cartwright's guard rushed in from the front and the rear, seized McKenzie and Whittaker, and carried them to a waiting carriage, which was then driven at full speed to the committee headquarters. Mary Floyd Williams adds vividness to her thorough narrative of these events by printing a curt order from the executive committee, dated August 22, to Captain Cartwright, directing him to detail a guard to "arrest two Prisoners to-wit—Sam Whittaker & R. Mackensie and bring them, into custody of the Committee of Vigilance," and the report of August 24 on the execution of the order, which reads:

Agreeably to your orders above I detailed (30) Thirty men who proceeded in Three Divisions under the respective orders of Col G. W. White, Capt Calhoun & Mr Oscar Smith & in the short spaces of 5 minutes from the first charge the Prisoners above named were on their way to your Head Quarters.[28]

[28] Williams, *op. cit.,* p. 299.

As the carriage bearing the victims raced at forced speed through the streets, the bell of the Monumental Engine Company tolled its mournful tap, tap . . . tap, tap . . . tap, tap, which the populace knew meant a vigilance committee execution. Excited people ran after the carriage to the committee rooms, and crowds from every direction poured into near-by streets. It was a show occasion for San Francisco. Above two of the second-story doorways on Battery Street, intended for the reception of goods, were two projecting beams, each with a block and tackle at the end. Within seventeen minutes after the prisoners were brought in from the jail, they were hanging by their necks from these beams.

While the bodies of the executed men were still swinging in the presence of some six thousand persons, Sam Brannan, Stephen Payran, and others spoke the committee's apologia for the daring, melodramatic, and vengeful invasion of the precincts of established authority. The answering approval of an emotionally stirred crowd momentarily gripped by mob cruelty, and a historical understanding of how and why these events occurred, do not make them other than what they were: illegal murder and insurrection. That no effective action could have been taken by the authorities to punish the murderers without precipitating serious civil conflict is granted. It is plain that constituted authority was rendered helpless by an arrogant, arbitrary, and lordly, secret band, which assumed that it was the people, and that it therefore was above law.

This latest example of lynch law produced much hostile reaction to the vigilance committee and was its last "daring performance." An influential religious paper, *The Pacific*, declared that the act forfeited the confidence of the community in the vigilantes. A respected judge of the court of sessions, Judge H. S. Brown, had the courage to resign his position because of the universal indictment of the courts by some of the press. Before the grand jury, on the day after the lynching, Judge Campbell stated that his views in the present case were the same as those he had expressed at the time of Stuart's execution, when he called upon the people to decide whether or not they would abandon law and liberty to an unlawful secret organization, and at which time he denounced the illegal execution as an outrage and the perpetrators as murderers. Whether as a result of blows from without, such as those of honest Judge Campbell, or because of repentance from within, many vigilantes all at once came to feel that perhaps their critics were right, and that they had gone too far in rebellion and lawlessness. Certain it is that after the execution of Whittaker and McKenzie the flame of vigilantism in 1851 suddenly died down.

The Committee of Vigilance of 1851 did not formally dissolve. Soon after the hanging of Whittaker and McKenzie, some of the group argued that the excuse for the organization had terminated, since the emergency that had called them together had been relieved, even though some lawlessness continued and criminals were present. Others thought that the organization should be permanent. A small group wished to continue the influence of the committee leaders by placing them in public office at the election in September. The committee refused to endorse a nonpartisan ticket, but individual members pushed a list of candidates, with some success. These differences of opinion over the future of the committee underlay many evidences of disaffection in the organization. Little is known about the issues at this time, since there exist no known minutes of executive committee meetings from the date of the seizure of Whittaker and McKenzie until the middle of September, when the Committee of Vigilance was thoroughly reorganized. It is a matter of record that the executive committee on September 6 stated boastingly, or perhaps resignedly, that its labors had been completed, and that peace and security had attended its efforts for the public good. The report of the committee on reorganization, which was presented to a general meeting on September 16, appears in the minutes of September 17 and was presumably adopted on that day.[29]

[29] The closing events in the life of the committee are recorded in Williams, *op. cit.,* pp. 336–337.

Under the provisions of this report the general committee adjourned *sine die,* and an executive committee of forty was elected and its duties were defined. From September 17, 1851, to March 17, 1852, it held twenty-five weekly meetings, with an average attendance of sixteen, at which only routine business seems to have been taken up. On March 17, at the end of the six-month term of the reorganized executive committee, some three hundred vigilantes assembled at the old headquarters to elect new representatives. The adjourned general committee continued to exist. At a later date it was reorganized, so that all members were relieved from duty except a committee of thirteen, which had the obligation of calling together the general body should the need arise. Thus, the committee continued to be dormant for the next three years, until it was revived in the formation of the San Francisco Committee of Vigilance of 1856.

What had actually been accomplished by the Committee of Vigilance of 1851? Statistical records show, between August, 1851, and the middle of the year 1852, a diminution in crime, which, while not too impressive, deserves respectful attention. The deportations and lynchings carried on by that unlawful organization did for a time frighten robbers, thieves, and even murderers. To such an extent the experiment in lynch law was successful. Unfortunately, however, the criminals made their appearance again in a social system corrupted by strutting individualism, dominated by predatory purposes, and deficient in religious and ethical restraints.

Even while the vigilantes were enacting their parody of justice, despoilers, fundamentally far more dangerous than the thieves the committee punished, carried on without public disapproval. Their colossal sins of political and economic exploitation, being so much a part of the social pattern, were uncomprehended by the vigilantes and by many other people who were too much a part of what was going on to recognize the corruptionists for what they were. With penetration, Stanton Coblentz has described the state of affairs. After quoting from the *Annals of San Francisco* a description of the city's strange mixture of peoples, nearly all of whom came to the city as devout worshippers of Mammon and resorted to schemes and actions which "nice honor could not justify nor strict honesty adopt," Coblentz says:

In view of the prevalence of such a ruthless, acquisitive spirit, the Committee could at most scoop a little scum off the surface of the social cesspool. The fetid depths remained putrid with deep spiritual decay, vile with that grasping philosophy which places each man's desires above his neighbor's needs; and it was beyond the power of any group of men, however fearless and determined, to sweep away the abysmal source of corruption.[30]

Although the Committee of Vigilance of 1851 rid the city of a few criminals, it only temporarily improved the surface of the corrupted social body, and it therefore must be judged to be fundamentally a social and political failure.

[30] Coblentz, *op. cit.*, pp. 101–102.

IX

A Businessmen's Revolution

The business men therefore chose to calm the spirits of more excitable people . . . by organizing the most remarkable of all the popular tribunals, whereby was effected that unique historical occurrence, a Business Man's Revolution. For such was the second vigilance committee of San Francisco.—
JOSIAH ROYCE, *California*, p. 440

THE SPECTACULAR career of what is usually known as the San Francisco Vigilance Committee of 1856, and the traditional story of it as a reform movement carried on by the virtuous against the vicious, have obscured the revolutionary character of what the movement involuntarily became. What occurred was not in the complete sense what the political scientist means by revolution, though a number of the elements of a revolution were present. An extralegal body set itself up in San Francisco to administer what it called justice. In carrying out its plans, this independent body undertook to administer functions of government and regulate the exercise of power by the legally constituted authorities in accordance with its will. In assuming such powers, this body defied the governments of the City of San Francisco, the State of California, and the United States, asserting its independence of them. Thus, the movement was, in a sense, a "revolution."

The influence of "Judge Lynch's" triumph in San Francisco in 1851 was of short duration. Whether the surface good done by lynch law offset the evil attending the disregard of civil rights and the flouting of Anglo-Saxon justice in procedures is open to serious question. Whatever the answer may be, even before the end of the year 1852, daring men, experienced in many kinds of wrongdoing, began to take the places of the rascals driven out or hanged by the self-appointed reformers of 1851, while the social sins continued and grew worse. By 1855, the usual offenses of the criminal classes had increased to an alarming extent, political degradation had reached a great depth, and unscrupulous land speculations and huge business swindles and defalcations were common and were condoned too frequently, as were even the crimes against persons.

As early as 1854, some public notice began to be taken of the increase in social and personal crime, and at times vigilance methods were suggested. The first step toward correction of alleged evils was the formation of an "Association for the Protection of the Rights of Property, and the Maintenance of Order." [1] This organization was intended to check the personal armed conflicts that sometimes resulted from disputes over land. Although its enrollment reached about one thousand members, its life was brief and unsuccessful. The ruthless exposure, and at times emotional exaggeration, of San Francisco's growing wickedness actually was made through the pages of a newspaper, the *Daily Evening Bulletin*, that first appeared on October 8, 1855.

The editor of this paper was James King of William, as he styled himself, having added his father's given name to his own to distinguish himself from other James Kings in his

---

[1] Described in Mary Floyd Williams, *History of the San Francisco Committee of Vigilance of 1851*, pp. 392–393. This scholarly study by Miss Williams is distinguished for its thoroughness, literary quality, reliability in its presentation of facts, and sound interpretation.

native Georgetown, District of Columbia. Seeking a change of climate and activity, King had journeyed to California, arriving on November 10, 1848. After a short visit to the mines, he returned to Sacramento, and there became a partner and book-keeper in a mercantile firm. He next went to San Francisco, where he and Jacob R. Snyder opened a banking firm on December 5, 1849. From this time until he went out of business permanently, on June 29, 1855, King's series of banking connections brought him only frustration and disillusionment. While he was still in a pathologically embittered state because of his experiences with dishonest banking and his own business failure, the affairs of Adams & Co., involving tremendous frauds, attracted public attention. Having had connections with this banking firm and other financial concerns involved, the emotionally overwrought King complied with requests for articles on the situation. The effect on the public mind of King's direct Anglo-Saxon sentences suggested to some of his friends, and to him, the idea of starting a newspaper through which he could express himself freely. Thus was begun the *Bulletin*. The paper was, so to speak, James King of William, for when it was launched, King and the publisher, C. O. Ger-berding, agreed that the editor should be lord absolute of the editorial policies of the paper.

Thus, in the autumn of 1855, the conscience of San Francisco began to speak through King. It was a new conscience, hating not only personal evils such as robbery and murder but also social sins in the higher places of politics, finance, and business.[2] King assailed the institutions of gambling and prostitution and their alliance with and protection by government. He attacked the press as being weak and servile, particularly the San Francisco *Herald*, which he charged was tied hand and

[2] "The *Bulletin* was not yet a week old before its guns had been spouting fire at nearly every corner of the horizon; not only private individuals but public figures were to feel the fury of the editorial discharge." Stanton A. Coblentz, *Villains and Vigilantes*, p. 135. This quotation may be too rhetorical and journalistic, but it tells the truth. Coblentz obviously wrote his book to be read. It should be. It is interesting and reliable.

foot to Palmer, Cook and Company, declaring that its editor dared not open his lips except at the bidding of moneyed tyrants. He expressed deep contempt for business concerns which he regarded as guilty of fraudulent practices, and he venomously attacked men who to him symbolized the evils he would destroy. King's editorial war was basically a campaign against social crime. Disregarding his own personal interest and peril, he fought to destroy public evils and to build a sound society. With the backing of groups who previously had been voiceless, he had some success in his fundamental purposes.

That the *Bulletin* was not more successful in its war against social evils can be mainly attributed to its militant editor's sharp and often unjust personal attacks, as he held up to public scorn bankers, city officials, politicians like David Broderick, and judges. Not infrequently King vented personal spite against those he assailed; and his exaggerations, prejudices, and at times blind intolerance often obscured from the public his lofty idealism.[3] Unwittingly, he turned many of his followers from awareness of social sin to be eradicated to dangerous hostility toward the persons he denounced. In doing this he unconsciously sowed the seed for the growth of vigilantism, which he did not wish to see revived although he had been a member of the vigilance committee of 1851. Tragically and ironically, his social message was drowned out by the lawless activities and personal hatreds of a vigilance movement set off by the news of his violent death.

About a month after the *Bulletin* began publication and while the public mind was being emotionally stirred by the exposures King was making in the paper, an event occurred which started San Francisco toward another form of lawlessness than that being attacked by King in his editorials. The

[3] In his *California* (p. 432) Josiah Royce avers that King "was not free from selfishness in the conduct of his mission; since, as is plain, he not infrequently felt a good deal of personal spite against the public sinners that he assailed." Coblentz, *op. cit.*, p. 139, says, that King "perpetrated injustices," and "committed the common fault of the reformer in tending toward an intolerant extreme."

event was the murder of United States Marshal William H. Richardson, on Saturday evening, November 17, 1855, by the gambler, Charles Cora. The thirty-three-year-old marshal had been prominent in Democratic politics. The two men, on the previous day, had had an altercation, which had grown out of a quarrel, at a theater, between Richardson's wife and the rich mistress of Cora, Arabella Ryan, generally known as Belle Cora. On the evening of the murder, the men met in the Blue Wing, a saloon on Montgomery Street. They left the place together, arm in arm, with no apparent ill feeling between them, though Richardson was somewhat intoxicated and a little quarrelsome. Not far from the saloon they paused before a closed, wholesale liquor store, where Cora was seen to grasp Richardson's coat with his left hand, and with his right hand take out a pistol and shoot him. What was said or why the shot was fired is not known, but Richardson fell dead.

The murder of a prominent man reawakened the spirit of vigilantism. As soon as it was known that Richardson had been shot by a gambler who was kept by the wealthy prostitute Belle Cora, there were cries to lynch the murderer. Sam Brannan spoke to a crowd that evening at the Oriental Hotel, urging that Cora be lynched. On the next day, the *Bulletin* flamingly remarked that Billy Mulligan, the keeper of the county jail, and even the sheriff, David Scannell, should be hanged if Cora were allowed to escape. At the same time, its editor said: "We do not want to see another vigilance committee, if possible to be avoided." After Cora was brought to trial on January 3, 1856, and the jury had disagreed, King sharply charged back, "The money of the gambler and prostitute has succeeded." Belle Cora had spent money lavishly to defend her lover, among other things employing the noted lawyer and orator, Edward D. Baker, as chief counsel. In reporting the disagreement of a jury, the *Bulletin* took occasion to say again that it did not want another vigilance committee, and at the same time it covertly advocated lynch law by prophesying that such law would quickly become the desperate resort of a city in which legal means could not protect citizens from violence.[4]

The excitement resulting from the Cora case was not allowed to subside. Suggestions were frequently made that the Committee of Vigilance should again become active. King's continued virulent attacks aroused the hatred of the attacked and kept many persons, some of them innocent, in constant dread of possible exposure. The enemies of the *Bulletin* knew that there was no way to muzzle it or to destroy it except to get its editor out of the way, and King's audacity and recklessness seemed to be a challenge for someone to kill him in order to silence the newspaper. King knew that his life was in danger, and for protection carried a pistol, a fact which he boldly announced. He had issued a challenging statement to a gambler named Selover, who had threatened his life because he had refused to meet him in a duel: "Mr. Selover, it is said, carries a knife. We carry a pistol. . . . We pass every afternoon about half-past four to five o'clock, along Market Street from Fourth to Fifth Street. The road is wide and not so much frequented as those streets farther in town. If we are to be shot or cut to pieces, for heaven's sake let it be done there." Since this had appeared in the *Bulletin*, on December 6, it was expected that most anything might happen to King.

The long-awaited personal attack on him, as an answer to the reckless earnestness and egotistical spitefulness of his editorial challenges, came on May 14, 1856. An immediate result was the organization of the vigilance committee of that year. On that fateful day the *Bulletin* had published an article opposing the appointment of John W. Bagley to a position in the United States Customhouse. Not long before, Bagley had been in a disreputable election fight with James P. Casey, a member of the Board of Supervisors of San Francisco, in which Bagley

[4] According to Williams, *op. cit.*, p. 397, the *Alta California*, which in the past had opposed popular tribunals, now subtly encouraged lynch law by prophesying that it would become the desperate resort where law was helpless to protect from violence, a condition which it declared existed in San Francisco.

had been the aggressor. King wrote of the incident, "It does not matter how bad the man Casey had been, nor how much benefit it might be to the public to have him out of the way, we cannot accord the right to any one citizen to kill him, or even beat him, without justifiable, personal provocation." Instead of stopping with this unwise statement, King added these cutting words: "The fact that Casey has been an inmate of Sing-Sing prison, New York, is no offense against the laws of this State," and more that were offensive. The reference to Casey's previous prison record was a cruel and unnecessary thrust.

The papers, with King's insulting allusion to Casey, appeared on the streets about three o'clock on May 14. About an hour later, Casey burst into King's editorial office, excitedly asking the editor, "What do you mean by that article?" A few angry questions and answers followed. King then asked him, "Are you done?" and pointing to the door said, "There's the door—go! Never show your face again." There were more angry words. Casey finally said, determinedly, "If necessary, I shall defend myself." King then rose from his seat and repeated, "Go! Never show your face here again." [5] King's bitter heart and stubborn mind thus closed against an aggrieved and hurt man. Without saying another word, Casey walked out. About an hour later, King, with apparently no concern about possible assault, left his office. Near the corner of Washington and Montgomery streets, Casey stepped from behind an express wagon, muttered some words, and fired his revolver at close range into King's breast. King was led into the Pacific Express office near by. There, surgeons, quickly called, diagnosed his wound as mortal.

Without delay Casey gave himself up to, or was joined by, a deputy sheriff and a man named Peter Wightman. None too soon the three men hastened to the City Hall to give Casey protection in the police prison. In less than five minutes he was

[5] This conversation, which was overheard by two persons in an adjoining room, was reported in the *Bulletin* of the next day. See Coblentz, *op. cit.*, pp. 151–152; T. H. Hittell, *History of California*, III, pp. 478–479.

surprised to find that he had unloosed pandemonium in San Francisco. To save him from the excited crowd, which had quickly gathered about the prison and could be heard crying, "Hang him! Run him up to a lamp post!" the officers decided to move Casey to the county jail while there was still a chance. There, guards and friends protected him from the menacing crowd. Mayor James Van Ness attempted to quiet the mob by telling them that justice would be done,[6] but they exhibited so much hostility that he left the scene. The crowd finally became quiet and withdrew when word was passed around that a vigilance committee was being organized, and after some friends of King who had visited the jail reported that the prisoner was securely locked up so that he could not escape.

On several occasions King had insistently stated that he did not favor a revival of the old Committee of Vigilance. His words, however, unhappily served as a rallying call to the former committee members. His violent death brought about the revival and reorganization of the old committee. The vigilance committee increased in numbers and effectiveness until it became virtually an army, exercising an independence that defied the authority of the city, the state, and the nation. Just why the shooting of a man like King, who was far from faultless and whose indiscretions incited the attack upon him, rather than worse evils patent to any observer, should have so fearfully aroused the popular attention, is not easy to explain. All that is clear is that mob action seemed to be imminent, and businessmen chose to calm the spirits of the more excitable people by organizing what Josiah Royce characterized as a "Business Man's Revolution."

The reorganization of the vigilance committee took place on the day after the shooting of King. Some steps in that direction had been taken on the evening of the shooting, when several members of the committee of 1851 asked William T. Coleman to act as leader in establishing a new committee. A

[6] Hittell, *op. cit.*, p. 485, explains that no sooner had the mayor said, "Let the law have its course," than his voice was drowned by derisive and angry shouts of the mob.

call was issued for a meeting on the next day, Thursday, May 15, at 9:00 A.M., "by order of the Committee of Thirteen," a secret committee that had carried over from 1851.[7] Coleman reluctantly became the leader in the proposed reorganization after its proponents agreed to two conditions: absolute secrecy and unquestioned obedience to leaders. It was also agreed that no names should be used in the new committee; each member should be designated by a number only. Although great care was used in their selection, about fifteen hundred were admitted to membership before noon. The only groups excluded were Negroes and Chinese. The increased size of the new committee necessitated the removal of the second meeting to Turnverein Hall that evening. At this meeting the organization was completed. An important action taken was the creation, at the president's suggestion, of an executive committee with an eventual membership of thirty-seven, which should direct the whole association. Regular drill work was begun at once, under some military men who were members, and under former city policemen who resigned their positions with the city to join the committee. Thus, at the very beginning, the committee began to assume the military character which distinguished it throughout its existence. It became a dictatorial body engaged in rebellion.

The all-powerful executive committee began to act in its dictatorial capacity on Friday morning, May 16.[8] It endorsed, in large part, the constitution of the committee of 1851 and elected as permanent secretary, Isaac Bluxome, Jr., who was to sign himself "33 Secretary," a signature which became as potent as that of a feared tyrant. A resolution was passed, providing that at such time as the executive committee might direct,

[7] Williams, *op. cit.*, pp. 399–400, says that "the Committee of Thirteen remains to this day a shadowy and unnamed power" but that in 1856 its call for reorganization of the vigilance committee obviated mob murder at the time.

[8] The organization and early acts of the committee as narrated in Hittell, *op. cit.*, pp. 488–494, evidenced that assumption by a self-appointed body of arbitrary power above regularly constituted government and over the minds of men is revolution.

the committee as a body should visit the county jail, take James P. Casey and Charles Cora, give them a trial, and administer such punishment as justice might require. Another resolution provided that after careful investigation the executive committee should report to the general body the names of all persons who were notoriously and criminally obnoxious to the community, or dangerous to the property and lives of the citizens, in order that action might be taken against them. Very clearly exhibiting the dictatorial character of the committee was the resolution, passed almost unanimously, that all members of the committee should withdraw their support from the San Francisco *Herald* and try to influence their friends to do likewise, because its editor and proprietor, John Nugent, as an independent editor, had opposed the revival of vigilantism, which he had supported in 1851, and had published in an editorial of his paper on May 15, this statement:

An intense excitement was caused in this city last evening by the affray between Mr. James P. Casey and Mr. James King of William. . . . the editor of this paper sustained the Vigilance Committee in past time to the peril of life and fortune: but at a time when justice is regularly administered, and there exists no necessity of such an organization, he cannot help condemning any organized infraction of the law. . . . We wish to be understood as most unqualifiedly condemning the movement.

Coleman opposed the resolution against the *Herald*, courageously stating his belief in the freedom of the press, but he was overruled. The committee dictatorship virtually destroyed freedom of the press in San Francisco.[9]

Strangely enough, in the theoretically democratic society of San Francisco, a tide of public feeling rose overnight in support of vigilantism and its methods. Reason was submerged in a surge of emotionalism. Many people saw in James King a symbol of the forces of constructiveness and morality, and saw

[9] The merchants on Front Street, where nearly all the wholesale mercantile houses of the city were situated, gathered up all copies of the *Herald* they could find and burned them with curses and reprobation. Support was withdrawn from the paper, and the paper temporarily had to suspend.

in James Casey a symbol of the robber, the plunderer, and the murderer. To them, an agent of the lawless had shot in cold blood a representative of those who favored the practice of honesty and the observance of political and social rights. They were deeply moved by what they thought was true. Many well-meaning persons became hysterically intolerant and uncompromising, and favorable toward armed revolution. It did not matter to them that James King was not faultless, that his impetuous methods and reckless personality had in the natural course of things aroused resentment against him, and that vigilantism was unqualified lawlessness. To them it mattered only that their motives were good and that they believed their cause to be just.

In this emotionally charged atmosphere, there were some persons who were not immediately dispossessed of their reason by the sensations of the hour, and who, in their fear of popular tribunals, believed that a little law was better than none. To be sure, many of these were soon coerced by those who, with intolerant self-righteousness, advocated extralegal proceedings and who, in their name-calling campaign, characterized the men who spoke for law and order as politicians with a bad odor, lawyers in disrepute, criminals, and crime defenders. Before they were all but completely silenced or driven to cover, these law-and-order groups gave assistance to the sheriff and other officers in their almost helpless situation.

On the night after the shooting of King, a party of volunteers went down to two steamers then lying at the Pacific Street Wharf and from each removed a cannon, which they took to the jail and placed in position for use. The police procured muskets and other guns from the various gunshops and armories of the city, for arming the defenders of the jail. When the volunteers found out the strength of the possible attackers, many deserted their posts. Fearing for their own safety, several of the military companies also disbanded and went home. When the sheriff found himself deserted by some of the military, he issued a call for the male inhabitants of the county to meet him on Friday afternoon in the courtroom of the Fourth District Court. Of the persons who came and accepted service, a goodly number were lawyers. With the new recruits, the men on guard in and about the jail building numbered about one hundred. Among those attending the meeting in the courtroom was William T. Sherman, who, about a week previously, had been appointed major general of the second division of the California militia. If the military should be called out by the governor, who was on his way to San Francisco, Sherman would head those forces. After declining at the moment to give aid to the sheriff, other than to point out some weak spots at the jail, he left to meet the boat from Sacramento carrying the governor.

Governor John Neely Johnson, in response to a telegram from the mayor of San Francisco, arrived in that city late on Friday evening, May 16. He went at once to the International Hotel, where Coleman, on invitation, came to see him. When the governor asked what the vigilance committee wanted, Coleman replied that it wanted peace, and wanted to obtain it, if possible, without a struggle, but, "If need be," he said, "we will seek it even at the cost of war." Coleman defiantly told the governor that when prominent criminals were punished and bad characters had been driven from the state the committee would disband, and he heatedly assured him that, if he tried to cut down the movement by calling out the militia, as "the mayor and a class of people here" had urged him to do, "it cannot be done, and if you attempt it, it will give you and us a great deal of trouble." The chief executive of the state was thus placed in a subordinate position by the youthful head of a self-appointed committee, who told him that he should for the present leave to an extralegal body the work of administering justice in San Francisco. Coleman's account of the interview records that the governor slapped him on the shoulder and said: "Go to it, old boy! But get through as quickly as you can. Don't prolong it: because there is a terrible opposition and a terrible pressure." [10] With a feeling of triumph, Coleman left the hotel.

Immediately after this humiliating interview, the governor was joined by General Sherman, Cornelius K. Garrison, a former mayor of the city, and William Neely Johnson, the governor's brother. The three men explained to him what had occurred, told him of the smallness of the sheriff's forces, and then took him to the jail and showed him how indefensible it was. They pointed out that the illegal vigilantes were rapidly adding to their numbers and were supported by influential merchants and bankers. His courage bolstered by the men with him and the challenge of the situation, the governor now went to committee headquarters and told Coleman to let the regular officers handle affairs and to permit Cora and Casey to be tried by the courts. He pledged himself to see that the trial would be conducted swiftly and that justice would be done. Coleman continued his defiance, asserting that the committee would go through with the work that it had set out to do, and that no power on earth would be permitted to stop it.

All that came from this discussion was an unfortunate verbal treaty of appeasement, by which the governor granted to the vigilante leader the privilege of placing ten men in the jail to assist the state and county officers in providing safety for the prisoners, and in turn received a pledge that the men so admitted into the jail would not attempt to take the prisoners or make a move in that direction without first withdrawing the guard and notifying the governor. The citizen aids of the sheriff, most of whom were lawyers, learning of the concessions to the "damned rebels," became angry. Some handed back their arms and left in disgust. Realizing his mistake in making the treaty with the revolters, the much-confused executive went to the committee headquarters on Saturday noon. There he was snubbed by the vigilante leader, who would not see

[10] These fragments of conversation, based on the "Statement of William T. Coleman," *Century Magazine*, November, 1891, are quoted in Hittell, *op. cit.*, pp. 497–498.

him. Matters continued thus overnight, while the committee perfected organization and made plans for a bold stroke the next day.

About eight o'clock, on Sunday morning, May 18, Charles Doane, who had been elected chief marshal of the committee's military organization the previous night, reported that the forces under his command were ready for immediate and effective service. How the leaders organized, armed, and disciplined some twenty-six hundred men in so short a time is nothing less than miraculous. At half past nine, the committee withdrew its guard from the jail and formally notified the governor of the fact. Shortly after noon, having completely surrounded the jail with its military, the committee commanded Sheriff Scannell to surrender the jail. After wholesale desertions had left only about thirty defenders to face the fifteen hundred men who had marched to attack the building, the governor gave the sheriff permission to surrender the prisoners under protest.

About one o'clock, officers of the vigilantes entered the jail to remove Casey. He at first drew out a long knife and swore that he would not be taken alive. But on being assured that he would not be manacled or handcuffed, and that he would have a fair trial, he peacefully accompanied Coleman and Truett to a carriage. Guarded by a strong military force, he was taken to vigilance committee headquarters and placed in a cell, incommunicado. About an hour later Cora was likewise removed to the committee rooms. Mayor Van Ness, General Sherman, and Governor Johnson watched these revolutionary transactions from the roof of the International Hotel on Jackson Street. They saw Marshal Doane riding on his white horse as he commanded the forces, and saw the successful military operations and the approving crowds. They were amazed and impressed by the spectacle, and were humiliated by their helplessness.[11]

[11] See Hittell, *op. cit.*, pp. 497–508, for the story of governmental helplessness briefly summarized in this and preceding paragraphs.

On the morning of Tuesday, May 20, the day fixed for the trial of Casey and Cora, the vigilance organization further exemplified its revolutionary character by two actions. The first was the naming of a committee to wait on the governor of the state and on the mayor of the city, to tell them that the Committee of Vigilance did not intend to interfere with the ordinary execution of the law, and that it would be pleased to have the legally constituted authorities proceed in civil and ordinary cases as if the vigilance committee did not exist. This was a clear assertion of sovereignty and an audacious subordination of the state to the authority of an unlawful body. The second action was the resolving, before the trial began, that the decisions in the cases should be by ballot, that a majority might convict, that the verdict should be approved by a board of delegates, that during the trial there should be no recess of more than thirty minutes until it was concluded, and that each prisoner should have the privilege of choosing counsel only from members of the executive committee—an independent imposition of conditions, at variance with established procedures under common and civil law.

The trial was interrupted soon after it opened by the appearance of Marshal Doane to announce that King had died—a fact which the prisoners and those trying them had learned a few minutes earlier from the sad sound of tolling bells. Although King had said to the Reverend William Taylor, "If I die, I don't want them to kill Casey," [12] the prisoners undoubtedly knew that King's death had sealed their fate. The committee paused only long enough to hear Doane's announcement and to direct him to notify the people that the trials of Casey and Cora were progressing with proper deliberation. Each prisoner was tried separately, each was declared guilty by the executive committee, and the verdicts of guilty, as well as the separate penalties of death by hanging, were unanimously approved by the board of delegates. The executive committee

---

[12] Quoted in Coblentz, *op. cit.*, p. 181. William Taylor was a famous and respected Methodist street preacher of the period.

fixed Friday, May 23, at twelve o'clock noon, as the time of execution. Although the trial of the two convicted men was conducted in an orderly fashion, "and not in the passionate manner of the mob," it was carried on before an illegal court and without the safeguards for justice that have grown up through centuries of experience. Casey and Cora had committed unjustified crimes, but in the light of all the circumstances it is certain that unbiased courts would not have produced identical verdicts nor have imposed the same penalties.

At six o'clock on the morning of Thursday, May 22, the day of King's funeral, the executive committee met and decided that the execution of Casey and Cora should take place that afternoon between twelve and two o'clock, while the funeral procession of King was passing through the streets, instead of at noon on Friday, May 23, as originally planned. The execution was to be publicly held, in front of vigilance committee headquarters. The prisoners were informed of the committee's action and were directed to prepare for death. Arabella Ryan, Cora's rich mistress, and Cora were married, in the vigilance committee rooms, by a Catholic priest, and spiritual advisers were admitted to the cells of the condemned men. A great crowd of morbidly curious people gathered in the vicinity of the execution spot long before the appointed hour. About half past twelve, many persons rushed from King's funeral services to join the already assembled multitude, until the estimated crowd numbered nearly twenty thousand. The entire Committee of Vigilance was drawn up by companies in defensive array, with bayoneted guns, and with cannon to command the streets.

About one o'clock a dramatic spectacle began. As the hearse bearing King's body, drawn by four white horses and followed by an enormous procession, was making its way to the cemetery on Lone Mountain, the prisoners, dressed in ordinary clothes and with their arms pinioned, were brought to the platform that had been arranged for their execution outside the windows of the second floor of the committee headquarters on Sacramento Street. Cora was composed and imperturbable. When asked if he wished to speak, he shook his head and said nothing. Casey was nervous and hysterical. Some of his almost incoherent utterances, as they were pieced together by auditors, need to be considered in any judgment one makes of his moral and mental responsibility for his crime. He expressed concern for his aged mother in New York, whom he no doubt tenderly loved. In emotional outbursts, he protested being called a murderer. He hysterically referred to his childhood, when he was taught that it was his duty to resent an injury, which he said he was doing when he killed King.[13] After Casey had been quieted, the ropes were adjusted about their necks, and at a signal from within the building, the ropes holding the platform were severed, dropping the men to their death.

After an inquest by the coroner, the body of Cora was given to his widow. His funeral was simple, only six hacks making up the funeral procession. Casey's body was taken in charge by the engine company of which he had been foreman. In his funeral procession there were eighty-four carriages, eighty horsemen, and some four hundred followers on foot—an impressive procession made up of his friends and of opponents of the Committee of Vigilance.

The question now arose: should the vigilantes disband or continue? Several factors prevented disbandment. Foremost were their deep distrust of constituted authority and their unlimited confidence in the purity of their own motives and procedures. Also, the vigilantes were aware that they had so aroused the supporters of law, and the authorities, that dissolution of the organization at this time would have involved many leaders in serious legal difficulties. More decisive than anything else, however, was the belief of the central group of the vigilantes that they had a messianic mission to perform and that they must go on until their work was finished.

---

[13] Some of the doomed man's hysterical and pathetic utterances are quoted in Hittell, *op. cit.*, pp. 516–517, and in Coblentz, *op. cit.*, pp. 188–189.

The committee acted according to revolutionary pattern, after the execution of Casey and Cora, by attempting to purge from its ranks persons whose adherence to the leaders was not absolute. It began a complete reorganization of the executive committee; compiled a black list of bad characters to be rounded up, tried, and sentenced; and drew up and approved a draft of a constitution. Then the members of this self-appointed body, considering themselves the representatives of the people, with powers that belonged to the state, as presumed executors of the will of its citizens pledged their sacred honor to carry out the various functions of a government body as stated in the constitution which they had adopted.

That the extralegal body was in earnest was shown by the arrest, on Monday, May 26, and the trial on the evening of May 27, of Billy Mulligan, Yankee Sullivan, and Martin Gallagher. All three were promptly convicted of various crimes and were at once sentenced to leave the territory of the United States, under penalty of death should they return. In the next several days, seventeen persons, adjudged by the committee to be corrupt politicians and vicious manipulators of elections, were sent away. Yankee Sullivan was not among these. Upset by being deprived of drink, and haunted by fears, he committed suicide on May 30 by severing an artery in his left arm with an ordinary case knife.

While the committee was moving on its arbitrary and unlawful way, with few obstructions, a concatenation of circumstances and events was in process which soon made the existence of the committee uncomfortable and insecure. The rumor that Sullivan's death in his cell was murder added to the fear and suspicion felt by the advocates of lawful procedure. The action of the executive committee in conceding to the regular courts jurisdiction in crimes of passion, and in pursuing and driving from California politicians whom it accused of being grafters, increased antagonism to the committee by its implications of supremacy and by its political emphasis. It was clear to the supporters of law and order that the committee was simply making a choice of the criminals it would try, for the crimes of both Cora and Casey were crimes of passion. Fears of intended revolution were confirmed on May 31 when the service of a writ of habeas corpus for Billy Mulligan was prevented, at committee headquarters, by the removal of all the criminals, in disguise, from the building before the sheriff was notified that he might search the premises.

The constituted authority and its defenders possessed enough vitality and initiative at this time to make the vigilantes apprehensive of their opposition. Members of the law-and-order group gave evidence of planning ways to end what they considered a reign of lawlessness. David C. Broderick, Judge Alexander Campbell, Austin E. Smith, and others of this group were seen examining the rear of the vigilance committee's building from the windows of a store. A few days later, on June 2, the law-and-order party held a mass meeting which its promoters claimed was motivated by a desire to restore liberty as expressed in constitutional procedures, respect for the writ of habeas corpus, and trial by jury. This meeting, held under the shadow of the liberty pole on the Plaza and contemptuously called the "Law and Murder Meeting" by the rabble of the Committee of Vigilance, was attended by a large and mixed crowd. The executive committee of the vigilantes had given orders that the assemblage should not be molested and had posted placards asking that members of the vigilance committee avoid disorder by coming out of the square; but enough unruly persons were present, with their mob-minded followers, to cause a great deal of confusion. Judge Campbell, James Wade, Calhoun Denham, Colonel Baker, and others made addresses in the face of yelling and ribald jests. In spite of coarse interruptions and much disorder, the meeting passed the following dignified resolution before it adjourned:

Resolved, That it is the sense of this meeting that the reign of law and order should be resumed in the city of San Francisco, and that a termination should be put to the present excitement, and that every free citizen be remitted to those inalienable rights which a free constitution and equal laws assume to them.[14]

On the same day, Governor Johnson began to intervene in the San Francisco crisis by issuing an order to Major General Sherman to call upon the enrolled militia and those subject to military duty, to organize and act with him in the enforcement of the law. On the next day, June 3, he issued a proclamation declaring the county of San Francisco to be in a state of insurrection, and ordering all persons subject to military duty within the county of San Francisco to report immediately to Sherman. He further ordered that all organizations existing in opposition to or in violation of the laws of the state, particularly the Committee of Vigilance of San Francisco, should disband, and that the members should yield obedience to the constitutional laws of the state and to the writs and processes of the courts.

Unfortunately, the people, impressed by the violent and lawless action of the revolutionary vigilantes, loved or feared their power more than they did that of the state. This is evidenced by the smallness of the response to Johnson's appeal and by the disbanding of a number of volunteer companies of the National Guard. Members of the groups that disbanded based their action on the grounds that their arms had been taken from them by the adjutant general of the state, and that they would not willingly slaughter their fellow citizens. The weakness of the state in the face of vigilante opposition became utter helplessness, when Major General John E. Wool, commanding the Pacific Division of the United States Army at Benicia, refused to supply arms and ammunition on the ground that he was without authority to grant the request unless so ordered by the President of the United States.

In the meantime, a number of prominent citizens of San Francisco undertook to bring about some kind of settlement

[14] H. H. Bancroft, *Popular Tribunals*, II, 326. For descriptions of the meeting, see Royce, *op. cit.*, p. 458; Hittell, *op. cit.*, pp. 529–530. See Hittell, also, pp. 540–556, for other events and documents mentioned in this chapter.

between the governor and Sherman on the one side, and the Committee of Vigilance on the other. They obtained from the committee an agreement that thereafter it would hold no exhibition of its armed forces in the streets or other public places of the city, and that none of its members would forcibly prevent the serving of any writ of habeas corpus, if the governor's proclamation was withdrawn and the law-and-order forces were disbanded. Sherman arranged that the citizen's committee would meet the governor at Benicia on Saturday, June 7, and, if possible, prevail on him to withdraw his proclamation.

After Sherman and the committee reached Benicia and the boat from Sacramento had come in, he went to the wharf and found Johnson there in company with Judge David S. Terry, Volney E. Howard, Edward D. Baker, and a few others, all of whom Sherman knew to be violently opposed to the vigilantes. In a private conversation, Sherman assured the governor that the men who had come up from San Francisco were not vigilantes, nor partisans in the controversy, but were moderate men who represented the classes from which the chief executive and his supporters would have to derive their strength. At the same time, he reported to him the precarious situation with reference to enrollment and arms. When the citizens' committee from San Francisco went to the governor's hotel and sent in their cards, Terry and some others denounced them as no better than the vigilantes and urged the governor to refuse a conference with them. Sherman explained that they were not vigilantes and that one of them, Judge Thornton, was a law-and-order man who had borne arms in defense of the county jail. The citizens were admitted in spite of the protests, and reported to the governor the conditions existing in San Francisco. After he had dismissed them, he prepared a statement, with the aid of the counsel around him, and uncompromisingly refused to recede from his position, insisting that it was his duty as chief executive to execute and enforce the laws.

The failure of the conference disappointed Sherman. He no doubt believed that he could have brought the vigilance committee to a standstill and placed it in the wrong, if Terry and the others had not made the governor believe that the committee was already "caving in." Sherman, finding his situation untenable, resigned his command. Johnson immediately appointed the fiery Volney E. Howard, a former Texan, as major general in Sherman's place. After his resignation, Sherman wrote a long explanation of his reasons for it, and directed an appeal to the viligance committee to disband and submit to law. His appeal was too late to influence the committee's action.

The news of the Benicia conference led the vigilantes to publish an address to the public, outlining their future plans, and to go about rebuilding their organization for effective defense against any movement that might offer opposition. While not crediting at face value reports that the law-and-order group had enrolled as many as three thousand sympathizers, the committee was aware that even six hundred or eight hundred equipped men could dangerously threaten its authority in San Francisco. The boasts of certain law-and-order members that their new major general would drive the "sour flour and pork merchants," as the vigilantes were called by their enemies, into the bay at short notice, were not without effect. On the Monday after the Benicia conference, a new military organization was effected. Its rules required that divisions of it should be on duty twenty-four hours a day. Batteries were put out at strategic points, and minute arrangements were worked out for the assembling of the vigilance forces on short notice. The headquarters were fortified by piling up gunny bags filled with sand, to make a breastwork ten feet high and nearly six feet thick; hence the appropriate name, "Fort Gunny Bags." Quantities of the arms stored in the fort were ordered removed and placed in the hands of members or in private depositories, to be saved for effective use should the fort be shelled or taken.

Such preparations were not merely a defiance of state authority—they were revolution.

The governor's determination, expressed at Benicia, to maintain the authority of the state and make no gesture of appeasement—a theory that was sound enough in itself—together with his rude treatment of the committee of citizens honestly seeking to end a dangerous situation, indirectly caused public support of the revolution to increase. This came about through a carefully arranged meeting in the open space in front of the Oriental Hotel, at noon on June 14, where a crowd estimated to be about fifteen thousand assembled. Though the meeting ostensibly was called by the disappointed and apprehensive citizens' conciliation committee to justify its action in appealing to the head of the state to face grave facts and make a sacrifice for peace, it was evident that vigilantes had a hand in it. Promptly at twelve o'clock, Bailie Peyton was called to the chair, lists of prominent citizens named as vice-presidents and secretaries were read, and Peyton then proceeded as the chief speaker of the day. His graphic description of political corruption in the city, which, he asserted, the vigilantes were cleaning out in spite of the counterefforts of law-and-order forces, struck a popular chord. His adroitness in showing that the vigilance committee must either be sustained or put down, and that any attack on it by the state's authority would result in great bloodshed, influenced many to stand by the committee. The emotionally stirred crowd passed resolutions approving the appeal made by the citizens' committee to the governor, which had failed, endorsing the Committee of Vigilance as a people's organization, and expressing confidence in the constitution and laws of the United States and of the State of California,[15] though these were being flagrantly violated by the vigilantes. The governor's honest, legally sound, but un-

---

[15] At this meeting, Bailie Peyton's appeal for support of the vigilance committee was made doubly effective by his adroitness in attacking political corruption, which it was alleged the vigilantes were cleaning out in spite of the law-and-order group's efforts to prevent them from doing so, and in making it appear that corruptionists and antivigilantes were the same.

wise decision at a critical moment had thus increased popular support of the vigilance movement.

While these events were occurring, the vigilance committee busied itself with work on the black list. A number of persons on the list were tried and sentenced to banishment from the state. On Friday, June 20, after a series of persons had been sent away on steamers, T. J. L. Smiley, for the committee on adjournment, presented a report. This recommended that no new business should be taken up or considered after June 24, that an effort should be made to close up all the affairs of the committee before July 3, that on July 4 there should be a full parade of all the troops and members of the committee, and that the general committee should adjourn on July 5. At the same time, the law-and-order party persisted in a militant attitude, attempting to hold together and to build up its forces. Howard tried to rally support, and a number of military companies were ready to bear arms under his direction. Whether organization under him could have grown further will never be known, for a succession of events now occurred which changed the aspect of things.

The law-and-order party needed arms. General Wool had refused to grant munitions in general, but a quota of arms was due the state from the nation, consisting of six cases of muskets, which he felt might rightfully be delivered to law-and-order representatives. On June 19, these arms were placed in the hands of James R. ("Rube") Maloney and John G. Phillips for transportation to San Francisco and delivery there to the law-and-order party. Informed, by the captain of a schooner, that a quantity of muskets was hidden in a vessel in the bay, the vigilance committee sent John L. Durkee and Charles E. Rand, with some eight or ten men, to secure them. They seized the arms, along with Maloney and Phillips, on the morning of June 21, but released the two men at the waterfront. Other arms being sent by order of the governor from Sacramento to San Quentin to be repaired were seized also and taken to vigilance headquarters. The boarding of these ships and the seizure of property and arms was in the nature of brigandage, or perhaps of piracy. These acts indirectly brought a tragic climax in the life of the lawless vigilance committee.

On the same Saturday, June 21, 1856, the vigilantes were informed that Maloney and Phillips, whom they had released, were making the rounds of saloons and boisterously issuing threats against vigilance committee members. The executive committee commissioned Sterling A. Hopkins, a rough committee policeman, to arrest the two men. He discovered Maloney in the office of Dr. Richard P. Ashe, a naval agent of the United States and an officer of the law-and-order forces, with several other persons, including Judge Terry. When the judge announced his official position and forbade any arrest of the kind proposed, in his presence, Hopkins and the three or four men who had accompanied him withdrew and went for reinforcements. Maloney, Terry, and the three others in Ashe's office, knowing they were not safe, decided to go for protection to the armory of the San Francisco Blues. Before they reached there they were overtaken by Hopkins and some eight or ten men, who attempted to seize Maloney. Terry drew his gun, and Hopkins seized it. In the general scuffle which followed, Terry whipped out his bowie knife and drove it into Hopkins' neck. Hopkins was hurried by his companions into the Pennsylvania Engine House, while Terry and his friends found refuge in the armory of the Blues.

The news of the stabbing of Hopkins quickly reached vigilance headquarters. An order went out for the arrest of Terry. The alarm bell was sounded. Vigilantes hurried to their posts. Crowds filled the streets in numbers equal to those which gathered when Casey and Cora were executed. The armory of the Blues was quickly surrounded by armed vigilantes, who removed some three hundred muskets and other arms to the rooms of the committee. Terry and Maloney were arrested and transported to committee headquarters. Vigilance forces marched forth in battle array to every armory of the law-and-order party, surrounded each, and compelled it to surrender.

They stripped the armories of all arms and sent the persons in them, handcuffed as prisoners and escorted by more than a thousand infantry and cavalry, to the committee rooms. The arrested members of the military company were subsequently discharged, after being warned that heavy penalties would be imposed should they again arm themselves against the committee. As a result of a fortuitous happening, on a single day, "the 'law and order' party, at one audacious stroke, had been stripped of its power." [16]

On the day on which Terry stabbed Hopkins, the United States Circuit Court issued warrants for the arrest of John L. Durkee, Charles E. Rand, James Hutton, and William E. B. Andrews, for piracy in seizing arms from a schooner in the bay. On the next day, Sunday, when Durkee was arrested by the United States marshal and taken to his office, crowds of vigilantes stormed around the building containing the office, threatening to tear it down and rescue the prisoner. The executive committee, fearing the results that would follow an attack on the United States, not only took steps to prevent such a blunder but requested the other men for whom warrants had been issued to submit peacefully to arrest by the marshal. Contrarily, the executive committee defied the United States court by preventing the serving of a writ of habeas corpus on its own prisoner, Maloney. Realizing that the arrest of Dr. Richard P. Ashe, who was not only a captain of a California military company but also a United States naval officer at the port of San Francisco, might touch off an explosion, the committee was glad to comply with his request that he be allowed to go on parole.

Governor Johnson had become officially impotent while these events were happening. His blustering major general, Volney Howard, who was supposed to be able to drive the "pork barrel merchants" into the sea, had been deprived of his army by those in power in San Francisco and was left able only to make a written report of his helpless predicament to the

[16] Coblentz, *op. cit.*, p. 217.

chief executive. The governor himself, previously refused arms by General Wool, and naval aid by Captain David G. Farragut, and now defied by an unlawful military organization that had practically all arms of the state in its possession, had no recourse but to appeal to the President of the United States, from whom aid, if it were to be granted at all, would come too late.

The Committee of Vigilance, which a few hours earlier seemed to be in supreme control, now found itself in a puzzling entanglement. Judge Terry, by his violence, had unintentionally placed himself in a difficult and dangerous position, and his murderous act, which grew out of the lawlessness of the committee, involved the vigilantes themselves in their most serious predicament. Members of the committee later confessed that Terry was bigger game than the committee had expected to bag. James Dows of the committee is reported to have said, "We started out to hunt coyotes, but we've got a grizzly bear on our hands; and we don't know what to do with him." [17] The committee dared not release Terry. That would have been confession of error in the revolutionary course attending and following his seizure. Consideration of his possible execution caused serious-minded vigilantes to wonder whether their organization could survive the opposition that so rash an act would arouse among law-and-order forces, and among Terry's many friends. In the face of its dilemma, the committee followed the course it felt driven to follow. The result was of doubtful value and endangered the existence of the organization.

Within a few hours after Terry was arrested on Saturday afternoon, June 21, the committee decided to begin his trial the next morning at ten o'clock, and to proceed to its end with no recess longer than thirty minutes. But on Sunday only one small item of testimony was taken, a motion was passed to permit Mrs. Cornelia Terry to see her husband at any hour she might desire admittance, an indictment consisting of three charges was drawn up against Terry, and the trial was post-

[17] Quoted in Hittell, *op. cit.*, p. 588.

poned until the next day. On Monday, Terry wrote a letter asking for delay. The committee at first denied his request, but on the appointment of Miers F. Truett as Terry's counsel, it postponed the trial until Wednesday afternoon. On Monday afternoon, a committee of citizens was admitted to see Terry, and another delegation visited him on Tuesday. They persuaded Terry and his advising friends to agree that he would resign his office and leave the state. On Wednesday, the day fixed for the trial to begin, only rules of procedure were drawn up, and the trial was postponed until the next day. On Thursday, the trial was again postponed. Someone said, at the time, that the dilatoriness in proceeding may have been to give wavering committee members time to pray for Hopkins to live.

On Friday, June 27, the trial of Terry got under way, although the executive committee was doubtful whether its course was wise, and was apprehensive for its own safety. Producing or contributing to the committee's confusion of mind and spirit were several immediate facts or developments. First, written threats were being made, of death and destruction, if Terry were harmed. Second, with courage renewed, Terry repudiated his compromise about resigning and leaving the state, having been bolstered to take his position by Mrs. Terry's insistence that, because he was not in the wrong, he should refuse to leave the prison alive except as judge of the California supreme court. Third, Captain Boutwell of the United States sloop *John Adams*, anchored a short distance from Fort Gunny Bags, communicated with the governor about the Terry case and wrote to the committee indicating that it might be necessary for him to use the power at his command to save a citizen who had tried to carry out the law. In carefully considered statements to the governor and others, Boutwell, though expressing his disinclination to start something that could only result in civil war, made it clear that if Terry were condemned to die he would make an effort to save his life in a manner that would not offend his fellow citizens. The executive committee showed its consciousness of the menace in Boutwell's statement of purposes by making elaborate preparations for defensive war.

The trial of Terry proceeded, accompanied by an apprehension of impending difficulty such as had not been felt in other trials. The committee no less than the friends of Terry feared that there would be serious consequences if Hopkins should die and Terry were sentenced to death. Luckily, a surgical operation on Hopkins brought about his rapid recovery; this obviated the possibility of Terry's execution, but it did not relieve the committee of the serious problem of exacting a penalty from him. Unlike other trials, which were completed within a few hours, this one dragged on, with much wrangling, until July 24, when the committee on the subject of penalty reported its conclusions, and the executive committee passed upon Terry the following sentence:

> That David S. Terry having been convicted after a full, fair, and impartial trial, of certain charges before the Committee of Vigilance, and the usual punishment in their power to inflict not being applicable in the present instance; Therefore it be declared the decision of the Committee of Vigilance, that the said David S. Terry be discharged from custody. . . .[18]

Before Terry could be released, however, the board of delegates had to ratify the decision. Serious clashes occurred here, also. Agreement on some of the propositions was not reached until August 6, when the board of delegates concurred in the verdict of the executive committee by a vote of forty-four to thirty-six.

After the dangerous clash over the penalty to be imposed on Terry and the almost forced approval of the delegates, some members of the executive committee decided to get rid of Terry before they slept and before the populace awoke. After the late adjournment of the delegates, a meeting of the executive committee was hastily called about two o'clock on Thursday morning, August 7. A provision in the rules of the committee allowed about a dozen members of the executive

[18] Bancroft, *Popular Tribunals*, II, pp. 468–469.

committee to act as a quorum at night if danger or an emergency should necessitate immediate action. Terry was brought before this emergency body, and the resolution for his immediate discharge was read to him. About a quarter after two, Attorney M. F. Truett secretly took him to the home of one of his (Terry's) friends where his wife was waiting. The weary Truett then went home and to bed. About half an hour later Truett was aroused from his sleep by the secretary of the committee, who reported excitedly that as many as a thousand men were hunting for Terry. Truett at once went to Terry, who was quickly taken in secret to the wharf and carried by a small boat to the sloop of war *John Adams*. In the afternoon he was transferred to a steamboat, on which, in company with about one hundred men of the law-and-order party, he left for Sacramento.

Coleman and others had planned that Terry should be formally discharged in broad daylight, in the presence of the whole committee assembled for that purpose, with a military escort from his place of imprisonment. The early morning secret discharge of Terry created great dissatisfaction and nearly broke up the vigilance committee. The executive committee members were displeased principally over the method of Terry's discharge; having followed the trial, in all its complexities, they were resigned to its outcome. Not so were the thousands of members of the general committee and the additional thousands of sympathizers who knew practically nothing of the proceedings of the trial. They were shocked by the news of Terry's release.[19] Several thousand excited persons quickly gathered about the committee building and vocally gave vent to their disappointment and anger, the speakers characterizing the action of the committee as criminal and weak, and as a blow, perhaps a fatal one, to the reform move-

[19] Bancroft, *op. cit.*, p. 475, says, "Some were sorrowfully disappointed; others swearingly rampant. Their late idol, the Vigilance Committee, the people now cursed as traitors, weak and treacherous sycophants, who strangle smilingly friendless criminals, but dare not touch the august Terry's garments."

ment. Little were they aware that self-appointed adjusters outside the law and properly constituted courts are inevitably forced by men and circumstances to make decisions and perform actions for which they are not prepared and which eventually cause their undoing. The committee by its action revealed the fact that it had no sound foundation for existence. Thus, the Terry case was a fatal blow to a house that rested on a sand foundation.

While Judge Terry was being tried and after his release, the committee tried and executed two men for crimes of passion, though it had previously conceded that such cases should be tried in the established courts of law. A man named Philander Brace had been arrested before Terry had stabbed Hopkins, and his trial on the charges of robbery and murder had been postponed because of the committee's occupation with the Terry case. Brace was brought to trial on Sunday, July 27. On the next day he was adjudged to be guilty and was sentenced to be executed the next afternoon. The other man was Joseph Hetherington, who, in a fit of anger or of insanity, had shot and mortally wounded Dr. Andrew Randall in a spectacular gun fight at the St. Nicholas Hotel on July 24. He, like Brace, was found guilty and was sentenced to be hanged.

The execution of the two men was a sordid spectacle. A huge crowd filled the streets, every window, and even the housetops for blocks around, all eager to see the hanging of two ordinary human beings. The vigilance committee, in a gross exhibition of showmanship, assembled its four or five thousand military, with a dense square of soldiers deep about the scaffold, companies of infantry and cavalry, and loaded brass cannons of the artillery, properly set. There was an impressive procession, consisting of the executive committee, a company of guards composed of delegates from each company of the committee, and carriages from which the condemned men walked to the scaffold. A grotesque hangman's attendant, dressed in a long, ugly, muslin robe and cap, added ridiculousness to tragedy, as the pinioned men, with ropes about their necks, were suddenly dropped to writhe in the agonies of death.[20] This was the closing scene of the vigilante drama.

The high emotional temperature that had prevailed during the trial of Terry, and the surge of human emotions that had attended the illegal public hanging of the two unfortunate men, who were a product of the times, now began to subside. On August 7, the news of the Terry case debacle fell upon the fever-ridden community like a chill. What was there now left to absorb the interest or recaptivate the attention of the vigilance committee and to keep up the community excitement? The executive committee members were weary from their months of exciting and exhausting labor, and the organization they had headed had run its course or, as they maintained, had played its part in a great reformatory crusade. The time had now come to disband the extralegal government and surrender the power it had assumed.

By previous plan and with elaborate preparations for making it a great day, the Committee of Vigilance adjourned on Monday, August 18, 1856. The closing ceremony was a grand parade which was a triumph of showmanship. The demonstration purposely embodied many features of a conquering army. By displaying their numbers and armed might the vigilantes emphasized their military character and strength. For reasons it would have been difficult for them to explain, the people welcomed this glamorous ending of a perilous period. For days they had prepared for the occasion by decorating the streets and houses with gay flags and banners. On the day of the parade, in festive mood, but perhaps without any analyzed approval or disapproval of vigilantism, the citizenry lined the streets through which the procession was to pass, and filled every vantage point. The march was along an appointed route and then to headquarters, where the men deposited their arms. The spectacle was impressive.

[20] This closing scene of the vigilance-movement drama was an orgy of emotionalism. The sadistic performance is described in Hittell, *op. cit.*, pp. 611–616.

The committee leaders continued their skilled showmanship by keeping open for public inspection the headquarters of the committee on the two days after Thursday, August 21. Here on display to the public were the cannon, guns, and swords of their armament. The cells that had been occupied by the prisoners were proudly exhibited, as were their pistols, knives, and other weapons. The hats of the executed men, Cora, Casey, Hetherington, and Brace, hung on the walls. The curious citizenry who filed through the building could not fail to be impressed with a sense of the vigilance committee's power.

The executive committee planned to continue its sessions for a while, and to exercise its revolutionary influence upon the community. An open letter from the executive committee to the general committee was published in the newspapers on August 27. According to the executive committee, its justified though extralegal measures had been carried out with "rectitude of intention, loyalty to republican principles, and a devoted adherence to the true spirit of government and law." In its effort to perpetuate the revolution, on September 8, when a list of jurors had been made up for the various courts, the committee directed its secretary to post in conspicuous places the names of all jurors who were not known to the committee or were of doubtful character, with a request that members or others who could show cause why the persons whose names were posted should not serve as jurors so report in writing. Whether or not this system for a time improved juries is not clear, but at least they were in part chosen by vigilantes.

A move to remodel the Committee of Vigilance into something of a political-action committee was undertaken in July, when an effort was unsuccessfully made to secure the resignations of all incumbents of city and county offices. The purpose was to pave the way for the purge of all the officials of the old order at the next election. In pursuance of this policy, a political party engendered by the vigilantes got under way at a mass meeting on August 11, in response to a call signed by some three hundred business citizens. Out of this came a committee of twenty-one, which became famous in the city as a nominating body. After this committee had held secret meetings for nearly a month, under the name of the "People's Reform party," it presented nominations for state legislative, city, and county offices. For the election on November 4, the committee later designated men to watch the polls, and instructed them to send under escort to the recent vigilance headquarters any persons attempting fraud or interference with what was understood to be an honest election, and to send information to the executive committee by vigilance dragoons stationed near the voting places. Certainly, an election thus supervised by vigilantes would be a triumph for the businessmen's group, or "People's party," as it was called. The committee of twenty-one continued to function as a closed corporation for several years. Here was another political machine, but being new, it was cleaner than the previous ones.

The intimidating influence of vigilance power on civil and judicial officials, and the psychological effects of the superb showmanship of the committee on the people of San Francisco, made practically impossible any general prosecution of the committee or its members for their many acts of lawlessness. In the wake of the storm, however, a few personal entanglements in some of the revolutionary activities came to court, but the offenders were not penalized by law, because the judge or the jury found it expedient not to waken the sleeping dogs of power. In the cases of John L. Durkee and Charles E. Rand, who had committed the crime of boarding a United States vessel and seizing arms belonging to the State of California, and who were tried in the United States Circuit Court in September, the judge's charge clearly favored the defendant Durkee, and the jury, some of whom were members of the vigilance committee, took but five minutes to return the verdict "not guilty." The other defendant was speedily released thereafter without trial. As might be expected, some of those who felt they had been personally wronged by the committee, as many had been, began to take steps to prosecute a number of the vigilantes. These steps did not lead far, for both the state and federal courts accepted expediency as the best policy, being coerced by the knowledge of the possibilities that still lay in the ringing of a bell.

Attempted prosecution of some leaders of the committee when they were out of the state, notably William T. Coleman while he was in New York, resulted only in annoyance and expense to the defendants. Courts in the East usually declined to assume jurisdiction in such cases. After the board of delegates and the executive committee, on September 13, 1857, passed a resolution rescinding the then existing resolutions of expatriation and penalties, many of the exiles who returned had the courage to bring suits for damages against vigilantes and steamship companies. In only two of these cases were damages awarded by the United States District Court. The exiles had practically no success in the state courts, for courts and juries continued to fear those who had been temporary masters. The persistence in submitting suits, however, did cause much annoyance and considerable money loss to the defendants.

So much is indeterminate in the flow of history that it is impossible to state conclusively whether the "Business Man's Revolution" of 1856 was a success or was a failure; whether, in the long-range sense, California and the United States were made better by it, or worse; or whether the right actions of the movement outweighed its fundamental wrongs. It did rid the state of some undesirables; it temporarily improved the political life in San Francisco by the creation of an organization that determined the course of the political life of the city for a few years; and it awakened in many persons an interest, even though a distorted one, in the city's civic life. It failed, in that, acting arbitrarily and emotionally, it built a house of fear on shifting sands, which soon disintegrated. It failed in administering justice, also, by its methods of secrecy and hate and the disregard of safeguards for the rights of individuals, which had been worked out through the trial and error of centuries.

Not to any great extent did it lead the way to constructive reform. It was a menace to organized society; its formation was a tragic admission of failure such as practically always comes to a society that is theoretically democratic but in which business and other leaders bent on personal gain are blind to civic responsibility. It shockingly demonstrated the ease with which lawlessness in the form of mob or extralegal action rises when American citizenry are unwilling to control the destroying forces in social life by the successful operation of lawfully organized representative government.

X

The Gods and Men in the Politics of the 'Fifties

Sir, men may talk disunion as they may; . . . they may talk about a Southern Republic and a Pacific Republic, representing anything you please; but let me tell such men, and let me press upon them the fact, that they little understand the great heart of the people of California, which will always beat true to the Union.—CALEB BURBANK, CALIFORNIA SENATE, February 27, 1861

IN ITS FIRST decade of development as a state, California regarded itself as a more or less independent commonwealth. Yet at the same time it sought to benefit to the utmost from the federal union. It wanted material advantages, political privileges, and a right to act independently. On occasion, it covertly threatened to sever the ties which bound it to the federal body if the government did not provide the advantages it desired. Some Californians felt, and not without sound basis, that by the addition of the "thirty-first star" to the American flag a favor had been conferred upon the

United States, and that the state should be rewarded in proportion to its own estimate of its importance.

Under the circumstances, and because of California's geographical remoteness from the political center of the nation, the politics of the state were for the most part provincial and personal, obsessed with local issues and advantages, and concerned only incidentally with national questions. In California there were, to be sure, national party organizations with party activity. Conventions of the Democratic and Whig parties were held in the state in 1851, 1852, 1853, and 1854; of the Free Soil party in 1852; of the Democratic and the American parties in 1855; of the Republican, the American, and the Democratic parties in 1856 and 1857; of the Republican party, the Lecompton Democrats, and the Anti-Lecompton Democrats in 1858 and 1859; of the Republican, the Union, and the Democratic parties in 1860; and, still later, of the Douglas Democrats and the Breckinridge Democrats. The platforms adopted in the conventions contained planks on national questions; these were referred to in the campaigns but were not particularly stressed until the years 1859 and 1860, when there was sharp division within the Democratic party and between parties.[1]

Throughout the decade, the interest displayed in the success of rival leaders for national office was in proportion to their ability to turn the federal bounty to state advantage. The politics of the period were centered in, and for the most part were expressed through, the rivalry for leadership and control between two remarkable men of the dominant party— William McKendree Gwin and David C. Broderick—who had widely different backgrounds. The successes and failures of these men resulted, first, from the forces operating upon them out of the past which made them in several respects what they were; second, from the environment in which they were placed, which shaped their native abilities, for good or ill, and

[1] Winfield J. Davis, *History of Political Conventions in California, 1849–1892*, pp. 6–109.

assisted them to choose wisely or unwisely; and third, from fortuitous circumstances, or the "action of the gods," which put them in the right place at the right time or withheld from them such an opportunity, thus lifting them to heights of power or casting them down. The politics of the period were affected by similarly determinative forces.

The gods were beneficent to William M. Gwin, from the hour of his birth as the son of heroic parents on the Tennessee frontier until he began his political career in California. Educational opportunities were given to him; he took advantage of them. Andrew Jackson, a friend of his father, made him United States marshal in Mississippi. Elected to Congress from that state in 1841, Gwin became a friend of John C. Calhoun. The prophetic picture which Calhoun drew of San Francisco Bay and California when the area should become a part of the United States made a great impression on him. Because Gwin was a man of varied political experience, Secretary of the Treasury R. J. Walker selected him to superintend the construction of the customhouse in New Orleans, after he had taken up his residence there in 1846. When he heard of the gold discovery in California, Gwin visioned not riches but political opportunity. At once, he resigned his federal office, settled his accounts in Washington, and set out for the Pacific Coast. He arrived in San Francisco on June 4, 1849, the day after Governor Bennett Riley had issued a call for the election of delegates to a constitutional convention. He entered enthusiastically into the governor's election plans, and so impressed his personality upon the public that the San Francisco district elected him as its delegate.[2] In the constitutional convention, the well-prepared and experienced Gwin found opportunity to display his talents, and he ably showed the stuff of which he was made. Probably no other delegate exerted as much influence in the convention as he did.

Up to this point fortune had smiled upon Gwin, and he had

[2] For a record of the activities referred to in this and the next paragraph, see William M. Gwin, "Memoirs," *California Historical Society Quarterly*, XIX, pp. 1–4, 17–21.

done his part. After the convention, without partisan machinery, and with quiet skill and efficiency, he aided in the ratification of the constitution, the election of members to the legislature, and his own election to the Senate of the United States. There was little of partisan politics in his being sent to the Senate by the first California legislature, or in the early years of his extraordinary service as a Senator for the new state. In the less than three weeks remaining in the first session of the Thirty-first Congress, after Senators Gwin and Frémont took their seats, Gwin graciously kept himself in the background, and Frémont took the more prominent part in the proposed legislation of the session since he had been elected for the short term, which would end on March 1, 1851.

Gwin alone served California in the Senate during the second session of the Thirty-first Congress. Frémont was absent from his seat because he was engaged in promoting his candidacy for reëlection by the legislature, which met on January 6, 1851, and adjourned on May 1. Announcing himself as a candidate, he had set up a "free ranch" in San Jose, after the fashion of the time, where his supporters and others were supplied with "refreshments" to their stomachs' desire. It did not take him long to see that he could not be elected, and he withdrew from the field. The fight for the Senate seat was mainly a personal one, though there were both Democratic and Whig candidates. One hundred and forty-two ineffectual ballots were cast. No one was elected, and the seat remained vacant. Gwin alone, therefore, represented California in the Senate for two Congressional sessions.

The first bill Gwin desired the Senate to act upon was one that had to do with California land titles. He introduced, on December 9, 1850, a bill intended to subject the land claims of California to a rigid scrutiny, and he continued to press the measure until its passage by the Senate on February 6, 1851. He was also successful in his efforts to effect extension of the Coast Survey—which had charge of the erection of lighthouses and fortifications—to the Pacific Coast. In the same session numerous offices were created and filled. For the first time, United States district judges for California were provided for and appointed: Ogden Hoffman, Jr., in the northern district and James McHall Jones in the southern. Gwin had supported a bill, which Frémont had introduced in the previous session, to name three commissioners to make treaties with the Indians of California. Though he later disapproved of the work of the commissioners, in this session Gwin proposed an amendment to increase by $25,000 the original appropriation of $25,000.

Gwin, in this session, introduced a number of bills which were not passed until later sessions, as well as some which were never passed, though he pushed them for several years. Among those that were eventually passed was an amendment to a bill for increasing the pay of army and navy personnel on the Pacific Coast because of the high cost of living there. A measure which Gwin introduced at this time and urged unsuccessfully for years was the return of the civil fund to California. The only part of this fund which California had received was that which had been used by Governor Riley to pay the expenses of the formation of the state government.

Gwin interested himself also in the question of a mint at San Francisco. Frémont, when he was with him in the Senate, had offered an amendment to the civil and diplomatic appropriation bill which authorized the Secretary of the Treasury to make a contract with some well-established assayer to appraise gold, form the metal into bars, and affix its value, under the supervision of the United States assayer, a measure which became law on September 30, 1850.

Gwin's bill to establish a branch mint in California, introduced on February 8, 1851, passed the Senate on December 12, 1851, and became law on July 3, 1852. Another bill, which Gwin regarded as of prime importance among measures he introduced in the second session of the Thirty-first Congress, provided for the survey of the public lands in California and for the granting of donation privileges in the state. The measure was voted down at this session and at many subsequent sessions.[3] Although Gwin's disappointing defeat, in a matter he thought vital, brought some criticism of his ability to secure rapidly for the people what many wanted, his continued efforts to carry the measure through kept the favor of many of California's voters.

Immediately after the adjournment of Congress, Gwin returned to California, where he was warmly received by a united Democratic party. In a political statement to the people of California he pointed out that Congress had been reluctant to make ample provisions for the needs of the state, and that he had had to work hard to secure the favors that he had obtained. His addresses in conventions and mass meetings were received with enthusiasm. There is no doubt that these, supplemented by his adroit work in his "still hunt" about the state, did much at that time to effect the unity which he declared to be necessary in order to establish the party "on an immovable foundation and insure the prosperity and greatness of the state." In accomplishing this, Gwin demonstrated the political acumen and leadership of a man who, as James O'Meara described him, "stood among the multitude as one born to be a leader of men." [4]

Shortly after Gwin's return to California, the legislature, in a joint resolution, expressed thanks from the people of California to him "for his indefatigable exertions and zeal, his constant and untiring advocacy in the Senate of the United States of the just claims and interests of the State." Gwin's response to the resolution, addressed on April 30, 1851, "To the Hon. D. C. Broderick, President pro tem. of the Senate, and Hon. John Bigler, Speaker of the House of Assembly of California," expressed gratitude for assurance of the people's

[3] For a record of Gwin's services in the second session of the Thirty-first Congress, see Gwin, *op. cit.*, pp. 21–23, 157–166; Hallie Mae McPherson, "William McKendree Gwin, Expansionist" (MS thesis, 1931, University of California Library, Berkeley), pp. 150–180.
[4] For a description and characterization of Gwin, see James O'Meara, *Broderick and Gwin*, pp. 33–34.

confidence, thus manifested through their legislature, and indicated his purpose to "earnestly strive to merit a continuance of that confidence by my future efforts, securing to the State her best rights, as member of the Confederacy" (which, it should be stated parenthetically, Gwin firmly believed the United States to be). He included a statement of his realization that the difficulties of a representative in Congress from this "unprecedented State," in securing what the people had a right to expect, were made greater because the far-off government at Washington did not comprehend the needs of California.[5]

The first session of the Thirty-second Congress assembled in Washington on December 1, 1851, with Gwin again the sole representative of California in the Senate. On the first day of the session, he gave notice of his intention to ask permission to introduce eleven different bills. Some of these bills he later introduced a number of times. His notification of intention at this time was an indication of his alertness to the interests of California as a self-governing dominion. His bill providing for the establishment of a branch mint in California passed the Senate, as has been noted, on December 12, and passed the House toward the end of the session. His first bill for federal aid in the construction of a telegraph line from the Mississippi River to the Pacific Ocean, introduced on December 18, was less successful. Ten years elapsed before he succeeded in securing legislation on this subject.

On December 8, 1851, the Senate named its standing committees. Gwin was appointed to two very important ones, the finance committee and the committee on naval affairs. He was chairman of the latter and continued in that office until 1855. While on these committees, he made use of every opportunity to push measures of interest to the Pacific Coast.

As chairman of the committee on naval affairs, Gwin ad-

<hr/>

[5] Gwin's reference to the joint resolution of the legislature and his response (printed in full) are given in Gwin, *op. cit.*, p. 166. For the activities of Gwin in the first session of the Thirty-second Congress, described in the ensuing paragraphs, see McPherson, *op. cit.*, pp. 177–180; Gwin, *op. cit.*, pp. 169–173.

vocated the building of a fully equipped navy yard on the Pacific Coast, stressing the value it would have as a means of national defense and also as an instrument for the advancement of commercial prosperity. In answer to objections made to the expense, he showed statistically California's financial value to the nation in customs collections, and its economic importance, arguing impressively that means should be provided for the protection of this valuable asset. One of the first actions taken by Congress for Pacific Coast protection as a result of Gwin's urging was the appropriation of $100,000 for the construction of a floating dry dock. In December, 1851, Gwin introduced a bill to establish a navy yard and depot in San Francisco Bay, and as chairman of the committee on naval affairs, on January 6, 1852, he reported this bill from the committee. The provision for the navy yard was finally included in the Naval Appropriations Act of 1852. Mare Island was decided upon as the site. After delays, from week to week, in appropriating the amount of money the plant would cost, the bill passed, with a first appropriation of only $100,000. Gwin's persistence later brought the amount up to $845,000. Before the end of his first term in the Senate, additional sums voted for the dry dock had increased the total appropriations for the establishment at Mare Island to $1,335,000.

Another bill proposed by Senator Gwin at this session was one intended to provide for a monthly line of steamers from San Francisco, by way of the Sandwich Islands and Japan, to China. Gwin introduced the bill on April 19, 1852. It was passed by the Senate in several sessions, but it was never approved by the House. The last time Gwin called up this measure was on June 29, 1854. This bill was to provide for the establishment of a line of steam mail ships between San Francisco, California, and Shanghai, China, which would touch at the Sandwich Islands and Japan on the way. It was defeated by the "Third House," or lobby, which was bent on defeating any bill for a steamship line that did not make provision for an African line also. Gwin's interest in a steamship line across the

Pacific was in keeping with his vision of California and the Pacific as he had first seen it when he and Calhoun had talked about the subject fourteen years earlier, when Gwin was a member of the House of Representatives.

When the second session of the Thirty-second Congress began in December, 1852, Gwin was no longer the lone Senator from California. On the preceding January 28 the two branches of the legislature had met in convention to elect a United States Senator to succeed Frémont. On January 30, in a contest with David C. Broderick, a Democrat, and Pearson B. Reading, a Whig, John B. Weller, a Democrat, had been elected to that office. Weller had been a member of Congress from Ohio, had been an officer in the Mexican War, and later had been appointed by President Taylor to head a commission to survey the boundary between the United States and Mexico. When California was admitted, he resigned his place on the Boundary Commission to engage in law and politics in the new state. Although he was not the equal of either Gwin or Broderick as a politician, he was an able one. Broderick's violent antislavery attitude and Gwin's preference for Weller were factors in his selection by the legislature. Stung by his defeat at the hands of Gwin and Weller in this 1852 election, Broderick began to figure how he might coöperate with the gods to effect his election to succeed Gwin. Thus began the long and eventful contest between these two men and their followers, the "Broderick and Gwin fight," which dominated political history in California for the next eight years.[6]

Those eight years of feud within the Democratic party in California may be divided into the period in which Weller and Gwin represented California in the United States Senate, and the period from 1856 to 1859, when Broderick was Gwin's colleague in that body. In the first period there were times when Broderick was dominant in state politics, but there was

[6] H. H. Bancroft, *History of California*, VI, 659–663; Jeremiah Lynch, *A Senator of the Fifties*, p. 54; James O'Meara, *Broderick and Gwin*, p. 29; Gwin, *op. cit.*, p. 173.

never a time in the Senate, not even in the year when Gwin's Senate seat was vacant, when Gwin's leadership for California was not recognized in the nation's capital. In the sessions of the Thirty-second and Thirty-third Congresses, Gwin worked persistently and constantly on such problems as recovery of the civil fund for California, the surveying of public lands, and the providing of donation privileges for settlers, as well as on questions of annexation of Cuba and the Sandwich Islands, fortification of San Francisco harbor, coinage of gold pieces, weekly express mail, additional United States courts for California, and many others, including the question of a Pacific railroad, which was by no means the least important.

Gwin considered a railroad to the Pacific essential for giving Californians a sense of belonging to the Union. He took his initial step on the subject in the second session of the Thirty-first Congress, when he submitted a plan for two railroads. This plan was tabled, along with another bill to which it was an amendment. Gwin introduced a second bill on December 22, 1852, in the second session of the Thirty-second Congress; and as a special order it came up for consideration on January 13, 1853. The principle embodied in Gwin's bill was that of having one great trunk road, from San Francisco to Albuquerque, New Mexico, and three branch roads. One branch was to go from Albuquerque to St. Louis, a second one from Albuquerque to Memphis and New Orleans, and a third, the Oregon branch, was to commence east of Stockton on the grand trunk road and run to Fort Nisqually, Oregon (now Washington). Great was Gwin's disappointment, when an amendment, providing that none of the money appropriated in the bill should be expended within the limits of a state, proved fatal to the acceptance of the bill.[7]

At the beginning of the next session of Congress, which convened on December 2, 1853, Gwin introduced another railroad bill. This went through a number of modifications.

[7] This and other railroad plans of Gwin are described in McPherson, *op. cit.*, pp. 213–220.

Its discussion was extended into the following session, and the bill, after being again modified, finally passed the Senate on February 19, 1855—the first Pacific railroad bill to pass either house of Congress. With only two weeks remaining in the session, it failed to pass the House of Representatives. When Gwin was not reëlected to office, Senator Weller was appointed chairman of the select committee for the Pacific railroad in the first two sessions of the Thirty-fourth Congress. He worked ardently for the proposed railroad, but he was unable to bring to the project the necessary support for its passage.

The defeat of Gwin for reëlection, which interrupted his great work as a California Senator for two years, was brought about by his bitter and ambitious political enemy, David C. Broderick, who, like Gwin, rose to great heights and then fell, not only because of his own character, ability, and experience, but also because of the working of "the gods of chance"—of opportunity. Broderick and Gwin were both able men; each was a skilled politician in his way, and each came to California from the East in 1849, not only ambitious to become a Senator of the United States but determined to attain that high office. Broderick's background was more modest than Gwin's, and he had had less opportunity for education and the development of the social graces; he was also younger than Gwin. Broderick therefore began his political ascent in California from a lower level than that from which his more mature and farther advanced rival started.[8]

Though deficient in many refinements which education and a different environment could have given him, Broderick brought with him to California sagacity, wisdom, and a rich background of political experience unusual for a young man of twenty-nine years. In New York he had worked successively as a stonecutter's apprentice, a stonemason, and a saloonkeeper,

[8] For Broderick's background before his entrance into California politics, see Bancroft, *op. cit.*, pp. 659–661; O'Meara, *op. cit.*, pp. 5–6, 9–10, 14; Lynch, *op. cit.*, 30–40, 50–51, 67–72.

and at the same time was a member and foreman of a fire-engine company. As an active Democratic worker in Tammany Hall since before he had a vote, he had become highly skilled in the methods of the organization. In this period, through the influence and aid of two acquaintances, who saw in him the stuff out of which leaders are made, Broderick effected considerable intellectual progress by developing the habit of systematic reading, a practice he kept up sedulously to the end of his short life.

In politics, as a recognized leader among the common people, he was nominated for Congress in New York City but was defeated by the more aristocratic voters in his district. Just when he had decided that it would be unwise for him to become a candidate for Congress again immediately, because of the defeat of the Democrats in the national election of 1848, Colonel J. D. Stevenson, an old Tammany Hall friend, wrote to him from California, urging him to leave New York and come to the land of "El Dorado." Broderick hesitated until further news of the western gold arrived. The news affected him as it had Gwin, making him see visions and dream dreams. This saloon-keeper, as Broderick had become, who never drank, smoked, or gambled, emptied his liquor casks in the street, preparatory to setting out for California. When he bade his friend, General Daniel Sickles, good-by, Broderick told him that if he ever returned to the East he would return as a United States Senator from the new and untrammeled State of California.

Broderick arrived in the little town by the Golden Gate in June, 1849, sick and practically penniless. Fortunately for him, his friend Colonel Stevenson, who had been in California since 1847 and was now wealthy and influential, received him cordially, as did Frederick D. Kohler, another former member of the New York Fire Department. Kohler was a jeweler and an assayer. With the financial assistance of Stevenson, Broderick entered into a copartnership with Kohler in minting gold slugs and coins, a very profitable business with the gold situation what it was at that time. The partners sold the business to a man named Baldwin in December, 1849, but they continued for a while to coin the gold for him.

While getting his economic start, Broderick got in touch with a number of New Yorkers in San Francisco. Some of these had been friends and some opponents in New York, but in California nearly all joined in helping him to get a political start in their adopted land. Opportunity met the man when Nathaniel Bennett, one of the two state senators elected from San Francisco in November, 1849, resigned his office to become chief justice of the state supreme court. Broderick was elected to fill the vacant senatorship, and took his seat on January 24, 1850. Fortune soon smiled on him again, for, in this office, Broderick so impressed his colleagues that when Lieutenant Governor John McDougal, on Peter H. Burnett's resignation, became governor, the senate of 1851 elected Broderick to be its presiding officer and lieutenant governor of the state, an office he filled with a fair degree of satisfaction to political friend and foe.

Among the former New Yorkers whom Broderick met soon after his arrival in California were several Tammany friends. At once he began a San Francisco organization on the Tammany model, and by 1852 he had this well worked out. Since there was no other political organization to equal his, he quickly became dominant in the politics of San Francisco and other centers in the state. While working on his political plans, he used his spare time to store his mind with knowledge needed in his quest for political control. He built up for himself a library of carefully selected books, which he read in his secluded quarters night after night in a process of self-education. With the same ardor with which he pursued his political ambition he studied history, literature, and law. In time he was admitted to the bar and served for a short period as clerk of the state supreme court. He was constantly ready to accept the opportunities which presented themselves or which he made for himself.

Broderick became obsessed with the idea of securing a seat

in the United States Senate, in accordance with the purpose he had expressed before he left New York. In this he was perhaps spurred on by the ending of his career in the state senate, and certainly by his defeat by Weller, with the assistance of Gwin, in his first bid for the post. He planned and worked for it ceaselessly. Even though Broderick's character—his vehemence, unbending will, and political sagacity—was suited to the rough-and-tumble elements of politics in an exciting and turbulent period of California's life, and his courageous but rash personal encounters made him a hero to many of the people, he and his faction were confronted with a wall of opposition: the Southern Whig vote and a portion of the Democratic party were lined up solidly against him. Broderick was a bold and by no means scrupulous master of Tammany tactics, but there was general doubt of his ability to prevail against the popular methods of party management in which Senator Gwin had been bred. Broderick was not well versed in the higher and more dignified aspects of political life of which Gwin was the master, but he was determined to work his way to the Senate, and he saw that the only way to succeed in this was by defeating the dignified, talented Gwin and his admiring followers.

With this end in view, and determined to achieve it against all odds, Broderick proceeded to institute the Tammany system of organization in every county where he could get a foothold. He succeeded well, both in organization and in imperious domination of many persons. Unfortunately, disappointment or disagreements sometimes turned his zeal into hot wrath, which at times exploded in harsh abuse. As a result he lost adherents whom he most wished to retain as friends and supporters. As with many a dynamic person, his most difficult struggle was to master himself. Gwin, on the other hand, the man whom Broderick was resolved to succeed in office, was not only the admired leader of many men of high caliber, but was, above all, the master of himself. He was careful not to offend friend or foe. He was consistently gracious and dignified, a great leader who loved office for the prominence it gave and for its opportunities of service. The majority of men of Southern birth preferred him to any other. Many Western men supported him, as did numerous merchants and wealthy Democrats from New York and from other northern states. Broderick had strong backing in San Francisco and other places, through the Tammany organization which he controlled, but the anti-Broderick wing of the Democrats was the more powerful in numbers and influence throughout the state. In spite of the strength and character of the opposition he had to overcome, Broderick did not shrink in the face of the odds against him. He conceived a daring scheme. What he intended doing was in defiance of all past usage. It struck at the sanctity of precedent, and in doing this created political consternation.

An analysis of the political situation, both in Washington and in California in 1853 and 1854 makes Broderick's plan for succession to the United States Senate seem incomparably audacious. The election of Franklin Pierce to the Presidency probably advanced the welfare of the Democratic party in California, but it did nothing for Broderick, who was unknown to Pierce. The majority of the California representatives, on whom Pierce had to lean, were either hostile or indifferent to Broderick. Senator Weller was as much opposed to him personally as was Senator Gwin. Of the two elected members of the House, General James A. McDougall entered Congress determined to make his own way to the Senate at the expiration of his two years in the House. The other representative, Milton S. Latham, who had joined with the Broderick faction in the state convention for the nomination of Presidential electors in 1852, soon came into full accord with the Western members of the party, and did nothing to help Broderick or his plans. Major Richard P. Hammond, Collector of the Port of San Francisco, recognized Broderick as one of the Democratic leaders of the state but was much opposed to him as a candidate for the office of Senator. Hammond was closely in accord with a section of the party which supported the leadership of Gwin. In dispensing patronage in the customhouse, Hammond favored Southerners; Broderick, in his most spectacular wrath, denounced the customhouse as the "Virginia Poorhouse," and the issue as one of the Southern "chivs" against the "plebeians" of the North.

Broderick in thus presenting the case convinced many Democrats from the North that they were being discriminated against because of their place of birth. In this way, he drew to his side many disappointed aspirants and applicants for federal positions in various departments of the government service who, for selfish reasons, had been in the wing opposed to him, had gambled and lost, and now came over to him on the chance of gain. Broderick had the support of Governor John Bigler, a persistent antagonist of Gwin. Bigler's election for a second term, through Broderick's assistance, made it possible for Broderick, through the governor, to reward his supporters throughout the state. This, added to his mastery in the municipal governments of San Francisco and Sacramento, kept him powerful, but not powerful enough in the state as a whole to give him control of a majority of the senators and assemblymen for the ensuing legislative term.

Fully aware of the opposition to him in high political circles, and in spite of his uncertainty about the legislature elected in 1853, Broderick was willing to make a gamble with destiny in the session that would assemble in Benicia in January, 1854. He concocted a scheme for his own election to succeed Gwin, which created consternation in the Democratic ranks of the state, particularly among old politicians. Gwin's term in the Senate would expire on March 3, 1855. In the regular order, the legislature to be elected in the fall of 1854 would, on assembling in January, 1855, elect Gwin's successor. Broderick's daring and ingenious plan was to bring about the election of Gwin's successor in the legislative session that would assemble in January, 1854. Such a move was revolutionary, for United States Senators had uniformly been elected by the legislature just preceding the expiration of the term of the Senator whose successor was to be chosen.[9]

The fifth session of the California legislature convened at Benicia, on January 2, 1854. From the day of its opening, Broderick's plan was a chief topic of conversation in bars, hotels, and other places where men met to converse or intrigue. Broderick was present with a solid body of followers organized after the Tammany model. The absent Gwin, busy in Washington, also had loyal supporters, effective organization, and skillful leaders able to cope in debate and tactics with Broderick's men.

The Broderick election drama began on January 28, when a Broderick supporter introduced in the assembly a bill providing for the fixing of a day on which the legislature, then in session, should proceed to the election of Gwin's successor in the United States Senate. As a tactic, the election bill was tabled a few days later, with the idea of letting the bill await action in the senate and, if the senate's action should be favorable, taking the bill immediately from the table and passing it.

The final exciting scenes in the drama of the Senatorial election were enacted on March 6 and 7 in the courthouse at Sacramento, where the legislature began its sessions after having adjourned in Benicia on February 25. On Monday, March 6, the senate voted on the bill providing for the setting of a day for the election of a Senator to succeed Gwin. The assembly, after taking its bill from the table and hurriedly passing it just before the roll call in the senate, had adjourned to witness the contest there. The painful suspense and ominous silence attending the calling of the roll was broken by suppressed murmurs of anger and of joy as Senator Jacob Grewell answered "Aye," when the anti-Broderick auditors expected him to answer "No." When the resulting tie was broken by the presiding officer's vote of "aye" for the election bill, the Broderick men cheered, shook hands, and hugged one another, then rushed to congratu-

[9] For Broderick's scheme and its complications, see O'Meara, *op. cit.,* pp. 30–45; Gwin, *op. cit.,* pp. 260–261; Bancroft, *op. cit.,* pp. 681–684.

late Broderick, whose steel-blue eyes flamed with the ecstasy of victory.[10]

Such rejoicing was short-lived. A few antielectionists knew that the deciding vote in their defeat had resulted from the intimidation of the former Baptist minister, Jacob Grewell. After he was called to account and his courage had been bolstered by anti-Broderick leaders, he agreed to move reconsideration of the vote of March 6 on the next day. He did so move, and the motion carried. Then, a motion that the assembly bill should be rejected carried by a vote of 17 to 14. The election bill was now irrevocably lost. The rejection of the bill crushed Broderick's scheme to have that legislature elect him to the United States Senate and, incidentally, widened the rift in the Democratic party in California.

The extent of this division was clearly seen when, on July 18, 1854, the Democratic state convention met in Sacramento in the most sensational political convention ever held in the state, before or since. Here gathered irregularly and regularly selected Broderick delegates and also anti-Broderick, or Gwin, delegates. By virtue of his position as chairman of the state central committee, Broderick had rented the Baptist Church building on Fourth Street in Sacramento for the meeting. In a caucus of the Broderick managers, the seating of delegates, the procedure in naming the chairman, and the selection of committees had been arranged in such a way as to give control of the convention to Broderick. The opposing delegates, having learned of what had been done in the Broderick caucus, also held a caucus and concocted a counterplan. When Broderick called the convention to order, he found to his surprise that his design for organization had effective competition. Amid great excitement and confusion, each of the opposing factions elected a chairman and pushed him to the platform, where the two chairmen sat side by side while each attempted to preside over the meeting. With some six hundred people in the church,

---

[10] For the events described in this and the ensuing paragraphs, see O'Meara, *op. cit.*, pp. 67–81, 90–96, 113; Bancroft, *op. cit.*, pp. 684–695.

many of them armed, the session was a trying and dangerous one. Each of the opposing presidents held his ground. With each side refusing to recognize the rulings or words of the president of the other faction, confusion reigned until night began to fall. It was at last agreed that the two chairmen should lock arms and march together from the building, followed by pairs similarly made up from the hundred or more on the platform. In this manner the hostile factions adjourned to assemble separately, to nominate antagonistic tickets, and to carry the factional contest into every district and precinct in the state. The division of the Democratic party was complete.

From this time on came kaleidoscopic changes on the political stage that produced dramatic climaxes in the Gwin-Broderick play. The fall elections resulted in the outnumbering of the Gwin men by the Broderick men by two votes in the state senate, the Whigs being a hopeless minority; whereas in the assembly the Gwin men numbered 31, the Broderick men 14, and the Whigs 35. In the joint legislative convention of 1855 for the election of a Senator to succeed Gwin, on February 17, when the balloting began, 42 votes were recorded for Gwin; 36 for P. L. Edwards, the Whig candidate; 12 for Broderick; 14 for McCorkle; and 6 votes were distributed among five other candidates. Gwin at this time was pushing important legislation for California, but this made no difference to his bitter young rival, who held his supporters firmly against him. After thirty-eight ballots, with no important change at any time in the position of the three leading candidates, and no candidate receiving the 56 votes necessary for election, the first convention adjourned, leaving Gwin's seat in the United States Senate vacant.

Having been instrumental in blocking the reëlection of Gwin, Broderick now directed his efforts toward management of the primaries, in order to regain control of the Democratic state convention and thus put himself in a position to influence Democratic politics. He succeeded so well in this that he was able at the state convention to direct the nominations for state offices, including that of Bigler for a third term as governor. Although Broderick exercised control in the Democratic convention, he was not able to do so in the election. The Know-Nothing movement, which by this time had become almost extinct in the East, had mysteriously spread in California. Being an anti-Democratic movement, it virtually absorbed the Whig party. Anti-Broderickites and anti-Biglerites had to retaliate in some way, and they turned to the Know-Nothings. The result was the defeat of the Democratic party at the general election, and the choice of J. Neely Johnson, the Know-Nothing candidate for governor, with a vote of 51,117, over Governor Bigler, the Democratic candidate, who received 46,220 votes.

The Know-Nothing majority in the senate was small, but the party was predominant in the assembly. As the legislative session of 1856 opened, there seemed every prospect that this party would elect one of its number to succeed Senator Gwin. Both Gwin and Broderick hoped to prevent the choosing of his successor at this session, and that the Democrats would triumph at the next election of a legislature. Among the Know-Nothings in the current legislature, each had his friends, old followers, in whom he reposed faith to defeat any motion for a joint convention. The Know-Nothings as a whole did their best to achieve the naming of a Senator, but through the efforts of Gwin and Broderick, they were prevented from doing so in this session.

The legislature which was to reconvene on January 5, 1857, would be called upon to elect two United States Senators instead of one, as the term for which Senator Weller had been chosen would expire on March 3 of that year. Before that election took place, significant political changes had occurred in California. The Know-Nothing aggregation, which had been made up for the most part of hopeless Whigs and disaffected Democrats, had all but ceased to exist. The new Republican party was making rapid progress. The divided Democratic party had become temporarily united. Trusted friends of Gwin and Broderick, in a conference, had agreed that Broderick should withdraw his candidacy for the seat in the Senate to which Gwin aspired as his own successor, for the term which would expire on March 3, 1863. They had agreed that the two men would no longer oppose each other, and that each, as far as he was able, would induce his respective supporters to aid in a vote for the election of the other. Further, they agreed that their antagonistic supporting organizations should disorganize. In the Democratic convention of 1856 Broderick carried out this compact by seizing the two factions and welding them together. This resulted in the securing of Democratic presidential electors from California, and a Democratic legislature.

At the conference which had produced the results just noted, Broderick is reported to have said: "I am going to that Senate. I'll go if I have to march over a thousand corpses and every corpse a friend." [11] Gwin was too dignified and self-possessed to make such a statement, but he, too, was determined, if possible, to regain a Senate seat. The hope of each of securing the Senatorship was a basic factor in achieving an outward unity, though neither of the contestants had changed in character or in heart.

For the two Senate seats now to be filled, besides Gwin and Broderick there were several other aspirants. Naturally, former Senator Weller wanted to succeed himself. He was fairly popular with his party and had served in a dignified way as Senator, but he had accomplished little in that office. Another candidate was former Congressman Latham, who as collector of customs had a rather numerous following. Others who had some support were former Congressman McCorkle, with whom Gwin had fought a duel, B. F. Washington, Stephen J. Field, Frank Tilford, J. W. Denver, and A. P. Crittenden.

Before the convention met to select the Senators, Broderick demonstrated that he would trample under his feet the pact made with Gwin in order to attain his goal. His preconvention

[11] Quoted in O'Meara, *op. cit.*, p. 131.

analysis convinced him that he lacked but two votes to be chosen as the successor of Weller, who was at his post in Washington. At an arranged conference with Solomon Heydenfeldt, Weller's manager, Broderick informed him that if the Weller men could be depended upon to give him the two votes he needed, he would in return assure Weller's election to the seat for which Gwin was a candidate. Failing to get the needed coöperation in this double-dealing proposition, Broderick now resolved upon a bold stroke, which was to have the Democratic caucus nominate the successor to Weller first— that is, for the longer term—and then to choose the Senator for the short term. He had no doubt that, if he could influence the caucus to act as he desired, he would be chosen first and for the long term. He then bargained with some of Latham's friends for their support of his plan, intimating that he preferred Latham as his Senatorial associate, thus making his "choice" of a colleague now three persons instead of one. Next, he trickily planted one of his unscrupulous supporters as a colored waiter in a secret meeting of Weller's men on Wednesday evening, January 7. This man supplied valuable information that was used by Broderick and Latham as together they planned for the next evening's caucus action.

At the Democratic caucus on the following night, Broderick's well-oiled political machine ran smoothly. A motion to the effect that the members pledge themselves to abide by the action of the caucus was quickly adopted. A prepared resolution was next presented, which provided: "That in making the nominations for United States Senators the following order of business shall be observed: 1. The nomination of a Senator to fill the long term, to succeed Hon. John B. Weller; 2. The nomination of a Senator to fill the short term, to succeed the Hon. William M. Gwin." [12] The resolution was adopted by a vote of 42 to 35. When the vote was taken on the nominees presented for the long term—David C. Broderick and John B. Weller—Broderick received 42 votes and Weller 34. The

[12] *Ibid.*, p. 152.

nomination of David C. Broderick as a candidate for the long-term Senatorship was then made unanimous. The nomination for the short term was not decided upon by the caucus in the two ballots taken at this time.

On the next day, Friday, January 9, the legislature in joint convention elected David C. Broderick to be United States Senator for the term that would begin March 4, 1857, and expire March 3, 1863, as the successor of John B. Weller. Broderick's commission as Senator was at once made out by the secretary of state and signed by Governor J. Neely Johnson, and it was delivered to Broderick in person at his hotel on March 10, by his devoted friend, W. M. Lent. By assiduous labor, pertinacity of purpose, the sheer force of his own indomitable will, political duplicity, and fortuitous circumstances, Broderick had attained the position to which he had aspired since before he set out for California. In pursuit of his ambition, he had disregarded precedent, overridden usage, trampled on friends, and tricked his enemies. He had fought Know-Nothingism, vigilantism, the opposing elements in his own party, and political manipulation that at times had him prostrate. At last, he had won.

The election of Broderick to the Senate created excitement in the state capital, and wild speculation concerning his possible colleague. It quickly became evident that Broderick, as the master of the situation, was resolved to name the Senator for the short term. Disregarding his agreement to support Gwin to succeed himself, he kept the rival aspirants for the short term in uncertainty for days. Gwin and Latham were the leading candidates; the other three mentioned as contenders were little more than political pawns in the game. In the contest, national political issues played no part. The conflict was purely personal and as thoroughly local as if California were not in the Union. What Broderick would eventually decide was still not apparent after four more ineffectual ballots had been taken in the reassembled caucus on Friday evening, January 9.

As the groups of politicians moved about the different places of political rendezvous on Saturday, January 10, it became clear that something serious was disturbing the Latham camp. Two troubles had, in fact, come down on Latham's head from different directions at the same time. The first was Senator Frank Tilford's charge that Latham was responsible for the disappearance from his desk of Latham's written pledge to recommend him for the position of collector of the port of San Francisco in the event of Latham's election to the Senate. The second had to do with Latham's relations, as collector of the port, with the vigilance committee of 1856. The case against him was that, though as collector he had a revenue cutter under his control, he had permitted various injustices by an organization condemned by Democrats for its attacks upon Broderick and upholders of law and order; and that Latham's brother, while an employee in the customhouse, had served as an officer of a military company of the vigilantes, against the protests of law-and-order citizens. The circulation of these charges in printed form at this time, while the contest between Gwin and Latham was on, not only created excitement and angry feelings, but it also seriously damaged Latham's cause.

Latham's loyal friends rallied support for him on Saturday. McCorkle was prevailed upon to uphold him against Gwin; Tilford was even brought back to his support in the caucus; and Broderick appeared to be still ready to arrange terms. When evening came, Latham's managers seemed to have gained much confidence, although eleven inconclusive ballots in the caucus made it clear that the defections caused by the charges had not been overcome. The caucus adjourned after the eleventh ballot, to meet again on Monday evening.

Throughout Saturday night and Sunday feeling was tense. The headquarters of Broderick, of Latham, and of Gwin, were carefully watched, and reports were made of the movements of these men, and of visits to them. About midnight, after it was supposed he had retired, the desperate and dispirited Gwin made his way secretly to Broderick's apartment in the Magnolia

Hotel, where Broderick by previous arrangement received him.[13] The next day, Monday, January 12, Gwin appeared more composed and hopeful. That evening the Democratic caucus reassembled. Thirteen ballots were taken, with little change in the vote tallies. When the fourteenth ballot was ordered, and as names were called, many members rose to explain their votes thus far, and the change they were then making. The final result was: for Gwin, 46 votes; for Latham, 26 votes; and for McCorkle, 6. Gwin had received seven more votes than necessary for nomination. On motion of General James M. Estill the nomination of Gwin was made unanimous. On Tuesday, January 13, 1857, the legislature in joint convention reelected Gwin to his own seat in the Senate, for the new term which would expire on March 3, 1861.

Senator Gwin left Sacramento for his home in San Francisco on the day of his election, after having sent to each member of the legislature a written invitation to a simple, social gathering to be held at his residence on Thursday, January 15, in celebration of the election. The day after his departure from the capital, there appeared in the papers an address [14] directed to the people of California, in which Gwin, after giving grateful acknowledgement to friends whose fidelity remained unshaken fom first to last, referred to the hostility and abuse of maligners which had pursued his Senatorial career and had nearly cost him the endorsement of a reëlection to the United States Senate. To the federal patronage he attributed in great degree the malice which had been directed against him. In the closing paragraph of his address, Gwin gave credit for his election to Broderick and his friends in a statement which both surprised and angered many who had supported him. Some among the more dignified of Gwin's friends were so affected by anger and disgust, or by pain and

---

[13] In a secret, written agreement signed by Gwin and given to Broderick, Gwin promised Broderick the California patronage, if he (Gwin) should be elected. The letter to this effect is printed in Lynch, *op. cit.*, pp. 156–157.

[14] The address is in O'Meara, *op. cit.*, pp. 184–185; and in part in Lynch, *op. cit.*, pp. 154–155.

sorrow, because it appeared to them he had paid for his return to office, that they remained away from the well-attended social celebration at his home on Thursday. Although there was some jubilation at the gathering, the public statement Gwin had made of his subservience to a man like Broderick manifestly put a damper on the hilarity of his best friends who were present, for they felt that by it both Gwin and they had been humiliated.

With but little delay, Broderick also returned to San Francisco. It was a return in triumph. With processions, addresses, and the firing of guns, the whole city acclaimed him in a fitting manner. Here was a young man thirty-seven years of age, who, as a "mud-sill of the north," in the words of one Senator, within a period of eight years since his arrival in California from New York, had risen from the trade in which he had been trained, to be a Senator of the United States. In those years he had struggled unceasingly against great odds. The Committee of Vigilance had been hostile to him; time and time again he had been rejected by Democracy at the polls, in the state convention, and in the state legislature; but he had never accepted defeat as final. In spite of all this, by sheer persistence, lucky chance, and the volatile mixture of good and bad forces in his own character, he had finally attained spectacular success. In the legislative session he had come to victory by audacious shrewdness, surpassing men of greater maturity by means of perseverance, manipulation, and the trampling down of opposition, plus the "breaks" in fortune which play an important part in the success of every conqueror. The enthusiastic reception, in San Francisco, of this gloomy young man of proper habits, who seldom smiled, by the friends who loved him and whom he loved, and by erstwhile enemies who hated him and whom he had hated, was the American laudation of a conquering hero.

In the latter part of January, 1857, Senators Gwin and Broderick, accompanied by Governor Bigler, left San Francisco for New York and Washington by the Panama route, a trip requiring something less than a month. From New York, Gwin went at once to Washington to resume his former Senate seat. Broderick remained in New York long enough to receive the adulation of friends and politicians at banquets in his honor, and to be further acclaimed by resolutions of the municipal authorities welcoming him back. New Yorkers seemed to regard him as one of themselves and to consider his meteoric rise from lowly status to the Senate as an honor to the city. And those who delivered encomiums intimated that this rise was all in accord with their early expectations.

In Washington, Gwin found himself in a compromised position because both true and distorted reports of what had occurred in California had preceded him and Broderick to the national capital. Broderick, on his arrival to take his seat in executive session on March 4, found himself greeted with more attention than a new Senator usually received. Much of this attention came from old Whigs and dissatisfied Democrats who had turned Republican. Although the circumstances attending the election of the Senators may have exaggerated Broderick's power, and the rumor that he had dictated the election of Gwin and brought him "to Washington in chains" may have understated the still active and potential political strength of the older man, the situation temporarily produced humiliation for Gwin and exaltation for Broderick.

The realities of practical politics quickly brought Broderick down from the heights to which he had been borne by adulation, and plunged him to angry depths of frustration. This descent resulted quite as much from the naïve commitments which he had made to aid in his conquest as it did from the ways of politics in Washington.

As was natural, great pressure was exerted on young Senator Broderick for federal posts. He and his office-seeking friends innocently expected the President to accept willingly his nominations for the federal offices in California. Broderick was quickly disillusioned. In telling of the reception given him on his first visit to President Buchanan, he is said to have remarked, "It was cold outside the house, but it was ice within." [15] When Broderick was next received at the White House, the old and experienced executive, familiar with patronage evils, told him that he had adopted a rule requiring Senators and Representatives recommending persons for federal offices to submit the name of each applicant for an office in writing, with the endorsement of the Senator or Representative presenting the candidate. Since Broderick curtly refused to recommend in writing the person he wanted appointed collector of the port of San Francisco, and Gwin declined to submit a name, a policy which they followed in regard to other appointments, recommendations for the filling of the offices had to be left to others. Broderick's friends thus benefited little in the distribution of federal patronage, from which they had expected so much.

Actually, neither Gwin nor Broderick controlled the dispensation of the offices in California. Most of the appointments made by the President were acceptable to Gwin, but the records will show that Gwin did not himself recommend even one person from his own state for appointment to office. The President, however, did ask Gwin for his advice and counsel on California appointments, which Gwin frequently gave; and he resisted Broderick's attempts to control these appointments, partly because the stern, imperious young Senator seemed to the polished old bachelor President to demand rather than to request Presidential favors. Gwin had not deprived Broderick of patronage opportunities—the President would not accord them to him.

Fearful that his dominance in his state might be wrecked by the President's attitude toward him, and by his failure to control patronage, Broderick returned to California in April, 1857, to explain his lack of success in the patronage matter and, if possible, to obtain control of the state convention which was to nominate state officers. On his arrival he learned that Gwin's supporters were indignant at the fact that their leader had had to purchase his seat in the Senate by a bargain

[15] Quoted in Lynch, *op. cit.*, p. 160.

with Broderick, and he also became aware that many of his own followers sympathized with Gwin. He quickly discovered that the widely circulated news of his hostility to the administration was harmful to his cause. To combat these reports and conditions he issued a public letter on June 6, in answer to a letter of inquiry from two friends, in which he expressly declared that he did not return to the state to make war on the administration, nor would he make war on it in Washington. With regard to his election and that of Gwin, and the rumor of a bargain between them as to federal patronage, he declared that his own election had been accomplished "without bargain, contract, alliance, combination, or understanding with anyone"; and in regard to the distribution of patronage, he asserted categorically that between Gwin and himself there was "no condition whatever." [16] He said that he had not come to California to distract the party or to control its nominations. Nevertheless, Broderick's motive for all these denials and assertions was to effect unity and, if possible, secure control.

The politically astute Broderick was not long in discovering that, in spite of his broadcasting of denials and assertions, he was not popular in California, even within his own party. He found himself face to face with the hostility of Gwin and his organization, the unfriendliness of former Senator Weller, the suspicions of Latham, the disappointment of Tilford, who had been promised an office he did not get, and the disaffection caused by the rumors from Washington which had preceded him. Broderick was unable to secure the election of delegates to the Democratic state convention who could be molded to his purposes and governed by his will. In the convention which he had hoped to dominate, the anti-Broderick faction, by a vote of 264, nominated John B. Weller for governor; whereas Judge McCorkle, the nominee of Broderick and his supporters, received only 61 votes. The convention appointed a state cen-

[16] The quotations are from a letter of Broderick to two of his political supporters, General Alfred Redington and J. P. Dyer, under date of June 6, 1857. See O'Meara, *op. cit.*, pp. 197–198.

tral committee which for the most part was anti-Broderick, and generally ignored Broderick's friends in the nominations for state offices. His visit was a political failure. In the course of a single year's events, the unlucky man had been markedly deprived of power. His apparently grand victory over adversaries and rivals had become almost worthless. Not only had he little control of his party in California through federal patronage, but his opponents now controlled the state government and were fortified by the administration at Washington, which Broderick despised. Such was the political situation in which he found himself, when, as an embittered and disappointed young man, he returned to Washington to take his seat in the Thirty-fifth Congress, which assembled in December, 1857.

This session opened to Broderick an extraordinary opportunity to give vent to his venomous hatred of Buchanan and to express his deepest moral and patriotic convictions. The unfortunate Kansas question had advanced to the point where the admission of Kansas into the Union was being asked under the constitution framed at Lecompton in 1857. The administration and its wing of the Democratic party favored admission of Kansas with the Lecompton constitution; Senator Douglas and his followers opposed it. With all the vigor he possessed, Broderick, "the brave, young Senator," as Senator William H. Seward called him, took the Douglas or popular sovereignty side, which was consistent with his principles as he had stated them on other occasions. In December, soon after the opening of the Thirty-fifth Congress, Broderick made his first speech in that body. His purpose in delivering it, according to his statement, was to clarify his position on the Lecompton constitution and the President's relation to it. The speech, although evidently hastily put together, clearly indicated a complete political break with the President. Broderick's second speech, which he delivered in March, gave evidence of having been more carefully prepared; parts of it were even poetic. It revealed clearly his hostility to slavery and to forced labor.

His religiously deep sensitiveness and sentiment with respect to labor kept him dignified and restrained as he made answer to Senator J. H. Hammond of South Carolina, who had referred to the laboring class as constituting "the very mud-sill of society, and of political government." Broderick spoke of his own apprenticeship of five years at a laborious trade that had denied him the joys of life in his boyhood, and then said impressively:

But, sir, the class of society to whose toil I was born, under our form of government, will control the destinies of this nation. If I were inclined to forget my connection with them, or to deny that I sprang from them, this chamber would not be the place in which I could do either. While I hold a seat here, I have but to look at the beautiful capitals adorning the pilasters that support the roof to be reminded of my father's talent and handiwork.

After this reverential reference to his father, Broderick indicated that he himself had become a sad and lonely man, with no tie of blood binding him to any living person, and spoke of having left his old home to live and work among strangers in California, where labor was honored. From such thoughts he turned back, with unexpected bitterness, to his argument against the Lecompton constitution, concluding with these words:

I hope in mercy, sir, to the boasted intelligence of this age the historian, when writing of these times will ascribe this attempt of the Executive to force this constitution upon an unwilling people to the fading intellect, the petulant passion and trembling dotage of an old man on the verge of the grave.[17]

Thus Broderick showed himself as a man who, in one breath, could awaken a kindly respect for his lonely figure and a sympathetic admiration for his filial love, and in the next breath, give out personal venom—a poison which later would come back to him on arrows from the gods.

When Congress adjourned in June, 1858, Broderick at once

[17] The speech from which this and the preceding quotation are taken is given in Lynch, *op. cit.*, pp. 172–176.

returned to California, where he remained for about three months. Back in Washington at the opening of the new session, he found that he had been dropped from the important committee on public lands, of which he had been a member since he began serving as a Senator. This slight he attributed to the Southern faction who dominated Congress and the President, and whose ideas with respect to the railroad differed from his. Whether in Washington or in California—wherever he went— he found that he was out of step with the controlling faction of his party, which continued adherence to Lecompton or proslavery principles and supported Gwin. When the California legislature met in 1859, it passed resolutions vigorously condemning Broderick for not obeying the instructions given him by the preceding legislature, to vote for the resolution it had passed endorsing the President's Kansas policy, and denouncing his castigation of the President in the Senate as humiliating to the people whom he represented.

The almost barren record of Broderick in the Senate came to an end with the adjournment of Congress in March, 1859. As though he had a premonition of impending fate, in bidding farewell to a friend in New York, he said: "I don't know whether you will ever see me again." [18] He and Congressman McKibben returned to California to organize the Anti-Lecompton wing of the Democratic party in the gubernatorial election of that year. Gwin and Congressman Scott came back also, in order to seek endorsement for their action in supporting the Lecompton Constitution bill for Kansas, and to advance the cause of the administration, which both had supported.

The three political groups in regular order nominated candidates and passed resolutions. The Republicans met on June 8 and nominated a straight ticket, disregarding the advice of Horace Greeley, then on a visit to the coast, to coalesce with Broderick, who hoped for such a fusion. The Anti-Lecompton Democratic convention met on June 15. In their resolutions, the delegates condemned unsparingly the administration of

[18] Quoted in *ibid.*, p. 192.

Buchanan for its outrages upon the rights of the people of Kansas, and endorsed the course of Broderick. The Lecompton Democratic convention met on June 22. In addition to giving cordial and unqualified approval to the administration of Buchanan, the group expressed rigid adherence to the principle of nonintervention by Congress, with slavery in the states and territories, as declared in the Kansas-Nebraska bill. For governor, the Republicans nominated Leland Stanford; the Anti-Lecomptonites named John Currey, a Republican; and the Democrats chose as their candidate, Milton S. Latham.

Because of its political background, California, in the campaign of 1859, could have been a forum for the discussion of the leading issue of the day, the question of slavery in new territories; but it was not. Broderick, already a marked man with reference to the national contest, would have had the opportunity in such a forum to build a solid groundwork from which he might ascend to new heights in the national conflict ahead, if he could have subordinated personalities to issues. Instead, this able, resentful, nonjesting man moved with unaltered course into channels where, by the law of probabilities, fate would eventually corner and destroy him. He continued to denounce the President in bitter language. He accused his rival, Gwin, who succeeded because of his own character and accomplishments, of being prompted by venal motives, and of "dripping with corruption." Into his party platform he forced resolutions implying or directly charging outrageous conduct, depravity, and swindling by his Senate colleague and the President. The campaign, begun with personal animosity on both sides, was carried through with vicious charges and countercharges of a personal nature. Broderick lost his last great opportunity, for his career ended in tragedy as the campaign closed.

An important circumstance in the chain of events leading to Broderick's tragic end was his clash with Judge David S. Terry as the campaign began. Terry had been a political opponent of Broderick in the exciting convention of 1854 in the

Sacramento church, and in 1859 had criticized him unfavorably, in spite of the fact that while the Committee of Vigilance held Terry prisoner Broderick had paid $200 a week to newspapers to defend him. Although the two men differed widely in political beliefs, associations, and sectional prejudices, they had, nevertheless, a personal respect and admiration for each other. This, together with the fact that Terry had never been a supporter or personal friend of Gwin, makes it difficult to understand the attack which he made on Broderick in the Lecompton convention, so markedly influenced by Gwin, that had just refused to place Terry in nomination again for the supreme court bench. There, after referring critically to the Anti-Lecompton party in California, Terry uttered sharp and contemptuous words in criticism of Broderick.[19]

These words of the chief justice of the state, delivered three years after Broderick had paid. newspapers to defend him, greatly irritated the sensitive young politician, as he prepared intensively to wage what he must have known would be a losing campaign. Two days after Terry's speech, on the morning of June 27, Broderick saw the address in a newspaper, while he was at breakfast in the International Hotel in San Francisco. Becoming angry at what he read, he spoke caustically about Terry's performance, to a friend, A. A. Selover, Selover's wife, and another lady, saying, among other things, that when all others had deserted Terry, he had supported three newspapers to defend him in the days of the vigilantes. He characterized Terry as a "damned miserable wretch," because of his ingratitude. He then said, "I have hitherto spoken of him as an honest man—as the only honest man on the bench of a miserable, corrupt supreme court—but now I find I was mistaken. I take it all back. He is just as bad as the others." D. W.

---

[19] After referring contemptuously to the Anti-Lecompton party in California, Terry said: "They have no distinction they are entitled to; they are the followers of one man, the personal chattels of a single individual, whom they are ashamed of. They belong, heart and soul, body and breeches, to David C. Broderick." Quoted in O'Meara, *op. cit.*, pp. 218–219; Lynch, *op. cit.*, p. 201.

Perley, a friend of Terry who was present and overheard Broderick's remarks, after some sharp words between them, sent a duel challenge to Broderick. Broderick, in a long letter, declined the challenge on the ground that a duel might affect his own political rights but not those of Perley, who was a subject of Great Britain and occupied an inferior position.[20] This letter ended formal discussion of that particular question of honor until after the campaign had ended. In the more than two months which intervened Terry said not a word about the matter.

The campaign, once it got under way, was carried on with fury. Broderick for the first time in his career canvassed the state as a stump speaker, and surprised even his opponents with the effectiveness of his passionate appeals. He felt wronged, attacked, encircled, with opponents trying to involve him in difficulties or to destroy him in some foul way. He took Gwin's criticisms of his political actions as personal attacks intended to ruin him. Gwin's political replies to his diatribes he regarded as personally intended and designed to involve him in affairs of personal honor. He accused Gwin of being prompted by dishonorable, mercenary motives in his public transactions as a Senator, and then considered that he himself was viciously attacked when sharp answers were made to his charges.

On August 9, 1859, at Sacramento, Broderick undertook to prove by documents the venality of Gwin, Latham, and Tilford, beginning his speech to a large crowd of supporters by saying, "I come tonight to arraign before you two great criminals, Milton S. Latham and William M. Gwin." [21] In the same fierce spirit he repeated his charges at Yreka, Shasta, Quincy, Santa Rosa, and elsewhere. Although on June 6, 1857, he had published in a paper the declaration, "Between Mr. Gwin and myself there was no condition whatever in regard to the distribution of patronage," he now not only gloated that "old Gwin came begging at my feet for favor and help," but at

---

[20] O'Meara, *op. cit.,* p. 220, 221–222; Lynch, *op. cit.,* pp. 202–203.
[21] O'Meara, *op. cit.,* p. 208.

several places he read, in high anger, the signed bargain Gwin had made on the patronage. In this humiliating document, Gwin had said, "Provided I am elected, you shall have the exclusive control of this patronage, so far as I am concerned." [22] At Yreka, shortly afterward, the proud and badly wounded Gwin replied to Broderick in biting words, charging him with conspiracy and double-dealing without a parallel. In making public the bargain to which he was a party, Broderick was releasing a two-edged sword. The edge directed toward Gwin had already been dulled by Gwin's acknowledgement of his surrender of the patronage, in his "Address to the People," on the day after his election, and now documentary evidence proved that Broderick's previous declaration exculpating Gwin and himself for the election was a falsehood. All these factors acted unfavorably for Broderick.

In the state election which took place on September 7, Broderick and the Republicans were defeated. The election cast no light on national issues. These never had a chance. Although in this election neither Gwin nor Broderick had been a candidate for any office, they had struggled against each other for leadership and control in state politics. In the heat of the campaign both men had uttered bitter words of recrimination and semichallenging phrases. Since each had previously fought a duel, it was expected that a meeting of violence would occur between them. But here, as frequently happens, other influences worked in a surprising way to effect different ends.

Chief Justice Terry, of whom Broderick had spoken acrimonious words at the outset of the campaign, had kept silence for three months, in spite of his deep resentment at Broderick's indictment of his character as a citizen and his uprightness as a judge. On the very day that the campaign ended, Terry sent to the governor his resignation as chief justice of the supreme court of California. He went at once to Oakland, and on the following day, September 8, sent a letter to Broderick in which,

[22] This document, dated January 11, 1857, is printed in Lynch, *op. cit.*, pp. 156–157.

after explaining that he had deferred taking notice of the remarks until the expiration of the time limit fixed by Broderick himself, the duration of the campaign, he said, "I now take the earliest opportunity to require of you a retraction of these remarks." In an exchange of notes, there was some quibbling about the exact words of the offensive "remarks," and, after quoting the words as published in the papers, Terry, on September 9, added his demand: "What I require is the retraction of any words which were calculated to reflect on my character as an officer or a gentleman." [23] In neither of Judge Terry's notes did he issue a challenge to Broderick. He merely demanded the honorable retraction of character-impugning language used by Broderick when he was deeply stirred by anger. Some of Broderick's trusted counselors, urging that a retraction of offensive language used in a sudden outburst of passion would be brave and honorable, protested against the draft of his second note, as it was being prepared to send to Terry. They thought it unwise to shut the door and thus make a hostile meeting practically certain. Broderick did not heed their counsel but took that of the more aggressive of his advisers. Unless he receded from his requirement, Terry could do no less than say to Broderick, as he did in his final note to him, "This course on your part leaves to me no other alternative but to demand the satisfaction usual among gentlemen, which I accordingly do." [24] In keeping with his own courageous spirit, on September 10 arrangements for the duel were quickly made by the seconds of the two men. The meeting was set for Monday morning, September 12, at half past five, at a selected place in San Mateo County, ten miles from San Francisco.

Descriptions of Broderick's condition and state of mind as he approached the ordeal of battle are seemingly contradictory, yet, considered together, they undoubtedly make a true picture of the man as he was then. When awakened in the dead of night at Leonidas Haskell's house at Black Point and faced

[23] For the letter from Terry to Broderick, September 8, 1859, see O'Meara, *op. cit.*, p. 227; for that of September 9, see *ibid.*, p. 230.

[24] September 9, 1859; see *ibid.*, p. 231.

with Terry's challenge, he seemed, according to the San Francisco *Bulletin*, "to have succumbed under the belief at last that, in his own person, either by Terry or someone else, he was to be made a sacrifice." Apparently convinced that fate was against him and he was now in great danger, he went about settling his personal affairs, giving attention, among other things, to his last will and testament. He acted as if he were aware that the crisis had arrived which he had foreseen when, on leaving New York a few months earlier, he had said to a friend: "Good-by. You may never see me again." But he appeared a changed man when he faced the immediate event. Courage and confidence are said to have radiated from his words and bearing. According to witnesses, he conversed with equanimity of manner and seemed confident of his own ability to sustain himself in every respect. In response to a remark of his intimate friend, John White, that he hoped for his safe deliverance, Broderick said: "Don't you fear John. I can shoot twice to Terry's once; beat him shooting every time." [25]

On Monday morning, at the hour set for the duel, the actors appeared on the scene, and several score of persons gathered to see the show. Officers of the law surprisingly appeared also and placed the duelists under arrest. Broderick and Terry were taken into court that day, but were discharged, as the court held that no breach of the peace had been committed. The next morning, the duelists, with the seconds and surgeons, together with some eighty spectators, went to the field for a second time. After the preliminaries had been taken care of, the two men stepped to their places and, at the word, fired. Broderick's quick-on-the-trigger pistol went off before "one" was spoken. As he raised the weapon, it discharged, the bullet entering the ground some nine feet from where he stood. Terry fired his shot just as "two" was called. The bullet entered Broderick's body just above the right breast, penetrating his lung. Almost immediately he sank to the ground. He was conveyed to Leonidas Haskell's mansion at Black Point, where he

[25] Quoted in *ibid.*, pp. 235–236.

had been when aroused at midnight three days earlier to receive Terry's challenge. After lingering another three days, in which he spoke only a few coherent phrases, Broderick died on Friday morning, September 16, 1859.

On Sunday afternoon, Broderick's body was taken to an improvised, draped stage on the Plaza, for the final obsequies. In the presence of some thirty thousand persons, Colonel E. D. Baker, eloquently and feelingly presented the good, the true, and the beautiful in Broderick's life. He said: "Fellow-citizens! the man who lies before you was your Senator." Then, after reviewing Broderick's remarkable rise and his public life, he thus described his character: "Temperate, decorous, self-restrained, he had passed through all the excitements of California unstained. No man could charge him with broken faith or violated trust. . . . Never, in the history of the State, has there been a citizen who has borne public relations more stainless in all respects than he." [26] In the funeral procession which made its way to Lone Mountain Cemetery were many distinguished persons, numerous societies, the fire department, a long line of carriages and every other kind of vehicle, and many citizens on foot. There, Broderick's body was buried in unconsecrated ground.

In life, Broderick had attacked, scorned, and crushed his enemies, often unfairly. In death, he became, in the eyes of many, a martyr to a cause. This fancied martyrdom, coupled with the forces of the time, was to endow him with greater strength in the grave than he had been able to achieve in life. Men cried out against the killer who, they asserted, had defied the laws and murdered a great and pure man. They insisted that he be punished. Terry's accusers were blind to the fact that Broderick had actually invited the duel, and that, had his pistol not gone off accidentally, he might easily have been the murderer, since he was a better shot than Terry. In the minds of many, the manner of his death purified Broderick; in memory

---

[26] See Bancroft, *op. cit.*, VI, 734 n., for the part of Baker's oration from which these excerpts are taken.

his faults disappeared and he became an incorruptible, earnest, brave man—a prophet of freedom. The rumors that a guiltless and brave leader had been hunted down because he had worked for decency in politics and for freedom now warmed the ferment of a national issue in the political mind of the self-governing dominion of California. After a few weeks it became apparent that the cause which had been tied in with Broderick's personal fight would triumph in the next year. Unquestionably, Broderick's death helped to demoralize the party with which he had been associated in his earlier years, and to give vitality and success to the principles for which he had confusedly stood.

When Senator Gwin was leaving San Francisco for Washington, in company with Congressman C. L. Scott, someone brandished in his face a large framed canvas on which was painted a portrait of Broderick and these words: "It is the will of the people that the murderers of Broderick do not return again to California." Below them was this statement, which Broderick was said to have made just before he died: "They have killed me because I was opposed to the extension of slavery, and a corrupt administration." [27] Gwin, on his arrival in Washington, found himself in an embarrassing position because of the events which had transpired in California, and especially because of his relation to his state and to the nation which had resulted from his personal convictions in the political crisis. As a Southerner with large property interests and family ties in the South, his sympathies were naturally with that section. Notwithstanding this, he loved the Union to which he had given years of faithful service. It was clear to him that his political fortune depended upon its continuance. He believed strongly that the Constitution was a compact binding together sovereign and coequal states, and that it was a grant of power from the states. In the first session of the Thirty-sixth Congress, which opened on Monday, December 5, 1859, he used every opportunity to emphasize that he was a representative of one of the sovereign states of the

[27] See O'Meara, *op. cit.,* p. 246.

confederation, whose people strongly favored the Union and its preservation.[28] At the same time, he maintained that the principles of the Republican party were destructive to the constitutional rights of the slaveholding states, and that the selection of a Republican President, and the attempt to carry Republican principles into practice which would follow his election, would endanger the Union he loved.

After Congress adjourned, Gwin and the other members of the California delegation returned to California and engaged in the Presidential election of 1860, the whole delegation supporting the Breckinridge ticket. They found that California politically had changed much within a year. In the face of the impending crisis, with Broderick's memory an active influence, and Gwin, in sympathy with the South, holding principles adverse to Douglas and to the Republican party, a political contest was being waged around national issues for the first time in California's history. This significant development, accompanied, as it was, by the rather general recognition that California could not stand as a self-governing dominion but only as an integral and dependent part of the United States, was actually a revolution.

The campaign of 1860 was a heated contest, and for Gwin and his principles, a losing battle. In the campaign he backed the Breckinridge ticket because he could not support the ticket of the Republicans and was opposed to Douglas' constitutional position. He supported Breckinridge's policy of state freedom with regard to domestic institutions, holding to the doctrine of the Union but regarding it as a confederacy. The proud Senator, once the supreme leader of his party in California, was attacked for his principles. His sympathy with the South, his alleged treachery to the state, his complicity in what Broderick had referred to as the "Lime Point Swindle," and his desertion of his party all counted against him. Quotations from his speeches, often removed from their context, were

[28] He said of himself and his constituents: "We revere this Union, and we desire to preserve it." Gwin, *op. cit.*, pp. 348–349.

used to condemn him. Newspapers, such as the San Francisco *Bulletin* and the Sacramento *Union*, assailed him savagely. On the other hand, there were friendly papers which called attention to his great services and spoke in complimentary terms of his forceful speeches in the campaign, that, in the words of one paper, "made his enemies quail." Gwin's candidate, Breckinridge, lost, receiving some three thousand votes fewer than Douglas, who received some seven hundred fewer than Lincoln. Gwin also lost. With this election, if not before, his political star went down, never to rise again.[29] When the legislature met in joint session to elect his successor, Gwin's name did not once appear.

Although the election of 1860 demonstrated clearly California's adherence to the Union, it also awakened again the possibility of a Pacific Republic, an idea which had had some support during the reign of the vigilance committee of 1856. Indirectly, the revived proposal combined with the election itself to make the self-governing dominion of California safe and solid in the federation of states.

Three statements indicating that influential figures saw the

[29] After the election Gwin returned to Washington, where he worked to prevent dissolution of the Union, or, if dissolution could not be prevented, a separation without war. Until shortly after the inauguration he continued to act as an intermediary between leaders in the South and Seward, in his efforts to avoid war. (See Gwin, *op. cit.*, pp. 363–365; McPherson, *op. cit.*, p. 240; Frederic Bancroft, *The Life of William H. Seward*, II, 25–26, 108.) On the last day before he retired to private life, Gwin said on the floor of the Senate, "There is nothing that can be proposed here, that can by any possibility tend to quiet the country, and restore the Union as it existed, that I will not sustain." Gwin, *op. cit.*, pp. 360–361.

On March 8 he went to New York, from there he went to Mississippi, back to Washington, and then to California. He left San Francisco for New York on October 21, 1861. On the voyage he and two companions were arrested as disloyal persons and then were paroled. They were arrested again in New York and were imprisoned in Fort Lafayette, but on December 10, 1861, were set at liberty by order of President Lincoln, on the basis of the report of Secretary Seward that "no one of the parties had any disloyal purpose in his journey." McPherson, *op. cit.*, pp. 241–244; Frederic Bancroft, *op. cit.*, pp. 264–265.

As a Unionist, a believer in the rights of states, a loyal American citizen with a strong heart pull toward the South, and with Northern and Southern lifelong friends now engaged in a fratricidal war, Gwin was veritably a man without a country.

rise of an independent republic on the Pacific Coast as a po-
tentiality were made in the early part of 1860 by three different persons. The first of these statements was a paragraph in
Governor's Weller's last annual message to the California legislature, in January, 1860, in which he said that if the wild spirit
of fanaticism which pervaded the land should destroy this
"magnificent Confederacy," California "will not go with the
South or the North, but here upon the shores of the Pacific
found a mighty republic which may in the end prove the
greatest of all." [30] The second was a phrase in a speech made
by Senator Latham in the United States Senate, on April 16,
1860, in which he said he saw "foreshadowed the idea of a
Pacific republic upon the dissolution of the existing Union."
In December, 1860, after the election, Latham retracted those
words as being premature, and declared it to be his considered
judgment that California would remain with the Union. On
this occasion he said that there was "but one thing which will
or can alienate the affections of the Pacific from the union as it
is, or as it may be, and that is, a failure to give them a Pacific
railroad." [31] The third statement was one made by Senator
Gwin, on the floor of the Senate. He said that he hoped "that
this Union will be imperishable; but if it is ever broken up, the
eastern boundary of the Pacific Republic will be, in my opinion,
the Sierra Madre and the Rocky Mountains." [32] It should be
emphasized that Weller, Latham, and Gwin, in these statements, were not so much advocating a republic as they were
predicting what they thought would come to pass under certain conditions.

As a result of the election of Lincoln in 1860, some persons
and newspapers in California brought into the open for a time
their advocacy of a Pacific Republic. In a letter from Washington dated November 22, Congressman John C. Burch
recommended that, as a means of avoiding the blighting effects
that would result from disunion and civil war, the people of

[30] California, *Senate Journal*, 1860, p. 60.
[31] Davis, *op. cit.*, pp. 128–129.
[32] Gwin, *op. cit.*, p. 355.

California, Oregon, New Mexico, Washington, and Utah create "a prosperous, happy, and successful republic on the Pacific slope." [33] Burch was careful to add to his statement, as a condition, "if the 'fates' should *force* us to this last sad resort." Representative C. L. Scott, on December 21, 1860, in a letter to the chairman of the Democratic state committee, followed suit. "If this Union is divided and two separate confederacies are formed," he said, "I will strenuously advocate the secession of California and the establishment of a separate republic on the Pacific slope." [34] For a time, independence for California was openly urged by a number of newspapers, such as the San Francisco *Herald*, the Sacramento *Standard*, the *Alameda County Gazette*, the Los Angeles *Star*, the Sonora *Democrat*, the Carson City *Silver Age*, and the Sacramento *Standard*.[35] While the advocates of a Pacific Republic were quite vocal, they were confined to the extreme secession sympathizers of the Breckinridge party, or supporters of it.

It is significant that of the many speeches made in the California legislature in 1861 on the "Resolutions upon the State of the Union," only a few advocated an independent state, and these few recommended it only as an escape from fratricidal war and what they considered to be unconstitutional coercion of states. A notable example of the oratory of the day was the much-applauded address made by H. I. Thornton on February 8, 1861.[36] Speaking in the state senate, Thornton ended his long speech opposing attempts to coerce seceding states, and thereby violate the Constitution, by expressing the hope "that, if certain areas in the East seceded, their people would come west to live and abide in this refuge, in this resting place, among the great pillars, and under the massive arches of

---

[33] Parts of Burch's letter are printed in Davis, *op. cit.*, pp. 129–130.

[34] See Joseph Ellison, *California and the Nation*, p. 182, for the greater part of Scott's letter from which these excerpts are taken.

[35] For quotations from these and other papers, see *ibid.*, pp. 183–187.

[36] California Legislature [Speeches on Resolutions upon the State of the Union], 1861, p. 15. Montgomery's speech of February 11 is in *ibid.*, pp. 14–15.

the constitutional edifice of a Pacific Republic, which will en-
dure for aye, and preserve and shelter it in all coming ages." A
corresponding speech on the same subject was made in the
assembly on February 11, 1861, by Zach. Montgomery. Toward the end of the speech, after opposing the giving of aid
in prosecuting "a wicked, unholy, unjust, black-hearted, Abo-
lition war upon my Southern brethren," Montgomery said that,

if war does come . . ., from the difficulties and perils of war, our
brethren, both from the North and the South, will seek California
as their home, and will come here with their families, with their
wealth, their enterprise, and their intelligence, and build up a great
and glorious country. They will establish a Republic which will
compensate, to some extent, for the loss of the one which seems
now upon the brink of ruin and destruction on account of the folly
of its own children.

These excerpts from the speeches of Thornton and Montgomery illustrate the extreme view of a small legislative minority, and even these speeches were not made as part of a
movement for an independent state but as incidental rhetorical
remarks within debate on the larger constitutional issues.

In replying to a minority resolution in the assembly, which
had stated that the people of California would not "even consent to become the ally of one section in waging a fratricidal
war against another section of our common country," and to the
Pacific Republic sentiments of Thornton and a few others,
other representatives pointed out that such an establishment
would not have the strength to continue as an independent
state because it would lack the incalculable values that inhered in the firm connections between California and the
Union. The greater part of the press of the state supported
this position. In both houses, legislators made many strong
speeches urging support of the Union, and passed, by large
majorities, resolutions pledging unconditional loyalty to it.
These resolutions, strongly and sharply worded, almost completely repudiated the Pacific Republic theory.

The resolutions passed, the activities of the respective political parties, and the results of the state elections in 1861 brought death—if indeed any seed planted had ever started on its way to life—to the Pacific Republic movement. With news of the outbreak of war, mass meetings with no party lines were held in San Francisco, Oakland, San Jose, and a number of other towns; at these, loyalty to the Union was always enthusiastically voiced. Although in party meetings vociferous raving against a Pacific Republic was seldom heard, the Republican party and that of the Douglas Democrats pledged support and unconditional loyalty to the Union. Thus they repudiated the idea of an independent state.

The Breckinridge Democrats were in a weak position. Their words and actions in their state convention, which continued for several days from June 11, 1861, were erratic gasps and struggles for life. They had not strength enough left to throw any weight in favor of secession or independence, even if a majority of them ever favored either, which is doubtful. In their desperate situation they feebly and hesitatingly declared that it was the duty of California, as a member of the Union, to obey all constitutional acts of Congress and legal acts of the Executive. They followed this declaration by a resolution condemning President Lincoln for violation of the Constitution and usurpation of power in borrowing money, raising armies, and increasing the navy, and asserting that his acts tended to convert the government into a military despotism. After the report stating the position of the Breckinridge Democrats was adopted, another resolution was introduced in which it was declared that California remained true to the Union and loyal to the Constitution and the Flag. Another resolution, after condemning both Northern and Southern agitators for plunging the country into sectional war, averred that California must contend for peace as "a question of policy *within* the government with whose destinies she is cast, and whose honor is our honor." [37] These resolutions occasioned bitter debate,

[37] Davis, *op. cit.*, p. 171.

but finally the conclusion was reached that, having stated their position in their platform, the party members saw no reason for added declarations of loyalty to the Union. Edmund Randolph, in a frenzied and damnable statement opposing the policy of Lincoln, then said: "If this be rebellion, then I am a rebel. Do you want a traitor, then I am a traitor! For God's sake speed the ball; may the lead go quick to his heart, and may our country be free from this despot usurper that now claims the name of president of the United States." [38]

In spite of extravagant declarations like that of Randolph in the summer of 1861, the Breckinridge party had run its course. In a meeting held at San Francisco on July 31, the people refused to listen to the speaker. The candidate for governor endeavored to make himself heard but only partially succeeded. Other meetings elsewhere in the state were disturbed and broken up. The party was going and was almost gone, even though in a way it declared for the Union. With its going, the movements for secession and for a Pacific Republic also passed. The newspapers which had formerly favored the independent state became silent on the subject. Nothing more was heard of the Pacific Republic idea after the gubernatorial election of 1861. California was firmly fixed as a state in the federal union.

[38] Davis, *op. cit.,* p. 173.

Bibliography

THIS IS NOT a comprehensive bibliography of the period but a partial list of books, articles in periodicals, and a few other works containing material for the study of the topics covered in this book. With a few exceptions, only works that are readily available to the general reader have been included.

BOOKS, PAMPHLETS, SCRAPBOOKS, AND A MANUSCRIPT

Bancroft, Hubert Howe. *History of California* (7 vols.; San Francisco, 1884–1890), Vols. VI and VII.

——. *Popular Tribunals* (2 vols.; San Francisco, 1887).

Bonsal, Stephen. *Edward Fitzgerald Beale: A Pioneer in the Path of Empire, 1822–1903* (New York, 1912).

   A loosely written biography of the originator of the Indian reservation system.

Browne, J. Ross. *Report of the Debates in the Convention of California, on the Formation of the State Constitution, in September and October, 1849* (Washington, D.C., 1850).

   A complete record of debates and actions of the convention, with an appendix containing important documents.

California Legislature. *Journals* of the Assembly, *Journals* of the Senate, and Appendixes to the *Journals* (San Jose, San Francisco, Sacramento, 1850–1860).

   The Appendixes were bound with the *Journals* for the first five sessions; from the sixth to the twelfth session (1855–1861) they were published separately.

California Legislature. *Statutes of California* . . . [1849–1860] (San Jose, San Francisco, Sacramento, 1850–1860).

———— and U.S. Congress. [Speeches on Resolutions upon the State of the Union.]

> Seventeen speeches delivered in the senate and assembly of the twelfth session of the California legislature are bound in one volume with "Speech of the Hon. Stephen A. Douglas, of Illinois, in the United States Senate, January 3, 1861." The California speakers were: A. W. Blair, Caleb Burbank, Alexander Campbell, S. H. Chase, John Dougherty, D. P. Durst, Henry Edgerton, Frank F. Fargo, W. D. Harriman, Robert Henderson, Charles H. Kungle, Thomas Laspeyre, Samuel A. Merritt, Zach. Montgomery, Murray Morrison, and Henry I. Thornton, Jr. The volume is in the Bancroft Library, University of California, Berkeley.

Caughey, John W. *California* (New York: Prentice-Hall, 1940).

> A single-volume history of California, of scholarly quality, readable, and with much bibliographical information.

————. *Gold Is the Cornerstone* (Berkeley and Los Angeles: University of California Press, 1948).

> A volume in the Chronicles of California series.

Cleland, Robert G. *The Cattle on a Thousand Hills: Southern California, 1850–1870* (San Marino: The Huntington Library, 1941).

> Chapters 1–3 and 6 give a valuable modern introduction to the land question.

————. *A History of California: The American Period* (New York, 1922).

> A well-written and interesting volume with chapters on the period embraced in this study.

Coblentz, Stanton A. *Villains and Vigilantes: The Story of James King of William and Pioneer Justice in California* (New York: Wilson-Erickson, 1936).

> An interesting literary presentation of the vigilantes, journalistic in its treatment, colored but not distorted, in the main accurate and historically reliable.

Colton, Walter. *Three Years in California* (New York, 1850).

> An interesting picture of California during the interregnum and the early days of the gold rush, by a Navy chaplain who served as alcalde at Monterey. His name has been perpetuated there in "Colton Hall."

Crosby, Elisha O. *Memoirs of Elisha Oscar Crosby: Reminiscences of California and Guatemala from 1849 to 1864,* ed. by Charles Albro Barker (San Marino: The Huntington Library, 1945).

Bibliography 317

A valuable source on the making of the constitution of California, the launching of the state government, and the work of the Land Commission. Crosby had much to do with the decision of the first legislature to adopt the common law for California.

Davis, William Heath. *Seventy-five Years in California* . . . (San Francisco: John Howell, 1929).

The memoirs of an important trader on the Pacific Coast. This work, originally published under the title *Sixty Years in California* (San Francisco, 1889) is of some value for the period of the 'fifties.

Davis, Winfield J. *History of Political Conventions in California, 1849–1892* (Sacramento: California State Library, 1893).

A complete and invaluable account of conventions of all political parties in the period covered.

Donaldson, Thomas. *The Public Domain: Its History with Statistics* . . . (Washington, 1884).

Ellison, Joseph. *California and the Nation, 1850–1869: A Study of the Relations of a Frontier Community with the Federal Government.* University of California Publications in History, Vol. XVI (1927).

A thorough study of the subject by a competent scholar.

Field, Stephen J. *Personal Reminiscences of Early Days in California* . . . (n.p., c. 1893).

Contains valuable material on the California legislature, and on David C. Broderick.

Fitzgerald, Oscar P. *California Sketches, New and Old* (Nashville, Tennessee: Publishing House of the M.E. Church, South [c. 1894], 1903).

Interesting observations on persons and events of the gold days by a minister who in his youth served in California. Included are striking descriptions and characterizations of William M. Gwin and David C. Broderick.

Frémont, John C. *Memoirs of My Life* . . . (New York, 1887).

Goodwin, Cardinal. *The Establishment of State Government in California, 1846–1850* (New York, 1914).

The most thorough study of the subject yet made.

———. *John Charles Frémont: An Explanation of His Career* (Stanford, California: Stanford University Press, 1930).

A sound biography, though critical.

Halleck, Henry W. *Report on the Laws and Regulations Relative to Grants or Sales of Public Lands in California* (Washington, 1850).

An account of the laws and regulations governing the granting of public lands before the acquisition of California by the United States. In it, the problems to which the grants would give rise under the American regime are also emphasized.

Hayes, Benjamin I. Scrapbooks: "California Politics," Vols. I, II, V (1850–1860); "Constitutional Law" (one vol.).

In a collection of some 138 volumes of newspaper clippings, speeches, reports, etc., in the Bancroft Library, University of California, Berkeley.

Hittell, John Shertzer. *A History of the City of San Francisco and Incidentally of the State of California* (San Francisco, 1878).

Hittell, Theodore Henry. *History of California* (4 vols.; San Francisco, 1885–1897), Vol. II.

A full and excellent history of political developments and of the struggle for order. The account of the vigilance committee is full, restrained, historical, and unsurpassed for penetration, comprehension, and understanding.

Hoffman, Ogden. *Reports of Land Cases Determined in the United States District Court for the Northern District of California . . .* (San Francisco, 1862).

Perhaps the most valuable book of reference for study of the Spanish-Mexican land grants and the decisions of the United States Land Commission and of the District Court.

Hoopes, Albon W. *Indian Affairs and Their Administration, with Special Reference to the Far West, 1849–1860* (Philadelphia: University of Pennsylvania Press, 1932).

A general work on the spread of the Indian-reservation system.

Hunt, Rockwell D. *The Genesis of California's First Constitution* (*1846–49*). Johns Hopkins University Studies in Historical and Political Sciences, Thirteenth Series, Vol. VIII (August, 1895).

Jones, William Carey. *Report on the Subject of Land Titles in California . . .* (Washington, D.C., 1850).

A concise, carefully prepared, accurate, and authoritative report on the subject with which it deals.

Lynch, Jeremiah. *A Senator of the Fifties: David C. Broderick, of California* (San Francisco, 1911).

Based to a large extent on original sources, which are not too skillfully used, this book is a valuable work on the subject. Fifteen illustrations assist the author in preserving from oblivion the deeds and memories of men who founded the State of California.

McPherson, Hallie Mae. "William McKendree Gwin, Expansionist." MS thesis (1931), in University of California Library.

This scholarly work is the most comprehensive study of Gwin that has yet been made. A bound copy of this MS is in Professor Herbert E. Bolton's collection of theses written by his students at the University of California.

Manypenny, George Washington. *Our Indian Wards* (Cincinnati, 1888).

Morrow, William W. *Spanish and Mexican Private Land Grants* (San Francisco: privately printed, 1923).

Nevins, Allan. *Frémont: Pathmarker of the West* (New York: D. Appleton–Century Company, 1939).

Some of the superlatives used by Nevins in his earlier work (1929) have been eliminated.

———. *Frémont: The West's Greatest Adventurer* . . . (2 vols.; New York: Harper and Brothers, 1928).

Although fulsome in praise of Frémont, this is full of information.

O'Meara, James. *Broderick and Gwin: . . . A Brief History of Early Politics in California* . . . (San Francisco, 1881).

An informative journalistic account of the political contest of Gwin and Broderick.

———. *The Vigilance Committee of 1856* (San Francisco, 1875).

This reflects the law-and-order point of view.

Robinson, W. W. *Land in California* (Berkeley and Los Angeles: University of California Press, 1948).

Royce, Josiah. *California from the Conquest in 1846 to the Second Vigilance Committee in San Francisco* . . . (Cambridge, Massachusetts, 1886).

A literary and philosophical treatment of the period covered.

Scherer, James A. B. *The First Forty-niner and the Story of the Golden Tea-Caddy* (New York: Minton, Balch and Company, 1925).

The life of Sam Brannan. Contains much material on the San Francisco Committee of Vigilance of 1851.

Scherer, James A. B. *"The Lion of the Vigilantes": William T. Coleman and the Life of Old San Francisco* (Indianapolis: The Bobbs-Merrill Company, 1939).

——. Thirty-first Star (New York: G. P. Putnam's Sons, 1942).

Sherman, William T. *Memoirs* (2 vols.; New York, 1875).

> The author treats of the vigilance committee period in San Francisco from the law-and-order point of view.

Shinn, Charles Howard. *Mining Camps: A Study in American Frontier Government* (New York, 1885).

> A well-written account of the mining era from personal observations.

Shuck, Oscar T. *History of the Bench and Bar of California . . .* (Los Angeles, 1901).

> Biographies, accounts of legislative history and of extraordinary cases, comprehending the judicial history of the state.

Soulé, Frank; John H. Gihon, and James Nisbet. *The Annals of San Francisco . . .* (New York and San Francisco, 1855).

> A summary of the history of California and of the city of San Francisco to 1855, with biographical memoirs of many of its prominent citizens.

Taylor, Bayard. *Eldorado; or, Adventures in the Path of Empire* (New York, 1850).

United States Congress. *Message of the President of the United States Communicating Eighteen Treaties Made with Indians in California . . . 1851–1852*, 32d Cong., 1st sess. (Washington [1905]).

United States Department of the Interior. *Reports* of the Commissioner of Indian Affairs, 1856–1860, 1871.

——. *Report of the Secretary of the Interior*, communicating, in compliance with a resolution of the Senate, a copy of the correspondence between the Department of the Interior and the Indian agents and commissioners in California. 33d Cong., Special sess. (1853), Senate Ex. Doc. No. 4 (ser. 688).

Upham, Charles Wentworth. *Life, Explorations and Public Services of John Charles Fremont* (Boston, 1856).

> Somewhat subjective and uncritical, but on the whole written with understanding and an attempt at fair presentation of one who is looked upon as a hero.

Wagstaff, A. E. *Life of David S. Terry* . . . (San Francisco, 1911).

Willey, Samuel H. *The Transition Period of California, from a Province of Mexico in 1846 to a State of the American Union in 1850* (San Francisco, 1901).
   Informative and interesting.

Williams, Mary Floyd. *History of the San Francisco Committee of Vigilance of 1851.* University of California Publications in History, Vol. XII (1921).
   An excellent work that is both history and literature.

ARTICLES IN PERIODICALS

Auchampaugh, Philip G. "James Buchanan and Some Far Western Leaders, 1860–1861," *Pacific Historical Review*, XII (1943), 169–180.

Ellison, William H. "The California Indian Frontier," *Grizzly Bear*, XXX (March, 1922), 1, 3.

———. "The Federal Indian Policy in California, 1846–1860," *Mississippi Valley Historical Review*, IX (1922), 37–67.

———. "The Movement for State Division in California, 1849–1860," Texas State Historical Association *Southwestern Historical Quarterly*, XVII (1914), 101–139.

———. "Rejection of California Indian Treaties: A Study of Local Influence on National Policy," *Grizzly Bear*, XXXVII (May, June, July, 1925).

Field, Alston G. "Attorney-General Black and the California Land Claims," *Pacific Historical Review*, IV (1935), 235–245.

Florcken, Herbert G. "The Law and Order View of the San Francisco Vigilance Committee of 1856," California Historical Society *Quarterly*, XIV (1935), XV (1936).
   Principally from the correspondence of Governor J. Neely Johnson.

Gwin, William M. "Memoirs of Hon. William M. Gwin," ed. by William H. Ellison, California Historical Society *Quarterly*, XIX (1940), 1–26, 157–184, 256–277, 364–367.

Merriam, C. Hart. "The Indian Population of California," *American Anthropologist*, VII (1905), 594–606.

Royce, Josiah. "The Squatter Riot of '50 in Sacramento," *Overland Monthly*, n.s., VI (1885), 225–246.

Still, Bayrd. "California's First Constitution: A Reflection of the Political Philosophy of the Frontier," *Pacific Historical Review*, IV (1935), 221–234.

NEWSPAPERS

Sacramento. *Democratic Journal*, 1854–1856. *Democratic State Journal*, 1852–1854, 1855–1857. *Union*, 1851–1860.

San Francisco. *Alta California*, 1849–1860. *Evening Bulletin*, 1855–1860. *Herald*, 1850–1861. *Journal*, 1852–1861.

Index

Adams and Company, failure of, 234

Admission of California into Union: favored by President Taylor, 80, 84, 92; discussed in Congress, 83 ff., 171 ff.; accomplished, 98

Agricultural counties, demand convention, 181

Aguirre, Antonio, land claim of, 113–114

Alameda County Gazette, 311

Alcaldes, 4, 7, 11–13, 15, 20; chief officers in mining camps, 195

Alvarado, Juan B., 115

Andrews, William E. B., 257

Anglo-Saxon justice: administered in California, 13; flouted, 193; safeguards absent in trial of Berdue and Windred, 213; defied by vigilance committee, 233

Argenti, Felix, and other vigilantes enter home of Peter Metcalf, 221

Ashe, Richard P., 256, 257

Association for the Protection of Rights of Property, 233

Bagley, John W., 237

Bailey, Godard, 164

Baker, Edward D.: defends Cora, 236; opposes vigilantes, 250, 252; on Broderick's character and career, 306

Balls: at end of constitutional convention, 42–43; given for first legislature, 61

Bancroft, Hubert Howe: quoted, 34, 78, 100; on slavery advocates, 189; on vigilante committee, 261 n.

Banks and banking: action by constitutional convention, 32–33; dishonest character of, 234

Barbour, George W.: Indian agent in California, 144 ff.; makes treaties with Indians, 146–147

Barclay, John S., hanged, 200

Baylies, Francis, of Massachusetts, quoted, 1

Beale, Edward F.: on treaties made by Indian Commissioners, 149, 155; as Indian superintendent, 159–161; at Tejon reservation, 161; removed from office, 162

Bear Flag Revolt, 2–3

Bell, John, 84, 85, 96

Benicia: incorporated, 66; state capital, 74; Pacific Division, U.S. Army at, 251; conference between governor and vigilance

323

F
865
E5
1978

Ellison, William Henry.
   A self-governing dominion,
California, 1849-1860 / by William
Henry Ellison. -- Berkeley :
University of California Press, 1978,
c1950.
   xi, 335 p. ; 23 cm. -- (California
library reprints series) (Reprint of
the ed. published by University of
California Press, Berkeley, in
series: Chronicles of California.)
   Bibliography: p. 315-322.
   Includes index.
   ISBN 0-520-03713-8

   1. California--Politics and
                     (Cont. on next card)

SUPAT   B/NA A DO-572054   06/29/79

F
865
E5
1978

Ellison, William Henry.   A self-
   governing dominion, California, 1849-
   1860.   1978   (Card 2.

   government--1846-1850.
   2. California--History--1846-1850.
   3. California--History--1850-1950.
   4. California--Politics and
   government--1850-1950.   I. Title.
   II. Series.   III. Series: Chronicles
   of California.

F865.E5 1978   979.4/04
                          78-108655

SUPAT   B/NA A DO-572054   06/29/79